Shadow W

Praise for *Fit Mind: 8 Weeks to Change Your Inner Soundtrack and Tune into Your Greatness* by Pat Divilly:

'Completely transformative … a fantastic work by a very knowledgeable man, worth every penny and more.' **Audible review**

'A transformative guide for anyone looking to make a serious change in their life.' **Yung Pueblo, New York Times bestselling author**

'*Fit Mind* will change your life for the better.' **Geoff Thompson, Bafta-winning writer**

'A journey from the head to the heart … encourages all of us to learn to listen deeply, building trust and connection with ourselves.' **Dr Easkey Britton, surfer and author of *Saltwater in the Blood***

'Therapy in a book! The eight-week program is packed with practical insightful activities that unlocked my mind and helped me set up a daily, ongoing self-support system. Nothing else worked like this, not even 1–1 counselling. A MUST read!' **Amazon review**

'This book is amazing! It's so easy to understand and relatable to our everyday thoughts and feelings. The journal prompts each day helped me start 2022 in a fantastic way and I will use this book again and again in times of need. I discovered a lot about myself during the eight weeks and have made some changes as a result. I have just finished the 30-day challenge at the end and love this new routine as I feel more in control of my emotions and my aims and challenges each day. Roll on the next book!' **Amazon review**

'I am in my early 60s and have done a lot of 'healing work' on myself over the years and read many inspiring books. Pat's book is one of the best I've come across. I'm incredulous that someone so young could have such wisdom and insights. He has somehow managed to distill all of this and communicate it clearly in this book.

It is such a practical book and he uses probing and pertinent questions throughout, which help deepen our understanding of ourselves. He encourages us to write down the answers to these and then reflect on how or where we can use them to improve our lives. I did this over an eight-week period and found it both enlightening and helpful. And often challenging! I love his courage, vulnerability and honesty in sharing his story. It makes his book authentic. I cannot recommend this book highly enough if you want to heal and learn to love yourself in all your imperfection.' **Amazon review**

'This book is very user friendly, great if you're early in your personal development or if you're well established. I used it in combination with meditation guides provided by Pat … It's one of the few books that I will use consistently going forward.' **Amazon review**

'I absolutely loved this book. *Fit Mind* explains how to silence the inner critic, take actions aligned with my values, and does it all in a really clear and concise way. I related to so much of it.' **Amazon review**

'Brilliant … this book is easy to read, using every day examples of how to understand yourself and your actions better. It will guide you through your search for inner peace' **Amazon review**

Pat Divilly has been involved in the wellness industry for over 15 years as a coach, facilitator and educator in the areas of physical, mental and emotional wellness.

Since 2015 he has run hundreds of corporate and public seminars, workshops and retreats globally and released over 250 episodes of his popular podcast.

Pat now runs a six-month group coaching programme called Shadow and Light, and founded the Journey the Breath breathwork school and facilitator training. *Fit Mind,* his number one bestselling book, has been described as 'transformative' and 'life-changing'.

Learn more about Pat at www.patdivilly.com.

Shadow Work

A practical guide
to embracing
your shadow side,
tackling shame
and transforming
pain into power

Pat Divilly

GILL BOOKS

Gill Books
Hume Avenue
Park West
Dublin 12
www.gillbooks.ie

Gill Books is an imprint of M.H. Gill and Co.

9781804581889

Designed by Bartek Janczak
Edited by Esther Ní Dhonnacha
Proofread by Jane Rogers

This book is typeset in Minion Pro.

*The paper used in this book comes from the wood pulp
of sustainably managed forests.*

Printed and Bound in the UK using 100% Renewable Electricity
at CPI Group (UK) Ltd.

This book is not intended as a substitute for the medical advice of a physician.
The reader should consult a doctor or mental health professional
if they feel it necessary.

To the best of our knowledge, this book complies in full with the requirements
of the General Product Safety Regulation (GPSR). For further information and
help with any safety queries, please contact us at productsafety@gill.ie.

A CIP catalogue record for this book is available from the British Library.

5 4 3 2 1

Dedicated to my parents.
The older I get, the more I realise just how much you did for us.
You made it look easy, even in times I know it must have been
anything but. Thank you for everything.

Contents

Foreword   x

How to Use this Book   1

CHAPTER ONE: Origins of Shadow   11

CHAPTER TWO: Shadow Activation   42

CHAPTER THREE: Who Did You Become?   72

CHAPTER FOUR: The Mind–Body Connection   97

CHAPTER FIVE: The Inner Child and Inner Teenager   125

CHAPTER SIX: Shame and the Inner Critic   153

CHAPTER SEVEN: Anger, Boundaries and Needs   179

CHAPTER EIGHT: Change, Loss and Grief   213

CHAPTER NINE: Facing Fear   240

CHAPTER TEN: Shadow in Relationship   267

Afterword and Integration   296

Acknowledgements   299

Foreword

'If only it were all so simple! If only there were evil people somewhere insidiously committing evil deeds, and it were necessary only to separate them from the rest of us and destroy them. But the line dividing good and evil cuts through the heart of every human being. And who among us is willing to destroy a piece of their own heart?' ALEKSANDR SOLZHENITSYN

'Wisdom tends to grow in proportion to one's awareness of one's ignorance.' ANTHONY DE MELLO

I cringe a little as it comes near my turn to answer.

I am sitting with a small group of fellow students as we approach the end of a 28-day yoga teacher training on the small island of Koh Phangan in Thailand. The question being asked of me: 'Who are you?'

It's an age-old question asked in spiritual circles – 'Who am I?' – serving as a form of meditation or self-inquiry to contemplate and ponder. It's a question that philosophers, mystics and thinkers have sat with throughout time as an invitation to go beyond the surface level of the identity that we have created for ourselves.

When initially asked we might answer by sharing our name, though we could easily change our name in the morning and we'd still be the same person, and so we are more than our name.

Perhaps we might share what we do professionally, in an effort to explain who we are, but again we could change our career in the morning and still be ourselves, and so we are more than what we do.

I might have answered at that time that I was a 30-year-old Irish man, though now I am 36 and I am still the same person in a biologically older body, and so I am more than my name, my profession, my age and my body.

I pause before answering the question. I notice my judgements coming up about some of what the others have shared, in my head thinking, 'You do a 28-day yoga teacher training and now suddenly you think you're a wise philosopher with the perfect answer to the timeless question "Who am I?"' I also notice a part of myself that wants to be impressive or wise in my response or contribution to the group, and another part that wants to numb out and avoid having to contemplate such a big question on our night off. 'Can't we just have a beer and relax?!'

Sensing some reluctance to share, the group eggs me on. And so I take a breath and respond …

'I'm light and I'm dark. I'm good and I'm bad. I'm a nice guy and an asshole. I'm wise and I'm dumb. I am good and I am evil. I am the potential for all things.'

I feel a mix of relief and vulnerability after sharing, while I am met with silence and looks of confusion.

My answer is in contrast to some of the previous shares, which included:

'I am a vessel for pure love and light.'

'I am a beacon of compassion and positivity.'

'I am a loving and caring mother.'

'I am vehicle for peace and healing in the world.'

On the first night of the training, after the opening session, I walked into the kitchen and overheard one of my classmates say, 'He said he's only been to two yoga classes and can barely touch his toes. What is this guy doing at a teacher training?' I'm sure at this point she in particular was unimpressed with my 'non-spiritual' answer to the question of 'Who am I?'

With a few days left on the training, and not wanting to be alienated or exiled from the group after revealing that I'm light and I'm dark, I choose to elaborate and share a little more. 'Of course I believe I have the potential for love and light, for being a positive force in the world and for being a good person. That's what I try to be and hope to be … As part of that, though, I also believe it's important to acknowledge my potential for being the opposite of all of those things, for me to acknowledge my humanity and the realities of the sadness, anger, grief, shame, judgements and fears that I frequently experience. Some might see spiritual or personal development work as being about removing or transcending these darker aspects of the human psyche.

'To me, though, the real work in healing, growth or personal development is to acknowledge, get close to and understand all parts of ourselves, not just the pretty and positive aspects of who we believe ourselves to be. I am coming to learn that all parts of me have a purpose and hold hidden gifts. In cutting off or denying the parts that I have previously disowned or labelled as wrong, I cut off those hidden gifts and remain at war with myself.

'I believe that only people who know their own capacity for cruelty, greed or evil can regulate those aspects of themselves and choose to show up from a place of compassion, love and care. People who deny those aspects of who they are don't ever get rid of those parts: they just push them into the shadows, out of sight, to a place where they take on a life of their own. It is great to have aspirations of love and light, but I feel that to bring love and light to ourselves we have got to embrace the messiness of being human! When we reject parts of ourselves and project them onto others, we make others heroes and villains in an effort to ease the discomfort that comes with recognising that anything we see in others lives in us too. I think it's true of any part of ourselves we try to deny. Those parts end up unconsciously running our lives.'

One or two of my international comrades nod approvingly as I explain, while others look uncomfortable and double down on their commitment to the path of love, light and positivity. I can't blame them. In a world of social media highlight reels, filtered images and putting our best self out there, the idea of stepping into and owning our own darkness goes against the grain and might not sound very appealing or aspirational. Then going a step further and revealing that potential darkness to others brings a whole other layer of fear.

I know from my own experience, though, that I have spent long enough denying and rejecting parts of myself and long enough hiding how I really feel and what I am really experiencing. I also know that despite my best efforts to run from the parts of myself I didn't like, I have never managed to. I have actually become further disconnected from myself in the process.

For many years now I have been fascinated by the stories we tell ourselves and how the beliefs that we form in early childhood go on to shape how we see ourselves, others and the world. I have been fascinated by what drives us, what stops us and what causes us to say we want one thing but then to do the complete opposite or unconsciously sabotage our own best efforts.

In my early teens I picked up a personal development book for the first time and for many years I read about how to set and achieve goals, how to be more productive and ultimately how to become 'successful'. My interest and commitment to personal development supported me up to a certain point, but also unknowingly led me on a path of chasing goals and accomplishments outside myself in an effort to avoid the parts of myself that I had disowned or rejected in childhood. Whenever I bumped up against or came close to the darker parts of myself, I would try to figure out what I needed to achieve in order to find more of my light and quieten my inner critic for a while.

Sometimes the goal-setting worked great, though as much as I achieved in life, I ultimately sabotaged myself or acted out in ways that left me feeling like all of my efforts were in vain. At times my external results looked great on paper, but my internal reality did not reflect this.

I found it easy to be with myself and love myself when I was reaching my goals in life or receiving praise from those around me, but in the absence of achievement and validation, my loneliness, fear, grief and shame would show up, leading me to work more and work harder in an effort to outrun how I really felt about myself, or to turn to addictive tendencies to distract myself from my authentic feelings. Rather than being driven by a sense of self-worth and seeing myself as being 'enough' just as I was, I was largely driven by wounding, a deep-seated belief that I was inherently flawed, but that if I achieved all the goals I set outside myself I would eventually come to feel like I was enough and I was lovable.

We all come into the world with pure potential and authentic expression, though as we get a little older and become socialised we begin to take on messages about what and who we need to be to maintain the love and approval of those around us. We learn to look outward and seek feedback from our environment as to what wins us love, praise and approval and what leads to the withdrawal of love, praise and approval.

Influenced by our family and friends, our teachers and peers and the culture we grow up in, we develop a 'persona' – a mask that we present to the world, made up of all of the parts of ourselves that we have learned garner praise and approval. Our persona reflects all parts of ourselves that we are proud of: the light, the aspects deemed attractive or admirable by our environment.

This persona supports us in having our needs met by the people and environment around us at a time in our lives where we can't meet those needs for ourselves. Being a 'good boy' or 'good girl' ensures we do not stand out in a way that might threaten our safety, comfort or needs.

As we develop this mask, persona or self-image, we also unconsciously develop what Swiss psychiatrist Carl Jung called the 'shadow', which becomes the storage container for all of the parts of ourselves we fear might attract judgement or criticism. If I am celebrated for my work ethic, I perhaps reject my laziness (which upon closer inspection might actually be my need for rest) and push it into the shadows. If celebrated for my strength, I perhaps place my weakness (which with closer inspection may be the vulnerability that allows me to connect with others) into shadow. When

I am judged, shamed or ridiculed by others in childhood, to avoid future pain I will unconsciously repress the emotions, behaviours or beliefs that caused the pain into the shadows. They do not disappear, but instead take on a life of their own, accumulating energy and often playing out in unhealthy or unhelpful ways in our lives. Hidden outside our conscious awareness, our shadow often appears in explosive reactivity or 'out-of-character' moments.

Although we all mature biologically, at times we get stuck psychologically. I am 36 years old at the time of writing this book, though at times in which I feel shame or fear, unless I 'wake up' and see my patterns, I can easily find myself reverting back to defence strategies or reactions learned in childhood or during my teens in times of shame or fear. Many of us tried to cut off from certain aspects of ourselves in our earliest years and now, decades later, remain fragmented as we continue to deny those darker aspects that were once shamed or ridiculed.

The purpose of working with and moving toward our shadow is to allow ourselves to outgrow outdated defence strategies and 'grow up' psychologically, so that we can show up to life from a grounded and clear place and not a reactive place based on our past conditioning.

When we push emotions like fear, anger, grief and others into shadow, we not only lose touch with these feelings but also severely limit our capacity to experience the fullness of life. It's like locking certain rooms of our mind, believing they are too painful to enter, not knowing that within each of these locked rooms are gifts that will be required to live a life that is truly authentic and meaningful to us. The smaller and more conditional we are with the content of our inner worlds, the smaller our outer world becomes, as we cut off from the emotions that are needed to support us on our journey.

When we disown our fear, we confine ourselves within the boundaries of a very safe and 'secure' existence, avoiding situations that might expose our vulnerabilities and limiting us to the predictability of our comfort zone. In being disowned, our fear doesn't disappear but instead operates unconsciously from the shadows. The result is a life lived with a need for certainty and control, missing out on the adventures and growth that come with exploring the wider world beyond the comfort zone of our current experience. Paradoxically, trying to deny or avoid our fear leads to a life controlled by it. The same is true of all shadow material. 'What we resist will persist.'

Disowning our anger restricts our ability to assert ourselves and set healthy boundaries. We become people-pleasers, often sacrificing our own needs to maintain harmony. In overlooking or sacrificing our own needs and muting our own voice, we do not cut off from that anger but instead see it play out in shadowy ways, perhaps taking the form of resentment, passive aggression, mocking sarcasm or self-destructive behaviour.

Grief, when disowned, keeps us trapped in a state of numbness, unable to fully engage with life. We avoid the pain of loss by shutting down emotionally, which prevents us from fully experiencing joy and love. This is like someone who, after a significant loss, refuses to form new relationships, living a life devoid of close connections to avoid the potential for more pain. A willingness to grieve and let go is actually what allows us to live and love fully.

When we disown our sexuality, we cut off from a vital connection to a core aspect of our identity. Sexuality is not just about physical intimacy; it includes our sense of self, our desires and how we relate to others. Efforts to cut off from our sexuality will often lead to shame, repression and unfulfilled desires, affecting our relationships and personal wellbeing. Integrating our sexual shadow offers self-acceptance, empowerment, healthier relationships and a pathway to personal growth and fulfilment.

Other emotions like shame and suppressed desires also trap us within narrow confines of self-perception and behaviour. Disowning these parts of ourselves keeps us stuck in cycles of perfectionism, addiction or emotional repression. This can lead us to constantly strive for perfection, never feeling good enough and turning to addictive behaviours as a way to cope with the pressure.

Through shadow work, we take these hidden aspects out of the dark, shining light on them and transforming them into sources of strength and self-acceptance. This process is like opening the doors to those locked rooms of our mind, discovering that they are not filled with monsters but with aspects of ourselves that hold the key to our growth. It enables us to live more authentically and freely, embracing the full spectrum of human experience.

By integrating these disowned parts, we become whole. It is not that we reclaim our anger and become violent bullies, or that we make friends with our grief, thus falling into a pit of sadness we can't ever climb out of.

It is the opposite, in fact.

Anthony de Mello, a spiritual teacher, once said, 'What you are aware of you are in control of. What you are not aware of is in control of you.' This is how I think of shadow. What's left in the darkness out of sight controls us. When it is brought out into the light we take back some control.

We often hear of the importance of living an 'authentic life' or of being 'authentically ourselves'. 'Individuation' is the name given to the process of becoming our true selves by embracing all parts of ourselves, including our hidden or neglected aspects. The individuation process is about living fully and authentically, finding balance and wholeness by embracing both our dark and our light, our shadow and persona.

Making the brave commitment to meeting all parts of ourselves allows us to see both the strengths and drawbacks of each trait, emotion or behaviour and allows us to choose how we show up in the world. Getting to know and understand our fear allows us to embrace more uncertainty and adventure in our lives, to embrace the new and move past old patterns, habits and routines. Getting closer to our anger allows us to set healthy boundaries, express ourselves authentically and protect what is important to us. Befriending our grief can allow us to reclaim the energy that keeps us stuck in the past and unable to open our hearts again to the fullness of life.

In essence, in working with shadow we can come to transform the parts of ourselves we have shamed or shunned into strengths and allies.

This book is not about self-improvement; it is about self-understanding. You may be surprised as you come to see how much of our potential, creativity and authenticity lives in our hidden parts and how, by changing how we relate to them, we awaken new energy, new life and new possibilities. Shadow work is not an easy path. It is confronting, often messy, non-linear and never-ending. But when embraced and integrated, the ideas and exercises shared in this book can change the way you see yourself and others forever.

The rewards that come with this path are fruitful – reclaiming authenticity and full expression, moving beyond cycles of addiction and self-sabotage, and progressing from a life limited by childhood conditioning to one inspired by creativity and an authentic personal vision. Embarking on this journey is choosing the brave path of leaning toward your uncomfortable edges, meeting your disowned parts with acceptance and compassion and allowing yourself to reclaim and be all of who you are, moving from a conditional state of loving yourself toward unconditional love and acceptance.

Some avoid this type of self-inquiry all their lives, while others jump in with two feet and become consumed by it. I encourage you to find a healthy middle ground, allowing a little time every day for self-reflection and understanding. Let's approach this work from a space of curiosity and compassion. You are not broken and so there is nothing to fix! I hope that I can be a gentle and supportive guide on your journey.

Thank you for joining me and for committing to meet yourself in this way.

Grá mór,

Pat

How to Use this Book

Shadow work is not about getting rid of any parts of yourself or getting rid of certain emotions, but instead about changing how you relate to them so that they can be integrated in a way that allows you to become more of yourself.

In each chapter you'll find some prompts and exercises intended to help you consider how the themes show up in your own life. You will also find a number of practical exercises shared to help create a bridge between the content of the book and your own lived experience.

If you have a lot going on in your life right now or are in the midst of some big changes or transitions, it may be more supportive for you to stick to reading the book and not dive too deeply into the exercises until things settle down for you. Reading the book can in itself spark awareness and insight, while actively engaging with your own shadow material through the exercises provided can deepen the realisations and contribute to lasting transformation.

These exercises focus on both the body and the mind with a recognition of the strong connection between the two. Much of the personal development, mental wellness and popular psychology work we have seen over the last number of decades has focused on a largely cognitive approach, with an emphasis on exploring and challenging the disempowering thoughts or beliefs someone might hold. In more recent times it has become clear that equal merit must be given to the role of the body in developing improved mental and emotional health. Only when we feel safe in our bodies can we access perspective, compassion and curiosity.

Sometimes, unbeknownst to ourselves, we are walking through life with a body holding chronic tension that does not feel safe, and so we are unconsciously perceiving our environment as a threatening or unfriendly place (we'll dive deeper into the mind–body connection in Chapter Four).

So, alongside the cognitive exercises shared throughout the book, you will find body- and breath-based practices shared to help develop greater emotional awareness, authentic expression and capacity for emotional regulation and self-soothing.

You might read the book all the way through and then come back to the exercises, or allow it to be an 11-week journey in which you complete the exercises on a weekly basis, beginning with those shared at the end of this section, before moving to the next chapter. Whatever you choose to do, go gently, be curious and seek out support if and when you need it.

———— Best Practices and Self-Care ————

Knowing Your Anchors

In stepping into any form of inner work that involves reflecting on or exploring our thoughts, emotions and patterns, it is important that we are engaged in self-care and are well resourced with anchors that provide us with a sense of stability. This means ensuring we have the support systems, practices and tools in place to nurture and sustain ourselves through the process.

Our anchors are the resources – practices, tools, environments and people – that help us to remain grounded and help us stay centred during times of change, uncertainty or emotional turbulence. Self-care helps to create a stable foundation, allowing us to delve into challenging areas with resilience and compassion. Being well resourced might include anchors like having trusted friends, mentors or a therapist to talk to, engaging in a regular form of physical activity that you enjoy, practising breathwork or meditation, or setting aside time for rest and relaxation. Without adequate self-care, the work can become overwhelming, heavy and isolating. I am of the belief that the deeper the level of change or challenge we are experiencing in our lives, the more essential these anchors and support systems become.

Compassion for Self and Others

As you learn more about the shadow self you will come to see that the parts of yourself that you have disowned, rejected or tried to push away were exiled because at some point they were made wrong – that is, shamed or judged negatively. You learned somewhere along the line, probably in childhood, that it wasn't safe to show or express those parts of yourself. In response you will have consciously or unconsciously pushed those parts into the darkness (the shadow). Much of the shadow is made up of emotions like anger, fear and sadness that may have previously been deemed bad or wrong. In truth, there are no wrong emotions. Every feeling we have is natural and part of the human experience. The problem comes when we label certain emotions as unacceptable and try to push them away. Instead of rejecting or vilifying certain emotions, with this work we can learn to understand and accept them all. As you go through the practices and exercises in this book, you will undoubtedly meet some of your shadow and shine light on the dark for the purpose of better self-understanding and acceptance. As you bring light to your rejected or exiled parts, it is essential that you meet yourself and your shadow parts with compassion.

As you will come to see as you read through the book, all of your parts and emotions, even the ones that seem to want to sabotage your best efforts, are doing their best to protect and support you. In working with our shadow, our mission is to change how we relate to these parts and to find acceptance and understanding of their origins, roles, strengths and fears.

Alongside this self-compassion it is important that we extend compassion to others in our lives. In exploring the early influences of our family of origin, our community and our culture, we are not doing so in order to point fingers or blame. Instead, this exploration is to allow us to recognise that these early influences shape our perceptions and behaviours, often without our conscious awareness.

By examining our past, we can gain insight into the parts of ourselves we've hidden away, not to assign fault, but to understand the complexities of our identity.

Lean in and Find Your Own Edge

Shadow work involves leaning in rather than leaning away. It is important with this type of work to find your own edge. Only you can know where that edge is, a little outside your comfort zone but not so much that you become overwhelmed. It is the space in which discomfort and growth meet.

You cannot heal your emotional or psychological wounds overnight, rush through it or do it on a timeline that feels convenient to you. Equally, the healing will not happen by avoiding discomfort or challenges, and so it is essential to lean in and commit to the journey.

In the fitness world the concept of progressive overload is among the most important. Put simply, progressive overload involves gradually increasing the amount of stress placed on the body during exercise over time. There is an understanding that for the body to adapt and change it must be given a new stimulus to adapt to. Sometimes that means adding a little more weight to the barbell, or running a little further, or completing an extra few repetitions of an exercise. If there isn't new stress placed on the body it has no reason to adapt, though to place too much stress on the body too quickly is likely to lead to injury. Thus progressive overload promotes small marginal gains over time that allow the body just enough stress to respond and adapt positively to the new stimulus.

Similarly, with the exploration of shadow the wisdom of leaning in and honouring your own edge marries the eagerness to explore the unknown with the patience to navigate the complexities within.

Responsibility and Empowerment

In recent years, terms like 'narcissist', 'boundaries', 'avoidant or anxiously attached' and 'gaslighting' have become common in conversations around personal growth and relationships. While these labels can be valuable in certain contexts, there is a risk in using them too casually or flippantly. Sometimes these words are thrown around to avoid personal responsibility, to place the blame on others, or to create a narrative that absolves us of responsibility for our own behaviour.

This book is not about diagnosing or labelling others, nor is it about placing the blame on external factors. While much of our shadow was formed in childhood, shaped by the environment we grew up in and the people we loved, this is not a book about blaming parents, caregivers or anyone else in our past. Instead, it's an invitation to explore our own inner world with curiosity and compassion. This journey is about personal responsibility and empowerment, not about finding others to blame. While there is certainly space for understanding how certain behaviours or dynamics affect us, the focus here is on how we can take charge of our own healing.

And now, as we begin our journey, let's prepare with a few of the exercises that you will use throughout the book. Work through the exercises at a pace that feels manageable for you. There is not any rush with this work, though I would suggest blocking off a little time at least a few days a week on a consistent basis to reaffirm your commitment to yourself in prioritising your self-understanding.

Incomplete Sentences

Sentence completion provides a powerful means of connecting to the unconscious and gaining deep wisdom and self-understanding beyond what can be accessed from the conscious everyday mind. Each chapter concludes with a number of these incomplete sentences. It is suggested you read them aloud and complete the sentences with your first response, no thinking, just trust the first response that comes to you. A response of 'I don't know' can be a sign of resistance, and so be patient with yourself and try to trust yourself in your responses.

As we will discuss at length, we have all formed a strong identity, an ego that looks to keep us safe by strongly protecting how we see ourselves and keeping us within the constraints of the identity or self-image we created long ago. Sometimes the immediate response when completing an incomplete sentence conflicts with the ego's self-image and our need for control, thus showing us that we are more than we thought we were. Again, trust yourself and allow curiosity around your first response.

–I hide parts of me because …
–The place where I feel I need to hide the most is …
–Knowing I hide in that area makes me feel …
–Fully embracing myself means accepting and facing my …
–As a child, I hid my …
–I get triggered by other people when …
–A hidden part of me I would like to better understand is …
–I am ready for …

Journalling Prompts

After the incomplete sentences you will find a number of journalling prompts to support you in exploring the themes discussed. These prompts will play a key role in helping you illuminate your shadow, bringing the book to life and allowing you to capture new insights to support you in your day-to-day life.

Let your mind ask the question and your heart answer it.

This requires letting go of any aspirations of 'getting it right' when journalling on the prompts offered. These prompts serve as a tool for self-exploration and so you cannot 'get it wrong'. Taking adequate time with the prompts is important. Given five minutes to write about a given topic you will likely write a lot of what you're already aware of, but take 15–20 minutes to write about the same topic and you'll likely access lots of new insight and awareness.

So much of modern life can be spent looking outward or having our attention pulled away from ourselves toward the abundance of noise, stimulus and distraction in our worlds. Committing to a journalling practice is a commitment to going within and really prioritising your inner world, which promises an exciting and often surprising adventure. I would suggest getting a specific journal to capture all your reflections in one place. I am confident that, in time, when you look back over your notes, you will be amazed at the changes you see in your life as a result of what emerges from your journalling practice.

- Reflect on moments in your life when you've felt a sense of hiding or suppressing parts of yourself. Describe these instances and consider why you might have kept these aspects hidden from others.
- Think about aspects of yourself that you might have neglected or not fully acknowledged. What are these traits or behaviours? How do you feel about exploring these aspects further?
- Consider recurring reactions or emotions you experience in certain situations or around specific people. Write about these patterns and any hidden motivations behind your reactions.
- Recollect moments from your childhood when you felt encouraged to express or repress certain traits or emotions. How might these experiences have influenced what you show or hide about yourself today?
- Identify traits or behaviours in others that trigger strong reactions or judgements within you. Explore why these traits evoke such responses and if they might reflect hidden aspects of yourself.

———— Embodiment Practices ————

Shadow work is not solely a cognitive endeavour; in fact in many ways we can think about our body as being our shadow self. It is in the body that we feel our reactiveness, our emotional triggers and our resistance. It is our body that holds the tension or armour around emotions that we do not want to or do not feel safe to feel.

Working with our body and breath and not just our mind can help us access greater insight into our shadow self, allowing us a much greater capacity for self-understanding. Building self-trust requires a willingness to begin listening to the signs of our body and not push past its feedback. One of the fastest ways of shining light on unconscious beliefs, fears and patterns is to begin to pay more attention to the body and its reactions to certain situations or environments.

Through consistent embodiment practice you will develop the capacity to be with intense sensations and emotions, expanding your window of tolerance without becoming overwhelmed and going to autopilot reactivity, defensiveness or shutdown. The embodiment practices shared throughout the book aim to help you deepen your connection between body and mind, allowing you to become more aware of your emotional state at any given time so that you can come from a place of responsiveness and presence in life and not a place of reacting from old emotional wounds. Body movements, breath techniques and expressive activities are designed to release stored tension in the body and restore a healthy flow of energy.

Thinking to Feeling

Our first embodiment exercise is a practice of moving from stories to sensations and from thinking to feeling.

1. Find a quiet space where you won't be disturbed, and sit comfortably, either on a chair with your feet flat on the ground or on the floor with your legs crossed. Gently close your eyes and take a few deep breaths, inhaling through your nose and allowing your belly to expand, then exhaling through your mouth to release any tension.

2. Start by bringing your awareness to your head, noticing any sensations like tension or warmth, and slowly scan your body from head to toe. As you focus on each area – neck, shoulders, arms, chest, abdomen, back, hips, legs and feet – simply observe any sensations without judgement. If your mind begins to wander back to thoughts or stories, gently guide your focus back to the sensations, using reminders like 'I'm here,' or 'I feel.'

3. Once you've identified areas of sensation, take a deep breath and imagine sending your breath into those areas, visualising it as warm, soothing light that brings comfort and relaxation. After a few minutes, slowly bring your awareness back to the room, wiggling your fingers and toes, and gently open your eyes when you feel ready.

4. After completing the exercise, notice how it felt to focus on your body rather than your thoughts – and jot down any insights in a journal.

This exercise can be practised anytime you feel overwhelmed by thoughts or emotions, helping you cultivate a deeper connection to your body and promoting a sense of grounding in the present moment.

CHAPTER ONE

Origins of Shadow

'One does not become enlightened by imagining
figures of light, but by making the darkness conscious.
The latter procedure, however, is disagreeable and
therefore not popular.' CARL JUNG

'The role of the artist is exactly the same as the role of the
lover. If I love you, I have to make you conscious of the
things you don't see.' JAMES BALDWIN

——— Authentic Expression ———

Many of us have changes we would like to make in our lives, maybe
patterns or cycles we would like to move past, addictions or habits
we'd like to overcome or relationship dynamics we would like to
outgrow. On paper the changes don't look too challenging and
'should' be manageable. In practice, though, we can often find ourselves looping back to old patterns, frustrated by our struggles to
make those changes stick.

And so we try and try again, sometimes caught in cycles for
years or decades. Each time we commit to change, we try to be more

positive, more disciplined or 'better'. Despite these best efforts, something keeps us in old patterns and stuck in our past. Sometimes we may achieve temporary superficial changes in our external world, but when our internal self-view remains unchanged, we generally return to familiar habits and old behaviours. This disconnect between our external efforts and internal beliefs is what keeps us in cycles of self-sabotage. I am going to suggest that these cycles of self-sabotage are a result of us denying the shadow self.

To break free from old unhelpful patterns, it's essential to address and transform the underlying self-concept and deeply ingrained beliefs that drive our actions by exploring and integrating the shadow self, rather than rejecting or denying those aspects that long ago we labelled as 'bad' or 'wrong'.

We are all born into the world unique and hopefully get to experience the freedom to express ourselves authentically in our earliest months and years. It is not uncommon to see a baby cry hysterically for a few moments and then quickly shift into laughing hysterically with just as much enthusiasm and ease. There aren't yet any judgements on what emotions or behaviours are 'good' or 'bad' and so the baby and (hopefully) the baby's caregivers are unconditional in their love and acceptance of whatever wants to be expressed. There is a freedom, a purity and an emotional range and flexibility to the young child, a natural flow of energy, without obstruction. Emotions are 'digested' in real time, not seen as something to deny or avoid, but simply experienced as a movement of energy in the body. Rather than an emotional outburst being judged, it is generally acknowledged as a call for attention. If in response to the call for attention, the baby's needs are gratified by their parent or caregiver, the baby builds trust, knowing that their needs will be met. If the baby's needs go unmet, they experience emotional distress and the pain of separation. This pain leads to a sense of disconnection or abandonment. As a result the baby can experience feelings of loneliness, insecurity, and the belief that their emotions or needs are not valid or worthy of attention.

As the baby grows into a toddler or young child the socialisation process begins. During this time they learn what behaviours, emotions and beliefs are celebrated by those around them. They learn what is welcomed and appreciated as well as what behaviours, emotions and beliefs are unacceptable, unwanted or unlovable.

——— From Authentic to Adaptive ———

This socialisation process is an essential time for developing important social skills and understanding societal norms. It helps children learn how to interact with others, navigate social situations and build relationships. As the child takes on countless messages from family, community and culture, they begin to learn who they need to become in order to stay safe and maintain love in the world.

It is at this stage that a split begins to occur.

The child develops a sense of who they are and who they are not. Emotions, now labelled 'good' or 'bad', are no longer seen as a neutral and natural expression of energy but instead as something to pursue or avoid. While coming into contact with others, the young child's personality forms, and the aspects of the self that are not deemed acceptable are pushed away, hidden, denied and repressed in the shadow. In blocking or hiding certain emotions, the freedom of energy in the child diminishes and the authentic expression begins to become dulled. The child moves from freely expressing what they are feeling in their body to going to their head to figure out how they 'should' express or present themselves.

The more is pushed into shadow, the more conditional the child becomes with themselves, desperately seeking to demonstrate the 'good' aspects of themselves while avoiding or hiding the 'bad'. It is as though they unknowingly push themselves into a smaller and smaller box over time in order to ensure they stay within the range of what is acceptable in their different environments.

So much of the child's authentic expression, emotion and desire gets hidden away over time that as an adult, they can be left feeling lost, disconnected or at war with themselves.

Adapting to meet the expectations of those who support and protect us in our early years is a genius survival strategy. But after years of editing what we allow ourselves to show or share from our inner world based on what the outer world has welcomed or rejected, it isn't surprising that we might feel estranged from our authentic selves and caught looking outward for the answers rather than looking inward at the aspects of ourselves we have abandoned. It is also unsurprising that we might be stuck in repetitive cycles or patterns, as we have confined ourselves to a limited range of emotions, behaviours and beliefs.

Many of those traits, emotions and aspects of ourselves that were pushed into shadow have lain outside of our conscious awareness for years or probably decades now. When we find ourselves struggling as adults, we can often try to be 'better' or more positive, unaware that what we relegated to the shadows didn't ever disappear, but instead gathered energy and took on a life of its own and is now acting out in the background in unconscious and unhelpful ways. It is as though the parts of ourselves that we tried to cut ourselves

off from, and those parts that were denied expression or acknowledgment, came to their own way of being and gathered strength in
the background. They are now determined to undermine our conscious efforts toward health, wealth and happiness. As a result of
denying our shadow selves we can find ourselves tiptoeing through
life in adulthood, hoping to avoid any of the emotions or situations
that make us feel uncomfortable or unsure of ourselves.

Until we get to know our shadow, we might question why we
often say we want one thing but end up doing the complete opposite. We might wonder why we can't move past our addictions, or
overcome destructive cycles or patterns we find ourselves in. We
might be confused, frustrated or even angry at the self-sabotage
that seems to be omnipresent. We might notice the same interpersonal dynamics repeating themselves despite our commitments to
creating something different.

Throughout life we go to great lengths to try desperately to hide
the shameful parts of ourselves that we fear might make us unlovable to those who get close. The problem with concealing what we
are ashamed of is that it often leads to a cycle of increasing shame.
Our shame can drive us to engage in behaviours that temporarily alleviate our discomfort but ultimately reinforce our feelings
of unworthiness. As we continue to hide our shame, we create a
vicious cycle where our actions feed into the very shame we are
trying to escape, making it even harder to break free and heal.

Rather than lean toward the discomfort of the content of the
shadow self, many of us have been conditioned to look externally in order to numb, hide or avoid. The knee-jerk reaction of
looking externally for solutions to internal discomfort only further disconnects us from ourselves. Media, news outlets and

marketing companies prey on this tendency, bombarding us with messages that offer and encourage external solutions to our internal struggles.

By leaning into the discomfort and facing our shadow self with compassion and courage, we can break free from the cycle of avoidance and truly reconnect with ourselves and the life that we are inspired to live.

What is the Shadow?

It was the Swiss psychiatrist Carl Jung who first presented the idea of the shadow in the Western world, though the concept appears across many cultures and can be seen in religious texts long before Jung's time. Jung proposed that within each of us there are two parts that make up the whole. There is the idealised self – the person we want to be – and then there are the parts of us that go against this idealised vision of self: the shadow.

The shadow often encompasses the feelings, urges and desires that we experience but do not want to acknowledge or admit to. Jung suggested that because we are often unaware of the aspects of ourselves that we have rejected, we tend to distance ourselves from these aspects rather than confronting them.

Whatever is labelled good in us tends to become a part of our 'persona', derived from the Latin word for 'mask'. Meanwhile, our shadow self forms as we reject or disown emotions, traits or beliefs that have been shamed by the people around us. Disconnection is a painful experience and so we learn that to stay in connection and avoid the pain of separation it is important that we hide the parts that seem unlovable. From childhood onwards, the shadow becomes the container for all of the parts of ourselves that we reject, deny or want to abandon. This can also include painful memories and experiences.

American psychologist John Welwood once likened it to being born into an incredible castle with 1,000 rooms, each room representing an aspect of our being – our thoughts, emotions, desires and potential. At first we explore and appreciate the complexity and richness of the castle, but then as we grow older we meet others who place judgements and expectations on us, telling us which rooms should not be entered and instead need to be locked up and avoided at all costs. 'You're too emotional,' they tell us, or 'too loud', or 'too needy', and so slowly, little by little, we begin to shame and dismiss the parts deemed unworthy until one day we wake up and find ourselves living in a cramped, dimly lit corner of the castle, a tiny fraction of the potential that once was. We may even have forgotten that the rest of the castle exists at all.

Shadow work is about going back into the neglected or forbidden locked rooms and exploring the untapped gifts they hold so that we can integrate these forgotten aspects of ourselves and become more whole. In unlocking these forgotten rooms or parts of ourselves, we get to remember and reconnect to the complexity and richness of our authentic selves.

We'll go deeper into these questions in the coming chapters, but I want first to address two common queries that emerge with those new to this type of work: Why would I want to acknowledge or welcome the negative parts of me? Shouldn't we just focus on being more positive and better?

Many of the traits made 'bad' or 'wrong' were done so in childhood, at a time when we did not have the context or capacity for nuance. All traits have value in the right context but when buried or rejected will generally play out in unhealthy or unconscious ways. A young boy may see emotional expression as bad after being teased for showing his feelings, in response pushing his sensitivity and authentic expression into shadow, opting instead to be stoic, 'tough' and shut down emotionally. Though this may be a good survival strategy for the youngster in the short term and in the given context, if the situation is left unaddressed he will later become a man who has no idea how to express and communicate his emotions, leading to recurring challenges in his life and relationships.

In essence, shadow work involves going beyond the 'black' or 'white', 'good' or 'bad' labels we have given to certain emotions or traits and finding the grey. Shining light on all our traits is an essential step in gaining a greater understanding of ourselves, our fears, insecurities and unresolved issues.

Consider that every trait we view as negative, such as envy, anger, pride or stubbornness, might have a beneficial role or be a gift in certain situations; disconnecting from the trait that we have labelled 'bad' cuts us off from that potentially beneficial role or gift. For example, envy could serve as the motivating force that pushes you to strive for success in a certain field, turning it into a source of inspiration. Anger, which is often seen as a 'negative' emotion, can be the fuel for positive personal or cultural change, providing the energy and determination to confront unjust individual dynamics or societal oppressive regimes. Stubbornness might be what keeps you rooted in your beliefs when facing opposition or criticism. Pride, meanwhile, which is often viewed negatively, can lead an individual to strive for excellence or mastery in their work.

Alongside losing the potential gifts in these previously labelled 'negative' traits, we will often overidentify with the opposite of the trait, not seeing the potential drawbacks in defaulting to these opposites. Someone averse to envy may overidentify with their generosity and find themselves over-caring for others and overlooking their own self-care and needs. The person who cuts off from anger perhaps overidentifies with patience or forgiveness and may find themselves stuck in passivity and/or inaction. Someone who has pushed stubbornness deep into their shadow may take great pride in their open-mindedness, not recognising that an overidentification with being open-minded can lead to a lack of discernment and being susceptible to manipulation. The person who cuts off from pride may overidentify with modesty and find themselves resorting to self-deprecation that slowly erodes their confidence.

Overidentifying with one trait while rejecting its opposite is like going to the gym and training only one side of the body. It works up to a certain point, until it doesn't. Overuse injuries and imbalances begin to appear in the body if we only focus on the 'beach muscles'! Similarly, focusing solely on what we've labelled 'good' throws us out of balance and is hugely detrimental to our long-term health and vitality.

Often when we have made an emotion wrong we find ourselves swinging between the polarities of underexpression or overexpression of the emotion. Using anger as an example, the underexpression of anger may be seen in the 'nice' guy or girl who doesn't ever speak up for themselves, put boundaries in place or ask for what they want or need. From the outside looking in it looks as though they have no anger in them, but often it is being directed toward themselves, resulting in toxic shame, or builds and builds internally until it moves from underexpression to overexpression in the form of rage that seemingly comes from nowhere.

Shadow work is about integrating these parts and finding a healthy expression for them so that, rather than swinging between the extremes of under- or overexpression of any given trait or emotion, we have a healthy connection to the trait or emotion and can use it when we need it. We go from being controlled by our traits or emotions to having control over them. We go from seeing traits as being good or bad, black or white, to being contextual.

I have trained in martial arts throughout my life and have found the martial artists I have met along the way to be among the most disciplined and gentle people I know. This might seem a paradox in that they spend their lives learning combat, but their intimate connection to violence and understanding of their potential for causing harm allows them to relax and not feel the need to under- or overexpress these aspects of themselves. Instead, they know that if or when there is a time when they need to tap into that part of themselves, they can. This is in contrast to someone who denies or buries their potential for violence, and then has it build like a pressure cooker in the background, eventually leading to an explosion of rage that is uncontained and destructive. We might think of our own reconnection to our different shadow parts as being similar to the disciplined martial artist, who knows the power they hold and thus can discern when and how it should be used.

In integrating aspects of ourselves we previously made wrong, we learn to contain those aspects and express them in healthy ways. Perhaps in the above example you can see that the 'good' or 'bad', 'positive' or 'negative' judgements we placed on certain traits, emotions or behaviours in younger years are not as black and white as we once thought. Moving toward the parts we may have rejected can yield great gifts and potential if we are willing to be open and curious.

If we had a friend or family member whom we only made time for when they were in good humour and being positive, they would most likely feel unsupported and unloved, and that could be considered a very superficial relationship. The same is true for ourselves. To focus solely on being more positive or being better would be to have a very superficial understanding or relationship with ourselves.

It is only by acknowledging and recognising how we relate to all of our aspects that we can come to a true sense of self-acceptance and resilience.

Finding the Grey

Here is a little exercise to begin to help you to see beyond a polarised 'black and white' view of certain traits.

On one side of a page write down three traits you are proud to demonstrate in your life. These make up aspects of your persona, the version of yourself you like to outwardly express and present to the world.

On the other side of the page write down the opposite of each of these three traits. These are possible aspects of your shadow. For example, if I wrote being compassionate, curious and adventurous on the side of the page representing my persona, I might write down being indifferent, apathetic and cautious on the other side.

Now, I am going to challenge you to consider what or where each of the persona traits may have drawbacks.

Next, I challenge you to see where each of the shadow traits may be useful or advantageous. The more polarised you are in how you see these traits, the more difficult it may be to find the drawbacks or benefits, but stick with it and allow your mind to stretch a little!

An example of a drawback of overidentifying with being kind could be neglecting your own needs or allowing others to take advantage of you. An example of a benefit of being selfish could be setting healthy boundaries and ensuring your own wellbeing, which ultimately enables you to be more present and helpful to others.

Going beyond a black and white view and embracing the grey areas can begin to soften the judgements we have around how we 'should be' and help us to understand that our traits are not inherently good or bad; it is what we do with them and how we integrate them into our lives that matters.

What Gets Pushed into Shadow?

Anything that is not welcomed and threatens to lead to disapproval or the withdrawal of love gets pushed into shadow. When we get things 'right' as children we experience loving energy directed to us. When we get things 'wrong' we typically experience the opposite. That removal of love is hugely painful for a child and so it makes sense that we would alter our behaviour going forward.

Some of what is typically rejected or pushed into shadow includes:

Gender norms

Gender norms have evolved over time, pointing to how men and women 'should' or 'should not' conduct themselves. Traditionally girls have often received messages like 'smile more' or 'be more lady-like' and have been discouraged from being assertive, independent or competitive like the boys, which can often lead to these aspects being pushed into shadow. Meanwhile, boys have been discouraged from showing vulnerability, expressing their emotions or seeking support, leading them to repress these natural aspects of their personality.

Sexuality

Societal taboos, family beliefs or religious influences will often deem nudity or sexuality as inappropriate or unacceptable aspects of the human experience, leading to a suppression of sexual feelings into the shadows. This might include children learning that nudity, the human body or aspects of sexuality are something to feel guilt or shame around. In other cases it might mean taking on messages that certain sexual orientations are bad or wrong.

Dark impulses

Impulses, thoughts or behaviours that are deemed socially unacceptable or morally wrong will be pushed into shadow.

Unacknowledged desires

Oftentimes the individual's genuine and authentic desires are pushed into shadow because they go against the values of their family, culture or community. Examples might be someone wanting to pursue a career that their parents do not agree with, someone with a passion for art rejecting that part of themselves because their family do not see it as a practical pursuit, or someone wishing to be vulnerable and open within a family, culture or community that values stoicism.

Unprocessed emotions

A child told that fear is bad might push that part of themselves into the shadows and then struggle in adulthood to connect to their authentic feelings of fear – or other emotions – because they have been numbed for so long. This suppression can lead to difficulties in recognising or appropriately responding to situations that genuinely warrant fear, potentially resulting in a lack of self-protection or difficulty empathising with others who experience fear.

Traumatic memories

In the case of deeply traumatic experiences, particularly in childhood, such as physical, emotional or sexual abuse, to cope with the pain and intensity of the experience the person may consciously 'forget' the event, though it does not go away and is pushed into shadow. Later in life these repressed memories can manifest in the form of nightmares or irrational fears, as projected by our disowned past onto our future through imagination.

—— Shadow Formation – The Three Filters ——

The First Filter: Family

Our first layer of 'editing' begins at home, with our family of origin. Every family is different and so in those earliest years we begin to adapt to meet the expectations of our own specific household. As we are completely dependent on our primary caregivers, we learn that to maintain the love and safety we so desperately need we've got to be a good boy or good girl.

How this looks will be different in every home. In one household being good requires providing entertainment and singing when family friends come to visit. In another household being good requires the opposite, staying quiet and out of the way when there are visitors to the family home. In one household creativity and artistic efforts are celebrated while in another they are shunned in place of logic and intellect. In one house the young child's tears are met with empathy and compassion while in another household the child is told to grow up and stop being emotional.

Much of what is celebrated or rejected in a household will have been passed down through generations. And so, to win and maintain love and safety in our own specific home, we show what is welcome and hide what is not. In other words, rather than authentically express what we feel inside, we adaptively suppress what is judged by the outside.

It's worth noting before I share a few prompts for you to consider that it isn't just the 'dark' qualities that we learn to hide in the early years. We also learn to disown some of the more 'light' qualities that we feel unworthy of or uncomfortable with. We'll often refer to this as the 'golden shadow', which is made up of the aspects of our greatness that we feel uncomfortable with. An example might be a child who demonstrates natural leadership being shamed for 'bossing their friends around' and then losing confidence in their ability to lead.

Consider: Your Family

Take a little time to consider what was celebrated in your home growing up and what was deemed unacceptable. Here are a couple of prompts to support you:

Family Expectations
Reflect on the expectations that were in your family and home growing up. What behaviours were praised, celebrated or encouraged? Were there specific rules that dictated 'good' or 'appropriate' behaviour?

Persona Traits
What were the traits that were most valued in your family? What aspects of yourself earned love or approval? Think about behaviours or characteristics that you learned to lean on for safety and approval.

Shadow Aspects
Consider traits discouraged in your family. What aspects of yourself did you hide to avoid judgement or rejection?

Emotional Responses
Reflect on how emotions were handled. Which emotions were embraced, and which were dismissed or considered inappropriate?

Communication Styles
Explore communication patterns in your family. Was there an emphasis on open expression? How were conflicts managed, and were there certain topics that remained unspoken?

The Second Filter: Community

Next, we take our first steps into the outer world beyond our family structure and into the wider community, perhaps beginning school, meeting neighbouring friends or joining a sports team or club for the first time. In this new environment there is a whole new set of expectations as to what parts of us are welcome versus what are not. Peer pressure kicks in and there are new influences that affect how we choose to present ourselves and what we choose to hide from those around us. We maybe base some of our persona on what we see in the 'cool kids' in an effort to fit in and be accepted. These early experiences in community begin to engrain ideas about where we might stand or fit in within the social hierarchy or power dynamics.

Knowing that to be safe we need to win and maintain acceptance from the 'tribe', we again stifle our authentic expression and instead present a filtered mask (persona) that will be accepted by our peers. More of the aspects of ourselves deemed unsafe to express or share become pushed into shadow, hidden out of sight, to prevent shame or ridicule.

Confusingly, at this stage some of what was celebrated at home is in opposition to what is celebrated amongst our peers. While performing well academically may be an expectation in your home environment, perhaps to be seen as smart or clever in school leads to ridicule or exclusion. The child begins now to develop different personas to be worn in different environments and likely presents themselves differently at home with their caregivers compared to how they present to the friends they meet in their community.

Consider: Your Community

Take a few moments now to consider what was celebrated in your community growing up and what was deemed unacceptable. Here are a couple of prompts to support you:

Home vs Community
Reflect on traits celebrated at home versus in your wider community and among your peers. Were there conflicting expectations, and how did you navigate the differences? How did this impact your sense of pride and challenges in different settings?

Persona Shifts
Recall instances where you adjusted your behaviour to fit into different social settings. What aspects did you emphasise or downplay, shaping distinct personas? Can you recall specific masks worn in different settings? How did the need for acceptance shape these personas?

Safety in the Tribe
Consider traits needed for acceptance in your community. How did fear of shame or ridicule influence what you revealed or concealed?

The Third Filter: Culture

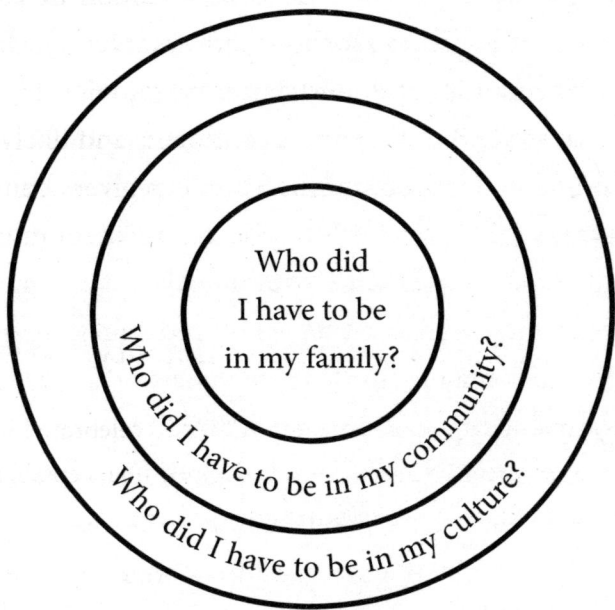

Then alongside the influence of family, friends, teachers and coaches we have the wider influence of the culture in which we are raised. This can include cultural messages related to gender, religion, media, cultural norms and geographical factors. Within all cultural and religious teachings are moral codes that dictate acceptable behaviour. We may find ourselves hiding certain desires, thoughts or actions that conflict with these codes, leading to an internal split. In many cultures, predefined gender roles serve as the basis of our self-presentation. Boys are taught to be assertive, stoic and unyielding, while girls are encouraged to embody nurturing, empathetic qualities.

The media, including television, movies and social media, often portray idealised personas that may not accurately reflect the diversity and complexity of real-life individuals. Characters and celebrities are presented with carefully curated images, showcasing specific qualities and lifestyles. This can create unrealistic standards that individuals may feel pressured to emulate, leading to the suppression of aspects of their authentic selves that do not align with these ideals.

In countries or cultures with a strong collectivist way of being, where there is an emphasis on harmony and cohesion among the group, individuals may forgo their own goals or desires and push their own authenticity and uniqueness into shadow in favour of meeting the collective expectations. Meanwhile, in more individualistic cultures such as in the Western world, there is often freedom to pursue individual goals and self-expression, though often other facets such as emotional expression or vulnerability may be perceived as weak and thus pushed into shadow.

Ethnobotanist Terence McKenna once famously stated, 'culture is not your friend', recognising how blindly following the cultural rules and expectations placed upon us can severely limit our human potential and the individuation process of becoming the truest expression of ourselves.

Consider: Your Culture

Take a few moments now to consider what was celebrated in your culture growing up and what was deemed unacceptable. Here are a couple of prompts to support you:

Cultural Persona Influences

Reflect on cultural messages related to gender, religion and geographical factors. How did these messages shape the traits and behaviours you deemed acceptable for your persona?

Moral Codes and Persona

Consider the moral codes within your cultural and religious teachings. Were there desires, thoughts or actions you hid due to conflicts with these codes? How did this contribute to an internal split in your identity?

Predefined Gender Roles

Explore the impact of predefined gender roles in your culture. How were boys and girls expected to present themselves? Did these expectations influence the traits and behaviours you integrated into your persona?

Media-Driven Ideals

Reflect on media influences, including television, movies and social media. How did idealised personas in the media shape your perception of acceptable traits and behaviours? Did you feel pressured to conform to these standards?

Emulation and Suppression

Consider instances where you suppressed aspects of your authentic self that did not align with cultural ideals. How did the pressure to emulate certain personas lead to the hiding of authentic traits?

And so, within our first few years of life, the countless messages we take on both implicitly and explicitly about what is acceptable and what is not from our family of origin, our community and the culture in which we are raised create a profound shift in how we see and present ourselves. Much of the editing that shapes our personality happens in the first seven years of our life, though later as we come into our teen years our persona becomes further influenced. Our teen years bring with them physical changes, hormonal shifts and an increasing awareness of social dynamics, including romantic and sexual interests. The image of self that we present to the world becomes more complex. Social pressures, peer relationships, media influences and cultural norms all play roles in shaping how we choose to express ourselves and present our identity to the world.

In Chapter Five, when we look at the inner child and inner teenager, we will explore further how your teen years have influenced who you became and how you show up in the world. For now, though, I encourage you to take some time to write and reflect on how the first seven years of your life shaped you.

Persona and Shadow Exercise

Taking into account the three spheres of family, community and culture that we looked at in this chapter and the notes you've taken from the previous exercises, write a little about what you learned in your earliest years about what was safe to feel and express. What was celebrated and garnered praise, love and approval within your family, community and culture? What was judged, criticised or shamed?

As a result of your early experiences, what are some of the aspects that made up your persona? In other words, how do you like to be seen and what traits or emotions did you place in the 'good' box?

Make a list on one side of a piece of paper of all of the aspects of yourself that you take pride in and on the other side of the page write down the opposite. What you are seeing on the opposite side of the page is some of your shadow, the things that you consciously or unconsciously put in the 'bad box'.

Beside each of the shadow traits you have listed, stretch yourself to see where they might have hidden gifts for you, or might be useful or appropriate in certain situations or scenarios. You can also look to see if you might be demonstrating any of these traits in unexpected or hidden ways.

To finish the exercise, set an intention to continue to explore your shadow self with curiosity, compassion and courage as you move through the book.

—— The Golden Shadow (Light Shadow) ——

For many people, it can be just as challenging to recognise and embrace their own magnificence and brilliance as it is to acknowledge and accept their darker aspects. Though this may seem strange at first, both positive and negative traits can be difficult to fully integrate into one's self-image. The 'golden shadow' specifically refers to positive qualities, talents or potential that individuals may unconsciously repress or deny within themselves. These are aspects that, for various reasons, they may not fully acknowledge or embrace.

In certain countries where modesty and conformity are highly valued by the collective, 'tall poppy syndrome' can lead to individuals being ridiculed, shamed or cut down for standing out, going in their own direction or excelling in certain areas. This can lead to a default of conformity in order to stay in connection and avoid rejection. The golden shadow therefore can encompass strengths, creative abilities and positive attributes that individuals possess but might find challenging to accept or express openly.

Embracing and integrating the golden shadow involves acknowledging and celebrating our positive qualities and capabilities. By recognising and accepting the positive aspects of the golden shadow, individuals can achieve a more balanced and authentic sense of self.

Consider: Golden Shadow

Overlooked Talents

What talents or strengths have you downplayed or dismissed, and why? Reflect on positive aspects of yourself you may have overlooked due to societal expectations or personal experiences. What fears or concerns were attached to expressing your capabilities openly? How have these fears contributed to keeping your golden shadow in the background?

Childhood Suppression

Consider messages in your early years that led you to hide positive attributes. Were there qualities you were encouraged to suppress as a child? How did these childhood influences shape your relationship with your golden shadow?

Cultural Impact

Examine societal norms that influenced your perception of positive traits. Were there expectations that led you to hide aspects like intelligence or creativity? Explore how cultural conditioning might have affected your golden shadow.

Repressed Achievements

Think about significant achievements you downplayed. What positive aspects of yourself have you unintentionally pushed into the shadows when acknowledging your accomplishments? Reflect on the reasons behind this repression.

Spiritual Bypassing

The term 'spiritual bypassing' describes using spiritual practices or beliefs to avoid facing our wounds, triggers, emotions, discomfort or pain. Although it can come from a genuine place of wanting spiritual growth or healing, it often leads to people 'bypassing the body' and the human experience, instead choosing love and light at all costs. We can think of it as a tendency to lean toward the light, enamoured by the upward journey of transcendence and avoiding the descent into darkness, the unknown and the messier parts of life.

The challenge in this bypassing of the human experience is the denial of the inevitable messy and perhaps darker aspects of being human. It is as though we want to live in the clouds rather than have our feet in the bare earth. We can see signs of spiritual bypassing in the avoidance of certain emotions, the avoidance of conflict at all costs, a denial of personal responsibility or in the use of excessive positivity. Though avoiding or suppressing certain emotions may provide temporary relief or comfort, it ultimately prevents the deeper potential for growth and healing in accepting and integrating some of the person's more difficult parts.

At the end of a therapy session with one of my mentors and elders, a deeply experienced shadow worker, he gave me some 'homework' to complete. Before our next session he encouraged me to write a letter (that wouldn't be sent) to someone I felt betrayed by, saying everything I needed to say to feel clear within myself and let go of the pain I had been carrying around the connection. I put all my frustration, anger and sadness into the letter and didn't hold back, though at the end before signing off I wrote that 'despite how things ended and how you lied I know you are a good person with a good heart and I wish you the best'.

Unexpectedly, in our next session he had me read the letter aloud as if reading it to the person, and stopped me at key parts, having me repeat them with more energy to connect to the emotion that I had been suppressing. When I got to the line that pointed to them being a good person with a good heart he stopped me.

'Why did you write that? Is how they treated you how a good person with a good heart treats someone?'

'I think everyone is a good person with a good heart deep down, but sometimes we just make mistakes or act out of fear or pain ...'

My discomfort with my own anger and my efforts to be 'spiritual' had me looking to deny what I was really feeling. My wanting to quickly move to the 'we all make mistakes' outlook was my effort to bypass. Anger wasn't something I had ever felt comfortable with, and so skipping straight to forgiveness eased the anxiety of being with the fiery energy of anger that I had always avoided by trying to be a 'nice guy'.

There would be space for this forgiveness in time, of course, but in that moment, I was bypassing my authentic emotions and abandoning myself and my genuine feelings. My mentor pointed out that while forgiveness and understanding are important, they should not come at the expense of acknowledging and honouring our true feelings. By prematurely labelling them as a good person and wishing them well, I was attempting to fast-forward to a place of peace without fully experiencing the journey of pain and hurt that I needed to go through first.

When we repeatedly deny our authentic emotions, we build a mound of unresolved feelings that over time can manifest as anxiety, depression or even physical illnesses. The emotions we fear are not the problem; it is what we do when overtaken by those emotions that can be problematic. In order to process or digest our experiences we must be willing to fully feel the emotions, not swallow them back down, deny them or make them wrong.

Throughout this book we will look at how we can give space to express our 'darker' emotions in a healthy and empowering way. Something I would love you to consider as you move through this book and the exercises presented is allowing yourself to hold space for multiple truths, emotions and experiences simultaneously. That might mean reflecting on childhood and being angry at your parents for splitting up while also having compassion for the challenges they were going through. Or it could mean feeling disappointed about a failed work project while also feeling relief that the stress of the project is over. Or it might involve acknowledging your fear of change while also feeling excited about new opportunities. Emotional maturity involves this capacity to hold these seemingly contradictory emotions and perspectives without rushing to resolve them or make them fit neatly together. This can be challenging, but can also be very liberating. It is about learning to see things as they are, not worse than they are or better than they are.

As you move through the book and the accompanying exercises I invite you to lean into your authentic feelings, allowing them space, while also noticing tendencies to bypass and dismiss how you authentically feel in an effort to be 'positive' or 'nice'.

—————— Summary: Gold in the Shadow ——————

- Shadow work involves going beyond a polarised way of seeing our traits and seeing that the traits are not inherently good or bad; it is what we do with them and how we integrate them into our lives that matters.

- In our earliest years, we picked up on all that was going on around us and learned what was safe to show and what was unsafe to show.
- As we engage with our family, community and culture, in order to stay in connection we begin to amplify the aspects of traits that gain praise (persona) and hide what is shamed, ridiculed or rejected (shadow).
- Bypassing our authentic feelings and defaulting to 'love and light' or positive thinking is us recreating a pattern of shaming our authentic expression.

Incomplete Sentences

Read the beginning of each sentence aloud and allow yourself to complete the sentence spontaneously in an unfiltered way. After completing all the prompts you can jot down any insights or reflections that stand out to you.

- It's important to me that people see me as …
- Something I hide from everyone is …
- Growing up, I received love when …
- Growing up, love was removed when …
- In school I learned to hide my …
- My culture taught me I needed to be …
- A way that I keep myself small is …
- Now I'm ready for …

Journalling Prompts

1. Reflect on a significant event or interaction from your childhood that you believe influenced the formation of your shadow. How does this memory still impact you today?

2. Consider the societal expectations and cultural norms that have shaped your understanding of what is acceptable or unacceptable about yourself. How do these influences contribute to your shadow?

3. Explore a positive trait or quality about yourself that you tend to downplay or suppress. How might embracing this aspect of your golden shadow enhance your self-awareness and personal growth?

4. Reflect on a recent experience where you felt a strong sense of pride or shame. What underlying beliefs or values contributed to these emotions, and how did they influence your behaviour or decisions?

5. Imagine how your life might be different if you fully embraced both your light and shadow aspects without judgement or suppression. What steps can you take to integrate and honour all facets of yourself?

Grounding Breath

This week's embodiment practice, and one that I would encourage you to engage with daily, even if just for a few breaths, is the 'grounding breath'.

One of the most important skills we can develop in life is our ability to stabilise our attention. By this I mean the ability to place our attention where we want it to be and not be constantly pulled away from ourselves with distraction, drama or noise. When we get triggered, stressed, overwhelmed or experience difficulties in life we often lose our sense of ground, leaving our bodies overlooked, with all our attention going to our heads or outside ourselves, as we focus on what or who we believe to be the source or stress or salvation.

In engaging with shadow work we can often be confronted with uncomfortable emotions or realisations. Learning to ground ourselves is a practice of anchoring back into the present moment even in the presence of the inevitable emotional storms of life or the emergence of uncomfortable feelings or realisations.

For the grounding breath simply sit comfortably with your back upright, your feet firmly placed on the ground and your chin slightly tucked in to elongate the spine. Feel your feet connected to the ground, your bum connected to the chair beneath you, and then bring your attention to the tip of your nostrils. If it feels comfortable you might gently close your eyes (though doing this exercise with your eyes open is perfect too).

Allow your tongue to rest on the roof of your mouth and place your hands softly down around your navel. Breathing in through the nose, breathe into your hands as if filling a balloon that sits in your belly. Then allow your exhale, again through the nose, to be twice as long as the inhale. Repeat for a minimum of 10 breaths and bring your attention to how it feels in the physical body to breathe deeply and slowly.

The more often you practise this breath, the more comfortable you will become with the skill of grounding and coming back into your body and the present moment, irrespective of the challenging thoughts or emotions you may be experiencing.

CHAPTER TWO

Shadow Activation

*'Until you make the unconscious conscious,
it will direct your life and you will call it fate.'* CARL JUNG

*'Whatever is happening at this moment, that is your life.
The future is not your life; it never arrives. What is actually
here is always only this moment.'* A.H. ALMAAS

—————— Recognising Hidden Forces ——————

Niamh's unaddressed childhood insecurities lead her to repeatedly sabotage promising relationships, recreating a cycle of heartbreak and isolation.

Meanwhile Mark's unexamined fear of inadequacy fuels a relentless workaholism, masking his deep-seated feelings of worthlessness with the veneer of success.

Jane projects her unresolved anger onto her colleagues, creating unnecessary conflicts and alienation.

Tom constantly undermines his own achievements by procrastinating and missing deadlines, driven by a deep-seated fear of failure that prevents him from realising his true potential.

These scenarios illustrate how our shadow selves, when left unchecked, steer us into patterns of projection, addiction, recurring relational dynamics and self-sabotage.

The nature of the shadow is that it lies outside our conscious level of awareness. It is aloof and looks to hide. In this chapter we will explore some of the ways in which we can know that our shadow has become activated. As we delve deeper, we will unravel the various defence mechanisms and addictive patterns that present when we feel threatened or triggered.

As a general rule, when our reactions seem disproportionate to the present situation, it's often a sign that a shadow aspect is at work – something deeper that needs our attention and healing. Noticing our reactions or triggers will be the first step in integrating our shadow so that we can show up in the present and not remain stuck in old unconscious patterns or cycles. The patterns, behaviours and emotions that we perhaps previously saw as obstacles can instead be viewed as being the way to greater levels of self-acceptance and understanding.

Why Do Shadow Work?

A common analogy used to describe the nature of the mind is an iceberg, with the small visible part of the iceberg above the water representing the conscious mind and the emotions, beliefs and actions within our conscious awareness. The much larger part of the iceberg, under the water and out of sight, represents the unconscious mind and the memories, emotions and beliefs that influence our behaviour without our conscious awareness. Carl Jung is quoted as saying 'until you make the unconscious conscious, it will run your

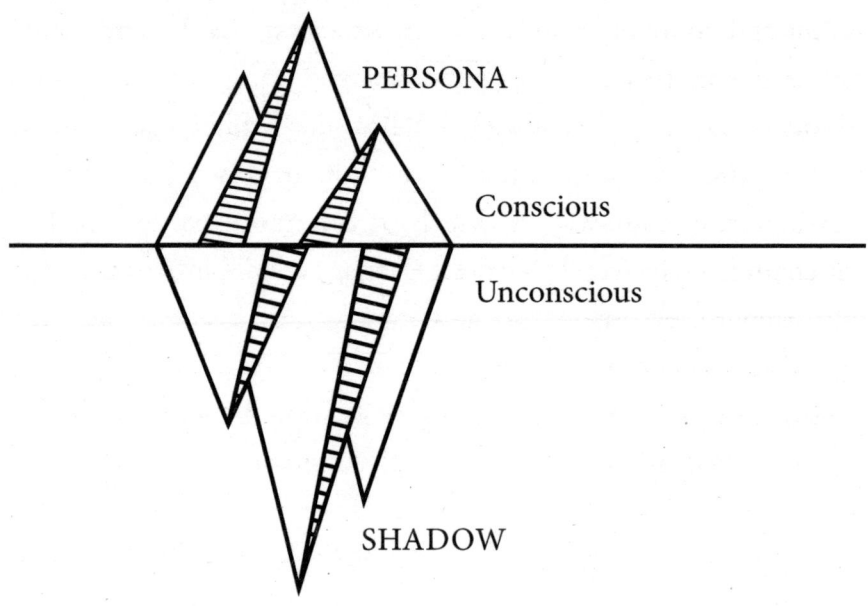

life and you will call it fate'. That is to say, until you become aware of your unconscious drivers and patterns you will often find yourself playing out the same repetitive cycles in life, perhaps believing that you will forever remain stuck. For example, a person may know consciously that they'd love to have an intimate relationship, but if there is deep-seated unconscious fear of vulnerability or rejection, that fear can significantly influence their behaviour and decisions.

On a recent trip to Phuket, Thailand (where I spent a few months training at Asia's top Brazilian Jiu-Jitsu gym) I hiked to the Big Buddha viewpoint, which offers incredible views of the island. I passed a number of elephants chained up for the entertainment of tourists, who fed them and took photos. I was reminded of a story I had heard about how these elephants are conditioned from the time they are babies. As babies the elephants are chained to a fixed object and confined to a very small area in which they can roam only a few metres. At first they try to resist the chain and move beyond their tiny area, but they soon learn that they don't have the strength and their efforts are futile. As the elephant gets older and bigger, of course it gets much stronger and could easily pull the chain from its fixed point, but despite its new-found physicality and strength, by this point it has become conditioned to compliance and resignation.

This pattern can closely parallel the experience of limiting beliefs we developed in childhood that keep us stuck as adults. Shadow work can allow us to recognise, explore and transcend the stories, thoughts, beliefs or emotions that have kept us chained and limited up to this point.

The Process of Individuation

Ultimately, shadow work is supporting the process of individuation, embracing more of who we are and becoming more 'whole' by exploring and integrating both the conscious and unconscious aspects of our personality.

Individuation is about embracing our true and unique self and gaining a greater understanding of our values, passions, beliefs and personal truths. It is about becoming an individual and embracing both our strengths and weaknesses and recognising our achievements and mistakes. In a way we can think of it as living a life from the inside out and listening to our own unique inner voice, as opposed to living from the outside in and being solely conditioned by the external environment.

The woman who proclaims, 'I'll never be like my mother,' is not choosing how she wants to show up in the world and not listening to her own unique voice, but instead reacting to the environment she was raised in and forming an 'oppositional identity'. Similarly, the individual taking over the family business out of a sense of obligation or guilt rather than a genuine sense of passion or purpose is not listening to their own unique inner voice and calling, instead emulating what they have seen growing up.

Rather than blindly emulating or rejecting aspects of our upbringing, the journey of becoming our true selves involves embracing our own uniqueness and individuality. This is an ongoing process. For that woman who has consciously or unconsciously committed to 'never being like her mother', rather than being like or not being like her mother, her journey of individuation would involve really getting to know all parts of herself so she can choose how she wants to show up in the world. Perhaps for the person who takes over the family business out of guilt and obligation, their journey involves finding the courage to communicate honestly how they feel with their family before stepping onto a path that feels more appropriate for them.

The poet Robert Bly once noted that it is as though for the first 20 years of our lives we hide away parts of ourselves in order to stay safe in the world, and then for the rest of our lives our work is to welcome back those parts that we have hidden. For many, the urge to explore and embrace more of themselves comes in midlife at a time in which they have ticked the boxes that they were taught they needed to tick for success. Perhaps after building a career or starting a family, the individual begins to question what else there is to life. Others are forced onto a hero's journey to find who they really are when life throws a curveball or plot twist that uproots the life they had planned and sends them into a period of uncertainty.

Midlife is a time when many start seeking more depth or answers as, perhaps for the first time, we become conscious of our own mortality. We may realise how much of our behaviour over the years has been driven by the desire to be accepted or approved of. I have heard the midlife crisis redefined as a possible midlife liberation, with the individual reaching a point of allowing themselves to be honest about their wants, needs, feelings and desires, possibly for the first time in their adult life. We sometimes see this in the archetypal midlife crisis, where a recklessness emerges in efforts to reclaim the feelings of youth with the individual reverting to teen-like behaviours. The man who leaves his wife for a much younger partner and buys a sports car in a desperate attempt to recapture his lost youth is a classic example of this phenomenon. This behaviour, driven by a fear of ageing and mortality, often reflects a deeper psychological struggle to reconcile one's identity and life choices up to that point.

The midlife crisis also emerges as the individual taking a deeper evaluation of the identity they have created and the purpose they have pursued in the world. We may see how our commitment to being a 'good boy' or 'good girl' all our lives has stifled our own authentic expression and led to us forgoing our own wants and needs. We may come to a point of realising for how long we have suppressed or buried our own selfishness, seeing it as bad, shameful or wrong.

Shadow work can offer a path to navigating this crisis of identity in a healthier and more conscious way that allows for true fulfilment and self-expression in a grounded and adult way.

Charles Handy, a well-known thinker in the management space, spoke of 'proper selfishness', that is, a mindset of prioritising our own needs and desires while also considering the impact of our actions on others and on the wider community. We might then think of proper selfishness as balancing self-interest and social responsibility. Shadow work can support us in finding this balance and integrating proper selfishness, rather than letting our shadow unconsciously take over and burn our current world to the ground in an act of rebellion.

For some, this process of individuation and inner work begins after raising their family, or after going through a challenging time in life or an identity crisis. While often uncomfortable or destabilising, a crisis of identity at any stage of life can be seen as a potential invitation to live in a more meaningful and authentic way. Regardless of when the individual commits, the process of individuation and moving toward wholeness becomes a lifelong journey.

Your Hero's Journey

The American writer and mythologist Joseph Campbell, who was strongly influenced by Carl Jung, spent his life studying and collecting stories and myths from around the world.

Perhaps Campbell's biggest contribution through his work was the framework he offered of the 'hero's journey' or 'monomyth', a common story structure found across all cultures and times. Typically the structure involves a call to adventure in which the hero of the story steps into the unknown and is met with a series of trials, tribulations and challenges. They meet mentors along the way, discover strengths they did not know they had, and eventually

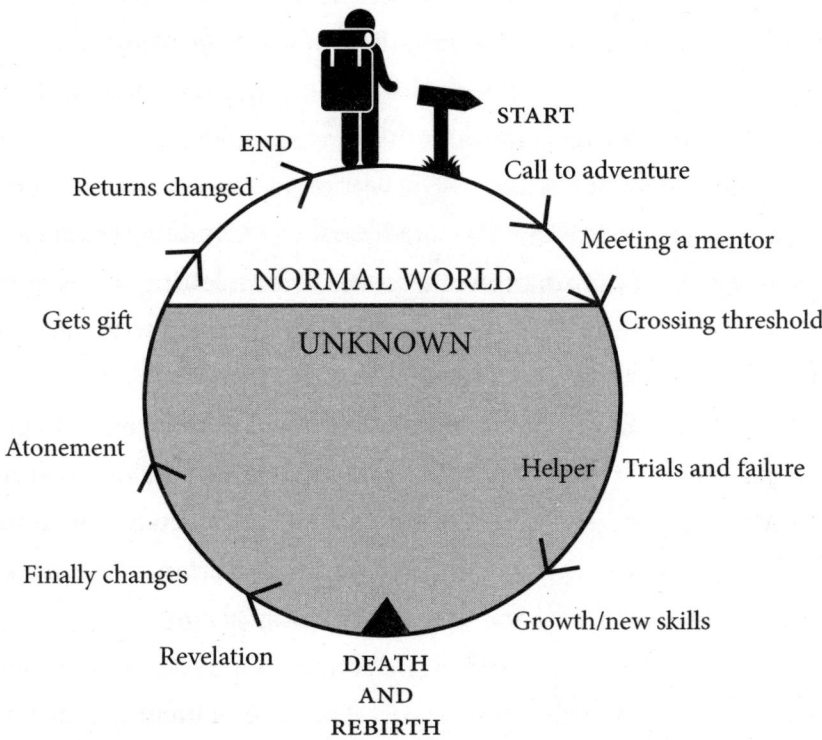

conquer these challenges and return to their village victorious, with gifts acquired on their journey that they can share with their community.

This structure that we see in so many myths and stories offers a metaphor or reflection of the process of individuation or self-discovery.

First we have our own call to adventure, either as a result of an external challenge or an internal calling that leads us to step into the unknown. As we take that step away from our 'ordinary world' we lose our sense of control and certainty and can be spun into a time of uncertainty and upheaval. While the heroes in our favourite books or movies might face dragons or demons as they step into the unknown, for us stepping into the unknown involves facing the parts of ourselves we have pushed away – aspects of our shadow.

Perhaps, in being made redundant after working in the same industry for decades, external change forces the individual onto a hero's journey of leaving their ordinary world and stepping into the darkness of the unknown. Perhaps after building a company for years and selling it, someone is left with an internal question of 'Who am I now?' which forces their hero's journey. The individual who has built massive career and financial success while neglecting relationships may find their own call to adventure involves dealing with the fears around rejection and intimacy while embracing their vulnerability through honest communication. The person who becomes single for the first time after spending most of their adult life in an intimate relationship is invited into the adventure of making peace with their lonely and codependent parts.

In essence we have all developed strengths and ways of being in the world, though, a little like only training one half of the body, eventually an imbalance and dysfunction can occur.

Consider: Your Call to Adventure

- Where in your life are you currently hearing the 'call to adventure'?
- This may be a challenge in your outer world that requires you to step into the unknown, or a calling from within that is telling you that something needs to shift. What does your instinct tell you?

—— Spotting and Meeting Our Shadow ——

Regardless of what inspires or triggers our hero's journey and call to adventure, stepping away from our ordinary world and comfort zone is guaranteed to involve meeting more of our shadow.

We all have an inner world and outer world. With much of our attention pulled to the outer world, we can sometimes put our focus there and forget about our internal experience, assuming that if we just keep our sights on where we are trying to go, we will eventually get to the promised land. I sometimes refer to this way of living as the 'I'll be happy when' lies.

What we might not be aware of is how small and limited our lives become when we have cut off half of who we are internally. When I cut off from fear, I'm reluctant to take risks. When I deny my vulnerability, I struggle to connect deeply with others. When I suppress my anger, I lose touch with my true feelings and needs. When I ignore my sadness, I miss opportunities for healing and growth.

I might set my sights on material goals I would like to achieve, but what will dictate whether or not I achieve those goals is how I relate to what is going on internally for me. Am I reactive to life or proactive in life? In other words, do I react and retreat to safety when I touch some of my shadow, those difficult parts I have avoided, or can I stay centred and work proactively with the shadow when it emerges?

With the shadow living outside our conscious level of awareness, working with shadow requires a commitment to looking out for some of the subtle signs that point to its presence. Let's begin now to outline some of the ways we can notice that our shadow is being activated. Take a little time to consider the following prompts to see how these patterns may play out in your own life.

—————— **Signs of Shadow Activation** ——————

Experiencing the same challenges in relationships

As we will explore later in the book, many of our psychological and emotional challenges emerge in our closest relationships. In Chapter One we looked at how we first become wounded in our early relationships when we are taught implicitly or explicitly that it is not safe to be our authentic selves. Later in life when people get close and we become vulnerable, our shadow can become activated and lead to us playing out defence patterns that keep us safe but deny the opportunity for intimacy, leading to feelings of disconnection and isolation. In response many will blame their partner and leave the relationship – only to find the same issues emerging in their next intimate relationship. Those who choose to stay in the relationship without consciously working with their shadow may experience the frustration and pain of the same issue emerging repeatedly, leaving them feeling unseen, unheard or misunderstood.

Take the example of a man raised in a household where emotions are suppressed. Later in life he ends up in a relationship with a woman who values open communication. As she looks to lean in and deepen connection, his fear of vulnerability leads to him pulling away and withdrawing. After the relationship ends he repeats the same pattern in subsequent relationships, unaware of the role his shadow is playing in creating the repetitive dynamic. To move past the dynamic this man will need to become intimate with his fear of vulnerability and learn to open up to others.

To become intimate with our emotions means being with them without being overtaken by them. We can allow ourselves to feel our emotions without immediately defaulting to trying to fix, change or get away from what we are feeling. Being with an emotion also recognises that the emotion is a part of our experience but not the entirety of it. It is the difference between saying 'I am angry', where we identify with the emotion, versus 'I am experiencing some anger', which informs us that that is not who we are but just a part of our experience.

Something I have noted in years of group facilitation and leading workshops is how many people will comment that they were surprised how easily they could be vulnerable and share with total strangers things they would not even share with the closest people in their lives. This doesn't come as a shock to me, seeing as much of the fear that will emerge in sharing our truth with a loved one is that we will be judged, shamed, rejected or abandoned. That fear of rejection or abandonment will likely be much stronger in our closest relationships than it will in sharing something personal with a stranger in a workshop. These foundational fears point to how much of our shadow can be wrapped up in our intimate and close relationships.

Bringing curiosity to the repetitive patterns that play out for you in intimate relationships, and working with some of the exercises I'll share later in the book, can support moving from conflict to connection and from 'shadow boxing' with a partner to 'shadow dancing'.

Consider: Relationship Patterns

- What is a pattern of pain or frustration you have seen play out repeatedly in your intimate relationships?
- What emotion might you be avoiding or protecting by going to this default pattern?

Self-sabotaging behaviours

'How's everything going?' asked a friend of mine who I hadn't seen in a while.

'Surprisingly well,' I responded. 'It makes me a little worried. Life and work feels weirdly easy and in flow at the moment ...'

'And where did you learn it had to be hard?'

We all have a self-imposed 'glass ceiling' on what we see ourselves as being worthy of. When we get near that glass ceiling we often go to unconscious behaviours to sabotage our efforts and put us back to what feels safe and familiar.

When our shadow becomes triggered we can find ourselves acting out of alignment with what we say we want the most and sabotaging our efforts by resisting positive change, turning to addictive behaviours to avoid the discomfort of feeling our feelings, procrastinating or succumbing to the voice of our inner critic. When we repeatedly engage in activities or behaviours that undermine our own happiness, wellbeing and success we are seeing the shadow play out, driven by deep-seated beliefs and fears in the unconscious.

The self-sabotaging behaviours, which are played out unconsciously and go against what we consciously say we want, are our shadows' ways of protecting ourselves and keeping us safe. A part of us may long for a promotion and advancement in our work lives, but feelings of inadequacy held in the shadows may lead to us sabotaging our efforts and downplaying our abilities for fear of being judged by our colleagues. An individual may have a deep and genuine desire to create positive lifestyle changes but hold a lot of fear around change and feelings of unworthiness around treating their body well. An individual with a deep-seated abandonment wound may long for a healthy and long-lasting relationship but unconsciously push their partner away in order to back up their unconscious belief that 'people always leave'.

In exploring how we self-sabotage our efforts and examining what we are trying to avoid during those times, we can begin to change how we relate to our uncomfortable parts, making the shift from being reactive in life to being responsive. An unconscious fear of intimacy may have led me to reacting by pushing people away when they get too close, while an awareness of this fear could allow me to respond in a different way, perhaps sharing my fear in a vulnerable way.

Consider: Self-Sabotage

- What do you do to self-sabotage?
- What triggers this behaviour?

Being stuck in old belief patterns

Ask a group of people at random to stand up and dance in front of an audience and many of the group may be quick to tell you, 'I can't dance.'

Were you to challenge or question their belief by asking when they last danced, they might respond by saying, 'Not since I was a kid'.

And so it might be more accurate for this person to say, 'I don't dance,' as opposed to 'I can't dance.'

Growing up, early experiences of being bullied and moving to a new school when my family moved from Limerick to Galway led me to the belief that 'I'm in this alone' or that 'I'm always the new guy on the outside looking in.' These beliefs and the insecurities I felt about not being enough drove a huge amount of my behaviour in my teens and twenties and influenced a lot of my drive to become 'successful'.

In my twenties, I fulfilled a childhood dream of owning my own gym, won entrepreneurial awards and built a life and lifestyle that my younger self would have been amazed by, though despite being surrounded by people who were supportive on the journey, my deep-seated beliefs remained 'I'm in this alone' and 'I'm always the new guy.'

Unconsciously my shadow self ran the show and I created experiences in my life that backed up these beliefs. As soon as people got too close I would eject and find a new social circle where I would be the new guy again. Paradoxically, our shadow often leads to us creating the very thing we say we fear or do not want to experience.

Recognising this pattern and story gave me the awareness to start noticing when this old belief was creeping in and looking to keep me stuck in my past. That awareness and a commitment to leaning into connection allowed me to start creating deeper, more meaningful friendships and relationships.

Consider: Old Belief Patterns

- What were some of the standout moments from your childhood and what beliefs did you form as a result of those experiences?
- How do those beliefs influence you today?

Repeating family dynamics

As children we are like sponges, soaking up countless daily messages implicitly and explicitly from our family of origin. Much of our worldview and life blueprint will be shaped in these earliest years, including deeply held beliefs, behaviours and judgements passed down through the generations. When we neglect shadow work we remain unaware of how old family dynamics play out in our lives and keep us in certain negative cycles.

If I grow up in a household in which conflict is avoided at all costs and difficult conversations are sidestepped, it is likely I will not learn to effectively communicate my feelings or needs, or resolve conflicts in a healthy way. As a result I may find myself repeatedly in interpersonal dynamics in which I end up resenting the other person for not meeting the needs which I have not been able to communicate.

Beyond the beliefs about ourselves we constructed at some point, there will likely have been a great many beliefs that we inherited from our family of origin. There is a story I heard a number of years ago about a couple sharing Christmas together for the first time. In preparing the turkey the man chops off both sides of the turkey before placing it in the oven. Curious about this, the man's wife asks why he's chopped off both sides. He shares that this is the way his mother taught him and how his grandmother taught his mother.

Her curiosity getting the better of her, the lady rings her grandmother-in-law to ask why she would chop off both sides of the turkey before placing it in the oven. 'Simple,' the grandmother responded. 'Growing up we had a very small oven in our house and the whole turkey wouldn't fit so we'd always cut off either side.'

This story shows how often we can inherit beliefs without ever thinking about or questioning them. Shadow work allows us to uncover old belief patterns we picked up somewhere along the line that continue to play out in our lives, impacting how we show up in the world. It allows us to become more intentional with how we show up in the world, giving us the chance to go beyond the blueprint we were handed in childhood.

Consider: Repeating Family Dynamics

- What did you learn from your childhood about intimate relationships? How have you seen this play out in your own life?
- What beliefs did you inherit? What beliefs have you carried throughout life that are not your own?

Experiencing recurring emotional reactions

Much of our shadow is made up of the emotions it was not safe to feel or express in earlier years. Take the example of a child who is shamed at school when they stumble over their words while reading in front of the class. The fear of being shamed again may lead to that child learning to 'hide' or avoid situations in which they may be subjected to ridicule. Years later, they may become frustrated by the grip that fear has on their life and how they find themselves hiding from life and the opportunities they would love to explore.

Becoming aware of and integrating our shadow allows us to better understand our reactivity and choose healthier, more intentional emotional responses as opposed to playing out old emotional autopilot patterns. In this way we become empowered, able to choose who we want to be in any given moment rather than unconsciously playing out old survival strategies.

Consider: Recurring Emotional Reactions

- What emotion was not safe to feel in childhood and needed to be buried or hidden?
- How do you react or what do you do today when that emotion starts to rise?

Working with Life

I have read books and taken courses around psychology and personal development for over 20 years now. There is a part of me that studies because I am passionate about this work, of course, though I know there is also another part of me that studies because it is easier to keep it academic and 'heady' rather than deal with the actual discomfort of certain emotions or experiences.

Personal development work, like anything taken to the extreme, can be another form of escapism. One of the ways we can look to find a sense of safety and comfort in the world and deal with anxiety or fear is to cling to control. One of my ways of clinging to control in earlier years has been to make plans and outline rigid goals as a means of masking my fears of the unknown and lack of trust in life's natural unfolding.

Often over the years I have worked with clients who have been very clear about an area they want to work on. For example, a client married for over 10 years might come with a very clear intention of improving their communication and deepening their connection with their partner. Without naming it specifically as their call to adventure, they will be clear that this is an area requiring some attention. In subsequent sessions I would often notice that when the client was checking in with updates on how their week had been, they would often have found 100 distractions or areas they would want to talk about other than the one thing they had said they wanted to focus on in our coaching. Sometimes they would tell me about new books they'd bought, courses they had signed up to or work projects they had taken on.

This type of pattern is common. The individual is clear on something they want to address. They are inspired and have uninformed optimism about addressing this area, but when the rubber hits the road and shadow appears in the form of fear, grief, anger or shame, it is easier to look externally for distractions or other areas to focus on or 'fix'.

In truth, our real inner work lies in working with whatever life is offering us in the form of the challenges or tension it is presenting. A belief system I lean on that I find supportive and empowering is that we all come into this world with a 'soul contract', made up of lessons we need to learn, experiences we need to have and people we need to be in connection with. Everyone will have a different 'soul contract' and so everyone will have different lessons to learn in their lifetime. I believe we keep creating the same experiences until we learn the lesson, then a new lesson is brought to us.

In Joseph Campbell's framework of the hero's journey he presented a stage after the call to adventure called the 'refusal of the call'. For us, this might be ignoring the voice within us that longs for fulfilment and meaning, and instead choosing safety and comfort. It might be ignoring the truth that we are unhappy in our relationship and turning to drink or drugs to distract ourselves, or perhaps longing to put ourselves out there in a public way but saying no to an opportunity to share a presentation at a local event.

How do we know what is in our contract and what we need to learn and embrace? By looking at what life is giving us and what is empowering or disempowering us.

Consider: What is Life Asking of You?

- We have all been conditioned to hold certain beliefs around what we need in order to be happy and successful. This can influence how we approach life, looking externally to figure out our direction rather than going inward and seeing what we really need for personal or spiritual growth that goes beyond the material.
- When you consider your life at present and look at both your outer world and inner world, what lessons do you feel life currently wants you to learn?

Alongside some of these signs of shadow activation, let's look at three more common ways in which we can begin to notice how and where our shadows show up in our day-to-day lives.

Projection – Heroes and Villains

Do you ever find yourself condemning certain characters in your life while celebrating or admiring others?

Carl Jung once stated, 'Everything that irritates us about others can lead us to an understanding of ourselves.' The same could be said of the people we greatly admire. Projection is a defence mechanism in which we place our own unwanted or unacceptable traits, thoughts or emotions onto others.

Someone who has perfectionist tendencies may project onto their boss that they are over-demanding and unreasonable. Here the individual is projecting their own internal pressure for perfection onto their boss, seeing in their boss what they fear to see in themselves. In another case the individual who unknowingly fears emotional intimacy and deep connection may project onto their partner that they are emotionally distant or emotionally unavailable, projecting their own fear of vulnerability onto the other person.

I know for years I was triggered by people who came across as assertive or very sure of themselves, labelling them as aggressive or domineering. Really I was projecting my disowned clarity and anger onto them because I was uncomfortable owning those parts within myself. Projection is a universal experience. In fact, Jungian analyst Marie-Louise von Franz once said, 'If we didn't project, we couldn't connect.' While projection can lead to misunderstandings and conflicts in relationships, it can also offer a means of connecting with others and exploring our own psyche.

At some point we have all found ourselves passing our disowned parts to others. Projection swings both ways, with us both handing our golden shadow to those we place on pedestals and also our dark shadow to those we place in the pit. In other words the traits we admire in our heroes mirror some of the traits we have rejected or not fully embraced in ourselves, while the same can be said for the things we judge about the 'villains' in our lives. Recognising who we are projecting onto and what we are projecting onto them allows us to get closer to recognising the parts of ourselves we have relegated to shadow.

A number of years ago a client I was working with told me how frustrated she was with how she was living. She noted that she was wasting hours every evening watching TV shows and felt her life was slipping away from her. When I inquired into the type of shows she was watching, she spoke about military-style reality shows in which former soldiers would put the participants through gruelling challenges and tasks. When I asked her what she liked about the shows and their characters, she noted their courage and passion for adventure. When we spoke further she could see how she had disowned these parts of herself and projected them onto the characters on her TV screen.

Another common outlet for projection in the modern age is in the form of pornography, with individuals projecting their unconscious desires and fantasies onto a screen. In this type of scenario the individual who may hold guilt or shame around their sexual preferences can externalise their inner conflict and create a little distance from their guilt and shame.

In working with our projections we begin to reclaim aspects of ourselves which have been rejected while simultaneously humanising those people we have made heroes or villains in our minds. It can be useful to distinguish between that which informs us from that which disturbs us.

As an example, consider a colleague who constantly challenges your ideas in meetings. Initially, their behaviour might disturb you, triggering defensiveness or irritation. Upon reflection, you might come to realise their criticism often leads to valuable insights or improvements in your work. In this case, their challenging nature informs you – it pushes you to reconsider your perspectives and refine your approach.

Conversely, imagine another colleague whose behaviour consistently triggers intense jealousy or resentment within you, despite their seemingly innocuous actions. This disproportionate emotional reaction points to shadow activation. Exploring why their success or demeanour disturbs you can reveal unacknowledged insecurities or unmet desires within yourself, offering an opportunity for personal growth and integration.

Celebrities, politicians and other well-known figures are often subject to a huge amount of projection and can allow the perfect distraction from looking at the totality of ourselves. When we put our favourite singer on a pedestal we may be handing them our disowned creativity and extroversion, which were hidden at a time when we were told we were being too much and we needed to 'quiet down and stop looking for attention.'

In the case of the people we judge harshly, our immediate instinct might be to say, 'I'm not like that. I would never do that.' Seeing a well-known politician take bribes might cause us anger and resentment and so our response might be to say, 'I wouldn't ever do that.' Though we might not be able to see ourselves acting out in the same way as the people we judge, if we dig a little deeper and consider the energy behind the given action we may potentially see a part of our shadow. For example, the energy behind taking bribes might be 'dishonest' or 'shady'. And so the question becomes, where am I or have I been dishonest or shady?

When we go beyond the specific behaviour or trait and look to the energy behind it we may come closer to a little piece of our shadow. Although the action or behaviour that we judge might be foreign to us, it is useful to look closer at the deeper driving force behind that action. The energy behind procrastination may be a fear of failure. The energy behind the 'attention-seeker' may be low self-worth. The energy behind aggression might be feeling fearful or powerless.

Heroes and Villains

A simple exercise I often encourage is to list three people whom you greatly admire and three people whom you judge harshly or look down on. It does not matter if you know these people personally or not.

We can think of these as the 'heroes and villains' in our lives. The heroes carry our golden shadow, while the villains carry our dark shadow.

Next list all of the traits you see in these people that 'activate' you. In the case of the people you admire, what is it you see in them that inspires, excites or pleases you? In the people you judge harshly, look to what traits these people show that lead you to judge, criticise or condemn them.

In a sense it is as though the parts of you that made you a 'bad boy' or 'bad girl' were handed to the people you now judge harshly in your life and the traits you showed when you shone too brightly were handed to the heroes in your life. In the case of the 'darker' traits that you see in the villains in your life, it can also be useful to bring some curiosity to how these traits might actually be of value at certain times. For example, if you judge people who are stubborn, you perhaps see no value in the trait of stubbornness. Upon closer inspection, though, we might see a link between stubbornness and persistence, a trait that can be really beneficial in the pursuit of meaningful visions or goals.

Finally, once you've got a list of all of these traits on paper, go through each of the traits and ask yourself: where have I or do I demonstrate this trait?

Reactivity

When we find ourselves caught up in reactivity, it is often a clear sign that a piece of our shadow has been touched. Our reactivity can act as a mirror, reflecting the parts of ourselves we have buried or hidden away in the depths of our unconscious. By pausing to acknowledge and investigate our reactivity – both underactive and overactive – we can gain a much greater understanding of our authentic selves.

I know that one of my reactions in social settings when I feel shame or anxiety is to deflect with humour. Another reaction I often go to before I even realise I have done so is to become defensive when someone pushes on something I am sensitive around.

In Chapter Four we will look closer at how reactivity manifests itself in the form of emotional triggers and how we can work with triggers to gain a greater understanding of ourselves.

Consider: Your Reactivity

When do you find yourself reacting with heightened emotion, aggression, defensiveness or perhaps humour? Consider how these reactions might be influencing your relationships and experiences.

Defence Mechanisms

There are countless other ways in which we look to protect or conceal the aspects of the self that seem unlovable, unacceptable and unsafe to share. Exploring these protective layers can help us bring awareness to aspects of the shadow so that we can bring about more integration and wholeness.

Addiction

Addiction often serves as a coping mechanism to deal with underlying emotional pain, trauma, or unresolved issues.

Renowned addiction and trauma specialist Gabor Maté poses a crucial question – 'Not why the addiction but why the pain?' This inquiry encourages a shift in perspective, urging us to explore the roots of addictive behaviours by delving into the emotional landscapes that often remain unexplored. As humans we all have needs, though when we are disconnected from our feelings we become disconnected from those needs and will often reach out to meet them in unconscious ways that take the form of addictions.

Repression

Repression involves pushing down unwanted thoughts, feelings or memories out of our conscious awareness. Hiding or pushing down these uncomfortable aspects of ourselves can create a protective barrier from emotional distress, though the repressed aspects of the psyche may well still manifest in other ways such as in our dreams, in slips of the tongue or in repetitive emotional patterns.

Rationalisation

Rationalisation is a way of cognitively trying to justify or rationalise a behaviour that may be inconsistent with our self-image or may go against our own moral compass.

Intellectualisation

Intellectualisation can be used as a temporary defence by leaning heavily on rational thought or analysis to avoid emotional discomfort. Despite the temporary relief it might offer, it does stifle the opportunity for genuine emotional healing.

Denial

Denying the existence of a problem or emotion can temporarily allow the individual to maintain the feeling of control or comfort in the face of uncertainty or threats to the ego. Denial might range from minimising the seriousness of a given issue to outright rejection of anything that is not in line with a person's own beliefs.

——— Summary: Gold in the Shadow ———

- By reclaiming and reintegrating the aspects of ourselves that we previously made 'wrong' we can show up more authentically and live a life from the inside out rather than the outside in.
- Becoming more accepting of our inner world makes us much less reactive to or fearful of our outer world.
- Individuation involves the maturation of one's identity, recognising and harmonising different elements within the psyche, including conscious and unconscious aspects.
- Being caught in our reactivity and defaulting to old defence mechanisms or coping strategies is a clear sign of the shadow becoming activated.
- If we can remain curious and create a bit of space around old reactions or patterns, we can come to greater levels of self-understanding and acceptance.

Incomplete Sentences

Read the beginning of each sentence aloud and allow yourself to complete the sentence spontaneously in an unfiltered way. After completing all the prompts you can jot down any insights or reflections that stand out to you.

–   My biggest fear about facing my shadow is …
–   The most common thing I project onto others is …
–   A recent situation where my reactivity surprised me was …
–   An addictive behaviour that I might use as a coping mechanism is …
–   A way that I often self-sabotage is …
–   One defence mechanism I often use is …
–   An unconscious pattern I've noticed in my life is …
–   Someone I refuse to be like is ...

Journalling Prompts

1. Reflect on a recent situation where you noticed yourself judging or criticising someone else. What traits or behaviours were you focusing on? Do these traits or behaviours reflect something about yourself that you are uncomfortable with or deny?

2. Can you identify any patterns of behaviour that you use to defend yourself when you feel threatened or uncomfortable? What are you protecting yourself from? Are there any connections between these defence mechanisms and aspects of your shadow?

3. Consider any addictive behaviours that you engage in. What feelings or situations trigger these behaviours? How might these addictions be connected to your shadow and what is it trying to communicate or protect you from?

4. Reflect on a recent situation where you had a strong emotional reaction. What triggered this reaction? How might this relate to aspects of your shadow that are yearning for recognition and integration?

5. What are some ways in which you engage in self-sabotage? Do you notice any patterns in these behaviours? How might they be connected to aspects of your shadow self that need to be acknowledged and integrated?

Cold Immersion

Often when our shadow becomes activated, we react and go to shutdown, freeze, defensiveness or withdrawal. In order to meet our shadow and integrate it we must be willing to lean toward it and be with discomfort without having to default to the safety of old patterns and behaviours.

This week I encourage you to face discomfort and stay open with cold showers each day. Rather than gritting your teeth and bearing it, the practice is to lean toward and remain present to the discomfort. This mirrors how we can approach the work we do in meeting aspects of our shadow that we have looked to hide, deny or push away. To meet ourselves and welcome these parts back we must stay open and welcoming, rather than closing off or withdrawing.

Begin by standing in front of the shower with the intention of welcoming discomfort. Notice any resistance that arises within you, this resistance mirroring the discomfort we often feel towards things we don't want to confront in life.

Notice how the resistance manifests in your body and in the stories you tell yourself. As you turn on the cold water, direct your attention away from the resistance and focus on your deep breath and feet grounded on the floor. Instead of tensing up against the cold, practise opening up and welcoming the intensity of the cold water as it hits your body.

Stay under the cold water for at least 1–2 minutes, staying present to the sensations. Aim to complete this exercise daily for the next week, observing how you respond to discomfort and cultivating a mindset of openness and resilience in the face of challenging experiences or interactions.

CHAPTER THREE

Who Did You Become?

'Parts are little inner beings who are trying their best to keep you safe.' RICHARD C. SCHWARTZ

'Awareness in itself is healing.' FRITZ PERLS

──────── **Outdated Strategies** ────────

'Sit down, now!' he roars over the microphone.

I, along with half the room, am stunned by the speaker's response when a woman stands to hug her friend, who has just broken down in tears. The crying woman continues to sob into the microphone, sharing with the full room how she thought she'd be married with kids by now but keeps finding herself in short-lived, bad relationships, repeating the same painful cycle.

I have travelled to a four-day intensive 'personal development' workshop in New York and there are thousands in attendance. I am in the cheap seats at the back and watching the drama unfold on the big screens as the lady in the more expensive seats seeks guidance from the speaker on stage.

'Can you see the pattern here?' he asks the lady. 'You cry, people come and hug you and tell you it's going to be OK, you get a hit of temporary relief, but then you repeat the cycle and nothing changes. I am sure the lovely lady next to you who tried to comfort you has the best of intentions but if you want to change this pattern you've got to do something different. You need to start showing up like the powerful woman you are and not a needy girl waiting to be saved. You need to start caring for yourself and not looking for someone else to do it for you. Then you'll be ready for a healthy relationship.'

At first I am unsure what to make of the tough love I have just witnessed.

It soon becomes evident he's known this lady for a while and has been working with her to help her see and move past whatever patterns have been keeping her stuck. She acknowledges that somewhere along the way, she learned that her tears brought people close and helped her to meet her need for connection, but she also recognised that this unconscious strategy, of wanting to be saved, was stopping her from getting the thing she wanted most: a deep and meaningful relationship with herself and with another.

Meanwhile the lady who had stood up to hug her shares that a pattern of hers, a strategy if you will, is to be the caretaker, the shoulder to cry on, the person everybody calls when they are feeling down. She says that throughout her life her means of getting connection has often been to take on the role of caring for others.

We have all developed strategies and ways of being in certain situations in order to help us meet our needs for love, connection, safety and approval. We will have certain strategies in our intimate relationships, in group dynamics, in familial relationships, in times of stress and in all other areas of our lives.

In intimate relationships, some may adopt the strategy of always being the pleaser, putting their partner's needs above their own to avoid conflict and secure affection. In professional settings, a person might take on the strategy of being the overachiever, tirelessly working to gain approval and validation from colleagues and superiors. Within family dynamics, someone might run the strategy of being the mediator, constantly trying to resolve conflicts and maintain harmony to ensure a stable and peaceful environment. During times of stress, an individual might turn to avoidance as their strategy, distancing themselves from problems or emotions as a way to cope with overwhelming situations. Socially, a person might adopt the strategy of being the entertainer, using humour and charisma to gain attention and feel accepted within a group.

Each of these strategies, while often helpful and healthy ways of being, can also become problematic when they are played out unconsciously, leading to burnout, resentment, or a lack of genuine connection and personal fulfilment. Recognising and understanding our patterns and the 'parts' that play out those patterns allows for a more conscious choice in how we meet our needs, allowing for healthier relationships with ourselves and others.

While we may view ourselves as one person, in truth we are all made up of a number of different parts, each with their own drivers, strategies and way of being in the world. In our early childhood experiences of learning 'good' from 'bad' and 'right' from 'wrong', we create an internal split between those parts of ourselves that we accept (persona) and the parts that we reject (shadow). As a result of this split we begin to develop different ways of being in different environments, with survival strategies that over time become sub-personalities. This is sometimes evident in how we hear people intuitively talk: 'Part of me wishes ...' or 'A part of me feels ...' Perhaps unbeknownst to ourselves, in this type of language we are pointing to the presence of our multiple internal sub-personalities.

Although we all mature biologically in life, many of us get stuck psychologically and find ourselves playing out old familiar patterns, particularly in times when we experience stress , discomfort or fear. As such, rather than showing up in the present moment, we find ourselves 'time-travelling', being reminded of experiences from our past and reverting to the strategies that kept us safe in those early childhood experiences.

Perhaps in childhood we developed a 'people-pleasing' part as a means of avoiding the discomfort of possible rejection from our classmates. Now, decades later, this part may still be very active in the workplace when you experience situations in which rejection proves a potential threat. Or maybe, learning early on that we got criticism and a temporary withdrawal of love when scoring poorly in exams, we developed a perfectionist part that continues to play out in our adult lives, leaving us constantly doubting ourselves or looking for where we are falling short. A child shamed for their sensitivity and told to 'grow up' perhaps develops a very serious and stoic persona which proves a barrier to intimacy and connection throughout their life until addressed and integrated.

Many of us beat ourselves up or shame ourselves for certain aspects of how we are. But upon closer inspection through a com-passionate lens, we will often come to understand that all of our different parts are looking to protect us and support us in their own outdated ways. By moving closer to and becoming intimate with our different parts we can come to understand our emotions, behaviours and beliefs and update outdated protective strategies. Many of the parts of ourselves that frustrate us are simply that: outdated strategies. Becoming a 'daydreamer' in the midst of a difficult home life as a six-year-old may have proved an essential strategy to handle the pain at that time, but as a grown man or woman, unconsciously living out the daydreaming aspect may become a limiting factor when left unintegrated.

To create changes to what parts of us are showing up, we must first shine light on the parts that have been showing up and gain a greater understanding of what has been driving those parts.

——— An Introduction to Parts Work ———

Doing a therapy piece publicly wasn't part of the plan when I clicked Record for episode 207 of my podcast back in 2021, but when the opportunity to do a piece of work with one of the world's leading therapists emerged I didn't want to miss it.

Dick Schwartz is the founder of Internal Family Systems (IFS), a form of psychotherapy developed in the 1980s. It involves seeing the mind almost like a family, with many different members or parts, all with their own thoughts, feelings, motivations and roles. Some of these parts may be really helpful and supportive, while others may seem to want to hold us back or get in our way. The goal in IFS work is to bring about a sense of balance and harmony internally by getting to know and understand our different parts, as well as their drivers and roles.

A notification pops up on my phone: 'Dick Schwartz has joined the meeting.' It's an hour earlier than I had expected, and so with

Dick in the States and me in Ireland, I must have got the time difference wrong. After rushing to my computer and logging on to the meeting, I click Record and we settle into the podcast conversation, where Dick talks about how IFS came to be and explains the basic premise of the model.

At its core there are three key pillars in IFS work: exiles, protectors and the self.

Exiles are the parts of our psyche that hold onto painful memories, emotions or experiences, often a result of past traumas. These exiled parts are generally hidden away in order to suppress or avoid future pain.

Protectors are the parts of us that try to shield us from the pain held by our exiles. In a sense they come in to shield us from the intensity of the pain we might feel from our repressed parts. These protectors act as a defence mechanism or coping strategy when we feel vulnerable, stressed or scared.

The self, unlike the exiles or protectors, represents a deeper part of us that remains stable in its compassion, curiosity and clarity.

Later in our podcast conversation, Dick offers to work with one of my protectors and asks me if there's a particular part I'd like to work with.

'I notice that I get into a nice workflow sometimes but I have a cycle of taking on too much and overwhelming myself. I'd like to look at this part that overworks and takes on too much. He knows it's going to be too much but says yes anyway.'

Dick asks me to connect with my body and see if an image or feeling emerges when I connect with this overworking part who can't switch off.

I tell him I can feel the sensation of a thick red ball in my gut.

'How do you feel toward that part?' he asks.

'I resent it a bit.'

'That makes sense. Can you ask the part of you that resents this overworking part to step aside?'

'Yes.'

'How do you feel toward it now?'

'I'm curious toward it and I can feel the intensity of energy easing a bit.'

'Now ask that part, what are you afraid would happen if it didn't do its job?'

'There is a fear around me not meeting my potential …'

'And what would it mean if you didn't reach your potential?'

'It would mean I wasn't enough …'

'So this overworking part is protecting the part of you who doesn't feel enough. How old does this part think you are?'

'Ten …'

'Ok, so something was happening then that led you to believe you weren't enough, and this overworking part came in to protect you when you were ten. Maybe you can let the part know you aren't ten any more and that you don't need it for that job any more. Before we finish, ask that part what it needs …'

'It says it needs a holiday!'

'That makes sense. It has been working hard! Finally, ask if it would be willing to allow you to work with the vulnerable parts it has been trying to protect at some stage in the future.'

This impromptu mini therapy session on the podcast helped me to better understand why I kept playing out this pattern of taking on too much, and the new awareness proved supportive in becoming better at managing my energy and boundaries. I got to meet a part of my shadow in connecting to the 10-year-old who felt he wasn't enough, and the overworking achiever part that came in in order to protect that younger version of me.

The value in this new awareness was the capacity to notice when the overworking part is taking over and seeing it as trying to protect my vulnerability and fears, as opposed to trying to ruthlessly work me into the ground. Now the presence of this overworking part allows a chance to check in with the fearful younger part of me who doesn't feel enough and allow it some reassurance and support.

A nice analogy that I have heard used to describe how our parts play out is to imagine a bus full of people. Each person on the bus represents one of our sub-personalities, and sometimes when we are scared or overwhelmed the hardest working of those sub-personalities, or the parts we are most used to defaulting to, take the wheel, running to the front of the bus and taking over.

If we have a strong people-pleasing part, that part takes the wheel when we are stressed or scared. If we are used to playing out the achiever in our lives, we may see that part take the wheel when we experience feelings of self-doubt or inadequacy. As we better come to understand our parts and what they are trying to protect, we can move past this reactivity and have more choice as to what parts of us show up. In essence, we can ensure the healthy sovereign adult drives the bus, not the scared and reactive youngsters.

Though parts work has been seen in previous modalities like Gestalt therapy, transactional analysis and voice dialogue for many years, from Dick's simple and natural way of working I could see why IFS has become such a popular form of psychotherapy in recent times.

The Chameleon Effect

From a young age we learned to take on different roles or play out different parts in different environments and relationships. We will have had certain ways of acting with our parents and maybe other ways of acting with our friends. Once we reach our pre-teens we perhaps begin to reject our more childish aspects and develop new ways of being within the different environments that we inhabit.

We are always shifting in and out of different roles, leaning on certain parts while repressing other parts. Perhaps when he's with 'the lads' a man represses his sensitivity, while in relationships with an intimate partner he rejects his machismo. We will most likely have a way we are with our family, a way we are with our colleagues, a way we are with our friends and a way that we are in group settings. Most of us might be a very different way while on holiday away from an environment in which those closest to us reflect back who we are. To a degree, we become a certain way based on our environment early on, and then going forward our environment reflects back to us that mask that we have created.

I found martial arts and weight training in my teens and that became a strong part of my persona, how I presented myself to the world. Having been bullied in younger years, I liked the confidence that I gained from learning judo and boxing and lifting weights. Then classmates and those around me would mirror back and reinforce this persona with encouragement or references to my training efforts and aspirations. How I felt others saw me heavily influenced how I saw and tried to portray myself.

This is summed up in a quote by Charles Cooley, an American sociologist from the start of the 20th century: 'I am not who you think I am; I am not who I think I am; I am who I think you think I am.'

This one took me a while to grasp when I first read it, but the essence of what is being pointed to is how influenced we are by the perceptions we think other people may have of us.

Consider: The Chameleon Effect

- How do you think you are seen by others?
- How does this influence how you portray yourself?

If you are someone who dresses in very plain clothing, you would probably get some funny looks from friends and family were you to show up in a flamboyant bright outfit with accessories, and so the fear of being shamed or teased may keep you in that same way of dressing all your life. Away from our day-to-day environment there is maybe more of a freedom and ease, fewer constraints put on who we allow ourselves to be and how we allow ourselves to express ourselves. Think of a student going on a gap year, coming back wearing elephant pants that they wouldn't have ever worn before their travels, being teased and then quickly reverting back to the way they were before.

The same thing goes for aspects of our personality.

At a retreat that I hosted many years ago I brought together a small group of 12 people from various backgrounds for a three-day deep dive into where they were in life, where they wanted to go and what stood in the way.

I noted that a man who had been heavily involved in sports all his life brought some 'locker room banter' and inappropriate jokes and comments to the group in the early hours of the retreat, but quickly came to see that that wasn't going to win him any friends. Rather than being supported by the environment, the persona he was presenting was ignored or rejected. Nothing had to be said as you could feel the energy sucked out of the room with his early comments, but it was clear to me early on that this was one of his own protective strategies or sub-personalities, being 'Jack the lad' and hiding his real self. As he dropped the façade and became more vulnerable and authentic over the following days, he won the hearts and respect of everyone there who appreciated the softer parts of himself that he had been hiding with this protective part.

Who do You Become?

In the last chapter we looked at some of the ways our shadow becomes activated. Now we might consider who we become in these times of shadow activation, or what parts take over. It is likely you have a few key parts that act as protectors for you when you get close to your vulnerability.

Who do you become when you get triggered in an intimate relationship?
Our triggers usually point to vulnerable feelings like fear or anger and so we will all have developed strategies to ease the discomfort of these feelings. Some become defensive, others become aggressive, others fawn and look to appease the other person.

What role do you shift into when triggered in a relationship?
Next, who do you become when accumulated stress pushes
you to the edge? Some become the victim, others the
perfectionist and others the avoidant. Do you go to one of these
aforementioned strategies or is it something different for you?

Who do you become in family dynamics?
I often speak with clients who share that when they step into
their childhood home they feel themselves shrink and revert
back to a childhood state. Despite lots of success in their work
lives and having grown up in many ways, stepping back into
the environment they grew up in can have them time-travelling
back to younger versions of themselves. Some instinctively go to
a position of being the rebel or black sheep, while others become
the peacekeeper.

Who do you become in social group dynamics?
Running and attending countless retreats and group events over
the last 10 years, it has been interesting to watch who people
become in new social or group dynamics in which they may feel a
little nervous or unsure of themselves. For some, the instinct is to
become the caretaker for the group, for others it is to hide in the
corner and for others still to become the group entertainer. Who
do you instinctively become to feel safe when in a new group?

—— Core Wounds and Vulnerable Parts ——

Let's dive into understanding who we became in order to stay safe
in the world, and how those parts have supported us as well as how
they may be limiting us.

First, we need to understand what we are trying to protect through our defence strategies, coping mechanisms and protective parts. Many, if not all, of us experience core wounds in childhood, deep-seated emotional injuries that come about from significant experiences which influence our worldview, our beliefs and our behaviours going forward. Left unresolved or unacknowledged in the shadows, these wounds can keep us in unhelpful or unhealthy patterns and dynamics in our lives, disconnected from our feelings, needs and authentic expression. There are many ways in which these wounds can present themselves, including but not limited to abandonment wounds, rejection wounds, betrayal or inadequacy wounds. In essence, things happen in our lives and we give them meaning.

As kids, we are egocentric and falsely assume that we are the centre of the universe, thus believing that whatever happens around us is a result of something we've done. We don't yet have the capacity to see the bigger picture. A tired parent struggling to give their full attention to their child after a long day's work is doing their best, though their child may come to the belief that the parent doesn't want to spend time with them, leading to feelings of rejection. Because they remain completely dependent on their parents for care, it often makes more sense to blame themselves and make themselves 'bad' or 'wrong', rather than blame their parents for the perceived rejection, and so a belief of 'not being enough' is formed.

These are some more examples of wounds and resulting feelings or behaviours.

Abandonment wound

In the case of a parent leaving the family or a child not having consistent emotional support, the child may develop an abandonment wound. As a result, they may carry with them fears of abandonment in relationships, difficulties in trusting others and feelings of insecurity.

Rejection wound

A child who is rejected by their classmates or family for being different may go on to develop low self-worth, fear of intimacy and people-pleasing tendencies in efforts to protect themselves going forward.

Betrayal wound

An individual who experiences betrayal by someone close to them may develop a betrayal wound and go on to have difficulty in trusting others, have a fear of vulnerability and a tendency to protect their heart at all costs, perhaps avoiding intimacy or closeness for fear of further betrayal.

Inadequacy wound

A child who is consistently teased, bullied, judged or ridiculed or held to impossibly high standards may develop an inadequacy wound and find themselves constantly fearing failure, experiencing self-doubt and feeling incompetent later in life.

The father wound

Our earliest and most formative experiences with those who represent the father or mother figures in our lives profoundly influence our development.

The father wound relates to the emotional, psychological or relational pain and wounding due to an absent, abusive, neglectful or critical father figure in a child's life. Sometimes the wounding is a result of a father who was cold and distant, other times the result of a father who was close and fiery, or potentially a mix of both. The father who is cold and distant may trigger the child into constantly striving for acceptance and validation at the cost of their own wellbeing. A father who is close but overly critical may trigger an inadequacy wound or inferiority complex in the child.

As a result, those who carry this wound may have anger and resentment toward their own fathers and other men of authoritative positions in life. They may also have difficulty connecting with male peers and find themselves in a constant state of trying to prove themselves to the world due to low self-esteem.

Consider: The Father Wound

- How was your relationship with your father or father figure?
- How do you feel this has influenced how you relate to the masculine in the world?

The mother wound

The mother wound similarly relates to emotional, psychological or relational pain and wounding due to an absent, abusive, neglectful or critical mother figure in the child's life. An overly critical or emotionally distant mother may result in the child feeling unworthy of love or affection. Another way in which the mother wound can occur is in enmeshment with the mother; that is, over-involvement and boundary violation, where the child does not have a chance to develop their own sense of self and identity. This can result in feelings of suffocation for the child, guilt in expressing their own wants and needs and emotional dependency on others.

Those who have experienced a mother wound may also have difficulty setting boundaries, a fear of abandonment and peo-ple-pleasing tendencies.

Consider: The mother wound

- How was your relationship with your mother or mother figure?
- How do you feel this has influenced how you relate to the feminine in the world?

Through shadow work all these wounds can become scars, and we can grow through the experiences, taking on wisdom to support us in meeting our needs and honouring our feelings going forward. But if they are neglected, these wounds can cause repetitive issues and challenges in our lives and leave us in unconscious patterns and cycles.

This can be particularly true in relationships. I often work with men who report having received a lot of criticism from their fathers in childhood. The pain of this as young boys led them to develop-ing strategies to protect their vulnerability.

For some the strategy will have been to appease their fathers, assigning blame to themselves and feeling shame for their short-comings. Now, years later, a hint of criticism from an intimate partner can trigger that same vulnerable part and lead to the same 'teenage' response of appeasing and making themselves wrong rather than communicating their own feelings and needs. Often a man who felt dominated by his father will have disconnected from his assertiveness and have a hard time expressing his authentic feelings and needs.

In understanding his different strategies and defence mechanisms, that man can begin to choose to respond differently. Rather than shrinking and making himself small and appeasing his intimate partner when criticised, he can instead check in with himself and respond with what feels authentic in the moment. In some cases that may mean taking ownership of his mistakes, in others verbalising that he does not believe the criticism is just or fair.

Consider: Early Wounds

- What are some of the experiences that stand out for you from childhood in which you may have been emotionally wounded?
- What happened and what did you take it to mean about yourself? In other words, what story did you tell yourself about yourself as a result of what happened?
- How has that wound played out since?

— Protective Parts and Adaptive Strategies —

Since my late teens I have enjoyed travelling and spent a few months of every year abroad. After staying home for two years during the Covid pandemic I was itching to travel again and see somewhere new. Wanting to go offline for a few weeks and do a pilgrimage of sorts, I began researching the Shikoku pilgrimage route in Japan, which involves visiting 88 temples while hiking 750 miles.

When I shared with my father my desire to go and walk 750 miles across Japan, he asked me if I had considered staying closer to home and walking the Camino de Santiago in Spain. He pointed out to me the part of me who always has to go against the grain, rebel or be different.

I immediately saw the truth in his reflection.

The rebel part of me that always feels the need to go against the grain came in early in life in an effort to be different to keep myself safe. During early experiences of being bullied, I rejected the values of the more popular kids and decided I would be a 'lone wolf' and do things my own way. If something was popular or cool I looked for the opposite, having made the association of popularity being tied to bullying, groupthink and inauthenticity. Being different allowed me to establish a sense of self outside of what the cool crowd were doing. I distinctly remember the day in secondary school when a popular girl in my class announced that she was now an Arctic Monkeys fan, and the rebel part of me decided the Arctic Monkeys were now 'too commercial'!

Having not integrated this aspect of myself, I was not being truly authentic, but instead defined myself by what I was not, much like the child who declares they won't ever be like their parents. As we discussed in the last chapter, the purpose of shadow work is to find out who we really are through the individuation process so that we show up in the present as adults, rather than being stuck in old patterns and defence strategies.

I recognised that it was my rebel part that was making the decision to go to Japan, seeing the Camino as something 'everyone else' does. Appreciating my father naming that part of me, I made the decision to fly to Spain and walk 900 kilometres of the Camino, though I compromised with my rebel part and chose to walk the northern route, a route that less than 10 per cent of pilgrims travel. During the final days, as we merged with the other routes and came toward the finishing point of the cathedral in Santiago, I felt the power of walking a route that had been walked by so many and had a new-found appreciation for the value of sometimes following the crowd.

Rather than continuing to unconsciously have my life run by my rebel part, I felt more integrated in recognising that part, allowing him a seat at the table, but not allowing him to take over. It is likely that we all have a handful of characters who largely run and control our lives with their protective strategies and drivers. We have certain parts that help us feel safe in relationships, others who help us feel safe in work and others who help us feel safe in other areas of our personal lives. As useful as these parts can be, they can also limit what is possible for us in life and keep us stuck in patterns or cycles for years or decades.

I see the integration of our parts as finding and being honest with ourselves about both the gifts and drawbacks of how we have chosen to show up and what we have rejected. In my case, the gift of the rebel has been a sense of courage, independence and creativity in my life, and the drawbacks have been a sense of isolation at times, sometimes recklessness and impulsivity. Meanwhile, some of the gifts I see in the conforming part that I rejected are reliability, connection to others and stability. The drawbacks of being too influenced by that conforming part might be rigidity, a fear of change and a follower mentality.

In a sense we are updating old scripts. I brought in this rebel character in my teens, maybe earlier, and just let him run the show for close to twenty years without ever getting to know and understand how much of a role he was playing in my life. With this more honest appraisal of the gifts and drawbacks of who I become and what I have rejected, I can now lean into different ways of being dependent on what will best support me and where I am trying to go.

Consider: Identifying Your Protectors

Who did you become to protect the wounded parts of you? How did you adapt and learn to defend your vulnerability? How has that part supported and helped you over the years and how might it be limiting or holding you back?

Meeting and Embracing a Protector

Allow yourself to find a quiet place where you won't be disturbed. Gently close your eyes and take a few deep, grounding breaths. As you breathe deeply and ground yourself, connect to a sense of curiosity and compassion. Choose one of your protective parts that you'd like to meet in today's session. See if an image or feeling emerges for you as you connect with this part. Notice first how you feel toward this protector.

Are you able to maintain this sense of curiosity and compassion or do you find yourself going into judgement? If there is judgement, ask the part that is judging to step aside and direct your compassion and curiosity toward your protective part.

Ask what they are trying to protect, or what they are afraid would happen if they weren't there for their job. Don't look for an answer, just wait and listen. Next ask them how old they think you are or at what time of your life they first emerged to keep

you safe. Again, wait and listen. Finally, ask them what they need
from you in order for them to feel they can relax and not have to
be so active in your life.

Listen for their response. If there are any other questions
for your protector, ask them before saying goodbye to them in
whatever way feels most fitting for you. You can journal about
any relevant or interesting insights that emerge as a result of this
exercise.

Anima and Animus

Alongside exploring our wounded parts and protectors to better
understand our unconscious drivers, we can look to the concepts of
the 'anima' and 'animus' to further understand what parts of us may
be hidden in the dark and playing out unconsciously. Carl Jung
offered the concepts of anima and animus to represent the 'inner
feminine' in men and 'inner masculine' in women. It is important
to note that in Jungian psychology when referring to 'masculine'
and 'feminine' in this context, we are referring to energies rather
than gender identities. Other terms we could use to describe these
energies are 'yin' and 'yang'. Regardless of gender, these masculine
(yang) and feminine (yin) energies exist within all individuals and
represent different parts of the psyche.

Jung believed it was essential for us to integrate both masculine
and feminine aspects of ourselves to avoid projecting them on to
others. At the time that Jung introduced these concepts it was a more
radical idea for men to embrace their feminine side and women
their masculine side, though in the modern day there is much more
of an understanding and acceptance of psychological androgyny.

For men, Jung believed the anima represented the unconscious feminine qualities such as compassion, sensitivity, emotional intelligence and intuition. An individual (regardless of gender) who has rejected these feminine aspects of themselves and placed them into shadow may find themselves struggling with their own emotions or in the presence of other people's emotions, living in their head and reliant on others to meet their emotional needs due to their inability to nurture themselves. This individual can take their feminine energies out of the shadows and integrate those parts by beginning to make space for and allow their emotions without judgement, seeing them as feedback and not as something bad or wrong. Self-care practices and mindfulness or introspection practices can support this development of self-awareness and compassion.

For women, Jung believed the animus represents the unconscious masculine qualities such as assertiveness, courage and focus. An individual (regardless of gender) who has not fully integrated their masculine energies may find themselves struggling to speak up for themselves, to hold healthy boundaries or to take decisive action. This individual can work on integrating more of their masculine energy by finding more direction in their life, practising courage by stepping outside their comfort zone and being more clear and assertive in their communication.

It is likely we will have a natural leaning toward one energy more than the other, though like all other aspects of shadow it is important that we have integrated both sides so that we can live authentically. There will be times when I wish to lean more on my sensitivity and compassion and other times when I want to tune into my focus and assertiveness. To only have access to half of who I am will be limiting and potentially harmful.

On a cultural level we can see the repercussions of these out-of-balance energies in the West, with priority given to 'masculine' qualities like logic, rationality and assertiveness over 'feminine' qualities such as sensitivity, compassion and empathy. As a result we see environmental degradation, addiction and emotional numbing, a mental health crisis and a huge amount of war and conflict, with decisions and behaviours driven by the head and disconnected from the heart.

Summary: Gold in the Shadow

- While we may view ourselves as one person, in truth we are all made up of a number of different parts or sub-personalities, each with their own drivers, strategies and way of being in the world.
- Sometimes these parts are hugely supportive and beneficial in our lives while at other times they can keep us stuck in old defence strategies and unconscious patterns.
- In beginning to notice when we default to our protective parts, we can begin to recognise when old wounds are being triggered in the present.
- As we begin to recognise our reactivity and repetitive cycles or patterns in life, we can become more intimate with the part of ourselves that plays out those patterns.

Incomplete Sentences

Read the beginning of each sentence aloud and allow yourself to complete the sentence spontaneously in an unfiltered way. After completing all the prompts you can jot down any insights or reflections that stand out to you.

–   When I feel vulnerable, I tend to … because …
–   The part of me that feels 'not enough' needs …
–   The part of me that takes over when I am exhausted is …
–   My protective parts are protecting my …
–   I learned I needed to protect these aspects of myself when …
–   To better understand my parts I can …

Journalling Prompts

1. Identify different parts of yourself that emerge in various situations (e.g. the pleaser, the achiever, the caretaker). How do these parts influence your actions and interactions with others? Which part do you feel most comfortable with, and which part do you struggle with?

2. Choose one of your sub-personalities and write a dialogue between this part and your 'self' or another part. What is this part trying to tell you? How can you address its concerns in a healthy way?

3. Imagine you are no longer controlled by your protective or limiting parts. How would you act differently in your relationships, work or self-care? Describe a day in your life living as your most authentic self.

4. Reflect on a childhood experience that significantly shaped one of your current sub-personalities. How does this experience continue to influence your behaviour and self-image today? What steps can you take to heal and integrate this part of yourself?

5. Reflect on your personal understanding and experiences of the inner masculine and inner feminine aspects within yourself. Consider how these energies manifest in your thoughts, behaviours and interactions with others.

Embodiment Practice: Shaking Practice

For this embodiment exercise, I want to introduce the practice of shaking, inspired by active meditation techniques that help bring people out of their busy minds and into their bodies. These approaches recognise that, especially in modern cultures, it can be challenging to settle directly into stillness due to our mental orientation. Shaking and dynamic movements are ways of softening this transition by allowing energy to flow freely and naturally.

Begin by standing comfortably with your feet shoulder-width apart, knees slightly bent. Close your eyes and take a few deep breaths, allowing your body to relax. Now, rather than consciously making yourself shake, allow yourself to surrender to the sensation of energy within you.

Let go of control and allow your body to shake naturally. Allow the vibrations to arise from deep within, moving through you spontaneously. Trust the process, letting the shaking happen without force or effort. You can offer a little encouragement to your body's movements at the start, though again the focus should be on allowing as opposed to doing.

As your body begins to shake, continue to breathe deeply and allow yourself to feel your body softening and tension melting.

Continue this for about 15 minutes, embracing the sense of freedom and flow that comes from the shedding of muscular tension or holding.

When you're ready, gradually slow the shaking until you come to a gentle stillness, standing quietly and feeling the after-effects of this short dynamic meditation. Look to complete this short shaking practice at least five times over the next week.

CHAPTER FOUR

The Mind–Body Connection

'Listen to your body, it never lies' WILHELM REICH

'Lose your mind and come to your senses.' FRITZ PERLS

The Body as Shadow

At the start of this book I introduced a simple practice called the grounding breath, a practice to help establish more of a connection between body and mind. In times of stress or reactivity our attention can often leave the present moment and bring us back to memories of past challenges or project us into the future, playing out worst-case scenarios.

When we lose our sense of grounding and go to the past or future in our imagination, we will often find ourselves going to autopilot defence strategies and coping patterns that keep us stuck in repetitive cycles of behaviour in our lives. For true transformation to occur we have got to learn how to come into the present moment and make choices from a grounded place and not a place of impulse or reactivity.

By recognising when we are caught in reactivity and coming back to a practice like the grounding breath or some of the other exercises I've shared, we can be reminded that our triggers often have little to do with what is happening in the present moment and are instead reminders from the body of painful experiences in our past. Only by pulling ourselves out of the story and creating a sense of safety in our bodies can we show up consciously in the present rather than playing out old reactions.

Shadow work and healing cannot just be a cognitive endeavour.

I came to a much deeper understanding of the significance of the body's role in healing seven years ago when working with a shamanic therapist and elder. I had worked in the fitness industry for close to 10 years at that point and so understood how important the health of the body is in overall wellbeing. I had also dived deep into cognitive-based therapies and coaching modalities that addressed the health of the mind. I just hadn't realised how strong a link there is between the two and how much the body, its holding patterns and its instinctive reactions or emotional responses could point to what is going on in deeper parts of the unconscious mind.

As myself and the shamanic therapist became acquainted in our first session he asked me how I felt. I launched into stories about what was working and what was not working in my life before he promptly but politely cut me off and explained that he hadn't asked for a story but had instead asked me how I was feeling. As I struggled to put words to how I felt, he had me close my eyes, breathe a little deeper and describe what I was experiencing in my body.

'My chest is tight and I feel a lot of energy in my upper body and very little in my legs or feet. Breathing feels a bit constricted and I feel some tension around my throat'.

'Good,' he responded, 'now can you just stay with your breath and stay with those sensations? Rather than push them away, lean toward them. What is the emotion connected to this tightness in your chest?'

'It's fear …'

'And if the fear could talk, what would it say?'

'I've taken on too much and I'm going to be found out …'

'What's happening in your body now?'

'The tension is melting a little and I can feel my breath opening up a little.'

In the weeks leading up to that therapy session I had replayed, dramatised and tried to outthink the stories and thoughts that were tormenting me. Now, in a few short moments of acknowledging the sensations in my body, I had connected to the fear that had been outside my conscious awareness and had brought a sense of calm that I hadn't been able to access in weeks.

Emotions are warning signs from the body, a collection of sensations experienced in the body that we give a name to. Sometimes we call the collection of sensations grief, other times fear, other times shame.

When our shadow becomes activated, as outlined in Chapter Two, and we experience these uncomfortable emotions, we often leave our body as a defence mechanism, disconnecting from uncomfortable emotions and sensations to avoid pain or perceived danger. This dissociation prevents us from fully processing the underlying wounds driving our reactions and keeps us stuck. In leaving the body and going to the head we are running away from the very part of us that is requiring some support – the body.

By understanding the mind–body connection and learning to stay present in the body using tools like breathwork, movement and mindfulness, we can regulate our nervous system and create a safe space for deeper emotional exploration and integration, allowing those protectors or sub-personalities we met in Chapter Three to take a break!

Top-Down Healing

Below our conscious level of awareness, all of us are experiencing a two-way conversation between body and mind at all times through the autonomic nervous system. It is the autonomic nervous system that is responsible for many of those automatic functions that keep us alive and healthy, such as our heart rate, digestion, respiration, sexual arousal and our stress responses.

When we talk about the mind–body connection, one way of describing it is to talk about the 'top-down' and 'bottom-up' approaches to healing.

Top-down approach

MIND

BODY

CHANGE HOW
YOU THINK

AND YOU'LL CHANGE
HOW YOU FEEL

Put simply, a 'top-down' approach focuses on how our thinking mind (top) affects how we feel in our bodies (bottom). A lot of counselling, coaching and talk therapy operate through this paradigm.

You might have noticed times in your life when you were comfortable and relaxed and then seemingly out of nowhere a disempowering or difficult thought popped up that quickly shifted the levels of comfort and ease in your body, perhaps leading to feelings of stress, fear or anxiety. Or maybe there was a time when you felt crippled by a difficult thought or belief, only to feel your whole body relax when you found out that the belief or thought wasn't true.

Here is a little experiment to demonstrate the power of our thoughts and this top-down perspective.

I am going to invite you to close your eyes and visualise a lemon in front of you on a chopping board. I would like you to pick up the lemon, to feel it, to smell it and then to place it back down on the chopping board.

After placing it down I am then going to encourage you to take an imaginary knife and chop the lemon into a number of wedges.

Seeing the wedges in front of you, I would like you to pick one of them up.

Now, imagine taking a bite of the lemon wedge, feeling the juice burst in your mouth and the sour taste making your mouth pucker.

You will probably notice how, even though there is no physical lemon, your mouth may have started to salivate and your face might have reacted to the imagined sourness.

This simple exercise shows how vividly our thoughts can influence our bodily sensations, demonstrating the profound connection between mind and body. Our thoughts, beliefs, expectations and stories directly impact our physical experience and the feelings that we experience in our bodies.

Cognitive behavioural therapy has been a hugely popular approach to working from a top-down perspective, with the basic idea being that if we can change how we think we can change how we feel.

Bottom-Up Healing

The bottom-up approach comes at things from a different perspective by recognising that how we feel (body) can have a dramatic impact on our thoughts (mind), influencing how we see ourselves, others and the world.

A simple way of thinking about this is to consider how different your thinking would be after 10 cups of coffee versus after attending a yoga class or doing a relaxing guided body scan meditation. Your external experiences could be the same, but how you feel in your body affects your thinking and perspective.

Bottom-up approach

MIND

BODY

AND YOU'LL CHANGE
HOW YOU THINK

CHANGE HOW YOU FEEL

After 10 cups of coffee, your body filled with caffeine and pump-ing out cortisol (a stress hormone), a message is sent from the body to the mind to say, 'We're in danger here,' and so the thinking mind begins to look for threats, challenges or problems in the environ-ment in order to keep us safe before defaulting to protective parts or defence strategies. It is very difficult, if not impossible, to access genuine positive thinking from this hyperaroused state. Therefore we cannot outthink difficult emotions and must work with the body to create a sense of calm and safety internally to allow us to regain access to our rational thinking mind. Then we can explore and challenge our difficult thoughts.

In contrast to the body's experience of 10 cups of coffee, after a yoga class in which you breathe deeply into the belly, move slowly and lie down for 10 minutes of relaxation at the end, you get up from the mat with the body informing the mind that it's a safe and peaceful world, allowing you to tune into thoughts of hope, possi-bility and gratitude.

I often ask people when they get their best ideas in life and gen-erally people respond by saying when they are in the shower, out walking, spending time in nature or in the moments after they wake. People don't get their best ideas during times of stress or overwhelm, when their wound-up nervous system keeps them in high-alert survival mode. In survival mode we do not have access to the neo-cortex, the thinking part of the brain, and so we are reactive rather than responsive. Our biology is always influencing our psychology.

This is where 'spiritual bypassing' or toxic positivity becomes problematic. Spiritual bypassing, as previously discussed, involves using spiritual practices or beliefs to avoid dealing with painful feel-ings, unresolved wounds or basic psychological needs. Similarly, toxic positivity is the overgeneralisation of a happy, optimistic state across all situations, leading to the denial, minimisation and invalidation of the authentic human emotional experience. Both spiritual bypassing and toxic positivity can ignore the critical connection between body and mind, suggesting that we should simply think positively without addressing the underlying physical and emotional states that inform our thoughts.

Because the content of our shadow self lies outside our conscious level of awareness, it often shows up in the body through physical sensations, tension or discomfort before we recognise it mentally. By adding a bottom-up approach to healing, we allow the body to guide us in uncovering these hidden emotional wounds, giving us access to deeper layers of healing that may not be reachable through cognitive approaches alone.

Perhaps in bringing curiosity to a clenching of our jaw, we come to realise we are experiencing some frustration that we can further investigate, or in noticing a tightness in our chest and sensations associated with fear we can explore what is going on for us. This somatic awareness can reveal unprocessed emotions and memories stored in the body, helping us bring unconscious patterns into conscious awareness for integration.

Trauma and shadow are deeply interconnected, with unresolved trauma often forming the core of our shadow self. The emotions, memories and beliefs that we suppress or dissociate from due to overwhelming or traumatic experiences become hidden in the unconscious, driving our shadow's reactions and patterns in everyday life.

Talking about our painful experiences often keeps us at a distance from them and does not allow us to process or digest the emotion. While in the past trauma was generally seen through a psychological lens, the more modern understanding looks deeply at the impact of trauma on the body's physiology. If you have a history of unprocessed trauma it is likely you will spend much of your day seeing through the narrow lens of your stories, beliefs and defence mechanisms. Somatic or body-based therapies, outlined later in this chapter, can be hugely beneficial to those with a lot of unprocessed trauma and can complement traditional talk therapies by addressing the physiological aspects of trauma that are often overlooked.

The Nervous System

In the wild we see animals go through a hierarchy of survival responses when met with external threats to their safety. An animal in its natural environment can relax in a state that allows for rest and recovery, play, reproduction, digestion and a host of other functions that support its health and wellbeing. The animal's breath, body and senses can relax. With no threats to defend against, all is well.

Now, imagine a threat in the form of another animal coming into the environment.

It is as though a switch flicks and everything changes in the blink of an eye. Rather than the animal's priority being rest and recovery, the only priority becomes survival. The muscles of the animal tighten, its blood thickens, breath shallows and vision becomes tunnelled.

If the threat in front of the animal is smaller or weaker than the animal, it will go to its first survival strategy, 'fight'. However, if the threat is bigger than the animal, it will move to a different survival strategy of 'flight'. If both of these strategies fail or the animal is met with an insurmountable threat it will resort to its third defensive strategy, 'freeze', playing dead in the hope that the predator will lose interest and leave.

Now mirror the above scenario to the human experience. When I feel safe in the world I can rest and digest, sleep and recover, play, be creative and be in connection with myself, others and the world. However, once threats emerge in my environment, I experience a similar 'fight or flight' response in which my muscles tense, breath shortens and focus goes to survival and to any immediate threat. If I feel I can handle the threat I will perhaps come with 'fight' energy. If the threat feels a little bigger I might 'fly' and if the threat feels even more overwhelming I may freeze or fawn.

In these survival responses to overwhelming or painful experiences, in order to protect ourselves from feeling the full pain of the experience, we push the uncomfortable emotions and sensations out of our conscious awareness and into the shadow. This repression helps us cope, maybe even survive in the moment. However, it also creates a divide between our conscious self and the aspects of ourselves we've buried. Over time, these unprocessed emotions – anger, fear, shame, grief – become embedded in the shadow, shaping our behaviour and reactions in subtle ways, especially when we encounter triggers that echo the original pain.

Some examples of the types of behaviours we might see during these survival responses include (but are not limited to):

FIGHT Aggression Defensiveness Control Intolerance	**FLIGHT** Avoidance Procrastination Hyperactivity Anxiety
FREEZE Numbing Isolation Dissociation Shutdown	**FAWN** People-pleasing Conflict avoidance Codependency Self-sacrifice

Consider: Your Reactive Patterns

Reflect on the survival strategies you've developed, such as the above behaviours related to fight, flight, freeze or fawn responses. Which of these feels most familiar to you? Where did you first learn this strategy?

When in any of these survival states, we lose access to our logical thinking mind, to our bigger-picture perspective and to our rationality. All that matters is survival and what needs to be done in the short term to ensure our preservation. In these reactive moments our shadow, shaped by past experiences of pain and trauma, takes over, driving automatic, often irrational reactions.

Notably, for animals the fight or flight responses are short-term defence strategies to combat actual life-threatening situations. The response is short, gives the animal what they need and the animal survives or dies. For humans this 'life-saving response' of fight or flight can be triggered by even a thought, and so rather than it being an acute short-term response that ensures our safety, for many of us fight or flight becomes a chronic response that leaves us in a constant state of hypervigilance. Anyone who has ever experienced chronic stress, anxiety or fear will know how activating it can be to the body and so this response, designed as a short-term strategy, becomes problematic and can lead us into a state of freeze or shutdown. This is something all too frequently seen in busy corporate environments where unrelenting pressure and stress eventually push people to burnout.

While in the animal kingdom freeze or shutdown can often be the animal playing dead, as humans it is more likely this response will manifest as dissociating from emotions, withdrawing socially, emotional numbing and avoidance behaviours to minimise further distress or discomfort. It can also show up in physical symptoms such as fatigue or lethargy.

In the animal kingdom we will often see an animal shake or tremble to discharge any excess of energy after the threat has passed; as humans we often try to talk our way out of these stressful feelings.

In recent years a young man who I was mentoring shared with me that he recognised how important using the punch bag at the gym was for him. Going through a lot of challenges at the time, he was experiencing a lot of anger, and he told me he could see clearly that if he didn't take that anger out somewhere consciously it would sit in his body and be directed in a reactive and potentially destructive way toward himself or the wrong person.

My friend Natasha shares a similar sentiment in her saying: 'If you don't use the energy, the energy will use you.'

Shaped by Experience

It is important to note that although every nervous system can engage in fight, flight, freeze or fawn responses, each operates differently because it is shaped by individual history and life experiences. What is familiar to the nervous system feels safe, while what is unfamiliar can feel threatening. Consequently, different people have distinct nervous system responses to the same challenging event, and a chronically dysregulated nervous system operates differently from one with a greater capacity or wider window of tolerance.

At a recent men's workshop that I organised, after doing some communication exercises and breathwork, I announced that we'd be finishing the day with a Jiu-Jitsu class. A little tight on time, I jumped into the class without giving too much context, naively overlooking the fact that the 10 men in front of me hadn't ever trained in this way before. It was interesting to watch and feel the energy in the room as the 10 different men's nervous systems responded in 10 different ways.

The nervous system acts like a security guard, thriving on predictability and familiarity, constantly on the lookout for potential threats or dangers in our environment. What is new or novel to our system can feel threatening, even when it is something that might be healthy or empowering for us. For someone who grew up around animals, the presence of a dog may elicit feelings of safety, connection and relaxation, while for someone who was attacked by a dog in younger years the presence of that same dog might lead to stress, fear and panic.

For someone who grows up in a household where care and presence are very inconsistent, a loving partner showing up consistently in a caring and present way may feel overwhelming at first, as it is unfamiliar. Because the nervous system has grown accustomed to unpredictability, it may interpret this consistent care as a threat of some kind. It might not make 'rational' sense at first, though on a deeper, unconscious level it makes complete sense. The shadow holds these hidden aspects of ourselves, and when faced with something unfamiliar – like consistent care – it may trigger defence mechanisms rooted in old wounds, keeping us from fully embracing healthy connection.

In the modern world, where most of us are exposed to a huge amount of stimulation, slowing down and reducing the amount of noise and stimulation coming in can actually feel threatening.

Can you think of what feels unfamiliar or threatening to your nervous system?

Of course, the nervous system can adapt over time as we work through our triggers and expand what feels safe for us.

Consider: The Security Guard

- If you think of something you would like to achieve or bring into your life that you have struggled to create up until this point, what might it be about that thing that feels unpredictable, unfamiliar and potentially scary?
- For example, maybe you've wanted to start a business, but the financial insecurity, risk of failure or new responsibilities may create fear for you. Recognising these fears and uncertainties can be the first step in addressing them and moving forward.

————————— **Triggers as Teachers** —————————

Working solely with the mind can help us come to greater levels of awareness of what has shaped us, though if we neglect the role of the body and nervous system on the healing journey we may find ourselves repeating the same struggles and cycles, in spite of our new awareness and cognitive understandings.

I noticed this in my own life working on a number of challenges during the global pandemic in 2020. Largely isolated and living alone, I worked through courses, journalling prompts and therapy training and garnered much greater insights into some of my patterns, where they came from and how they played out in my life. I spent a year becoming a training provider in Dr David Berceli's TRE (tension and trauma releasing exercises) and went through a year-long professional training in Dr Gabor Maté's psychotherapeutic therapy called compassionate inquiry. Both courses involved giving and receiving therapy sessions on a weekly basis and so I was deep in the work!

It felt at times like I had 'gotten past' certain patterns that I had played out for years and found new levels of confidence and self-belief, though in those times of isolation I was not in any environments or around people that might trigger the unprocessed experiences. As we shifted back into normality and back into more social connection, it became evident to me that 'knowing' was not enough. I needed to lean on my new somatic (body-based) tools and strategies for dealing with my triggers and the feelings of danger that would emerge in my body at times when it was reminded of difficult past experiences.

You might know cognitively that to overcome feelings of loneliness you've got to put yourself out there socially, but if your body becomes overwhelmed by the experience, a 'flight' survival pattern may kick in, with your biology bypassing your psychology in an effort to survive. The part of you that 'knows better' goes offline unless you can regulate and bring the rational, thinking mind back online.

In a similar vein, someone going to therapy and gaining a better cognitive understanding of their triggers will find it of little use without learning and practising tools for creating a sense of safety in the body when it reacts to experiences that trigger old memories. Most of our wounding was formed in relation to other people and so our triggers will also emerge in the same way, as will our potential opportunities for healing. How often in life have we felt ready to change but then reverted to old patterns, behaviours or reactions when we experience the discomfort of difficult feelings?

In the Western world, logic and thinking are often seen as the only form of intelligence, and so the wisdom and knowledge of the body can often be overlooked. From the time we begin school there is huge value placed on intellect and cognition. Before that time we are more emotional beings.

A child who experiences fear when seeing a spider is perhaps told by a parent, 'Don't be silly, it's only a spider,' and a strange disconnect or conflict occurs. On one hand the child is aware of the sensations of fear running through their body, but on the other hand the all-knowing superhero parent is saying the child's internal experience is not real. Perhaps this is when the child begins to disconnect from their feelings for the first time, lose trust in themselves and choose to live in the head rather than the body.

As adults we may find ourselves relating to our emotions in the same way as our caregivers did, and so the child who was told 'don't be silly' when experiencing fear may dismiss their adult fears with the same attitude. In adulthood, these suppressed emotions can resurface in unexpected ways, manifesting as anxiety or avoidance when facing similar fears, revealing the shadow's influence on our behaviour and decision-making.

Consider: Your Suppressed Emotions

- Which emotions are most difficult for you to be with?
- How did your parents or primary caregivers relate to this emotion in your younger years?

Despite the best effort of our ego defences, the body remembers what the mind forgets and to practise true self-care we must be willing to listen to the body and not try to outthink it or outsmart it.

Consider a scenario of a young child starting school, anxious and nervous but reassured by their parents that everything will be great. They settle in after a few days and meet some friends, but then something happens that leads to them being exiled by the group, surrounded by their peers, ridiculed and teased. In this moment of complete overwhelm the child's body tenses, their breath stops and they lose their voice. This memory becomes imprinted in the body. Our tissues store our issues.

In that moment two things happen for the child. On some level cognitively they have learned that 'it is not OK to be myself' and so they will develop strategies to hide whatever it was that led to the ridicule. As outlined in the last chapter, we develop different 'parts' or ways of being in order to shield ourselves from future hurt.

On a somatic (body) level, for the sake of safety, the child's body remembers the experience and will instinctively do its best to avoid similar scenarios in the future. The physiological response that the child experiences in this moment of fear is linked to the memory of the event, creating neural pathways which link the emotional experience with specific sensations. As a result the body becomes more sensitive to cues that resemble this original triggering situation and activate a 'fight or flight' response in efforts at self-preservation.

Looking back on early childhood experiences that at the time felt scary or overwhelming, it can be easy to dismiss those experiences as inconsequential or irrelevant, though if we step back into the shoes of the younger version of ourselves who felt a sense of overwhelm at the time, we can better understand the impact our experiences had on us. Take an example of a child losing their parents for a few minutes while at the supermarket doing the weekly food shop. What in reality may have only been a few minutes of separation can feel to the child like a case of life or death.

Working with Triggers

Emotional triggers are specific situations or stimuli that evoke a strong emotional reaction, usually based on past painful experiences or traumas. As is the case with all of our shadow work, the act of working with triggers involves leaning into discomfort rather than away from it.

In speaking about ways in which our shadow becomes activated in Chapter Two, I outlined reactivity as a clear sign of our shadow being touched. Our reactivity often takes the form of an emotional trigger in which we are reminded of aspects of ourselves that we have disowned or suppressed. Triggers can either lead to us acting out and losing our centre, or coming inward with a commitment to self-understanding. The following steps can be used as a mind/ body practice for gaining insight from your triggers.

Working with Triggers

1. **Identify a trigger**

   Consider a situation, thought, event or person who evokes intense physical or emotional sensations or reactions within you.

2. **Pause and breathe**

   Breathe a little deeper and allow yourself to tune into sensations within the body. If it ever feels too intense you can slow things down by making your exhale twice as long as your inhale.

3. **Explore the emotion**

   Get curious about the emotion that you are experiencing around this trigger and identify any sensations that you are experiencing in your body related to the emotion. Name the emotion, its location in the body and the accompanying sensations.

4. **Identify the belief**

   If this emotion had a voice, what might it say? What do you believe when this trigger is present?

   Trace it back. Get curious about the sensations, the emotion and the belief behind that emotion. What is the earliest memory that comes to mind related to this? How does it tie in with your core beliefs about yourself?

5. **Journal**

   Write a little about the origin of the trigger, the emotion and belief that it brought about and any insights or realisations that come to you in leaning toward this reaction rather than away from it.

6. **Integrate**

   Explore how you might be able to respond in future situations, rather than react, when triggered by similar scenarios. Explore practices that might support you in managing similar triggers more effectively.

Somatic Therapies

A simple definition of trauma is any experience that is too much, too soon or too fast for our nervous system to handle and integrate in the moment.

Trauma can also result from repeated exposure to stressors over time, or from neglect, with a consistent lack of emotional, physical or social care and support. In overwhelming situations our body's natural response is to shift into a survival state, directing the energy for us to either fight or take flight.

When neither of these options is viable and we feel overwhelmed or powerless, we instead experience a freeze state in which we become immobilised, often losing our voice, stopping our breath and tensing our bodies. Even when the threat or danger has passed, with trauma our bodies remain dysregulated and muscles hold the tension of the experience.

An example I sometimes offer is a soldier being at war for a number of months and having to remain in a hypervigilant and high-alert state all that time, watching out for potential threats or danger. Without finding tools to calm the body and regulate the nervous system, the soldier will return home to the safety of their family but still be on high alert looking for threats and danger, unable to connect and be present, compassionate and playful, characteristics of a nervous system and body that feel safe and grounded.

Of course this does not just apply to the extremes of a soldier spending months at war; something similar might be seen in an individual struggling to feel safe and relaxed with their family in the evening after returning from a busy corporate work environment in which being switched on or fired up is essential. We cannot just tell ourselves mentally to calm down and relax – we have to take steps to allow our bodies to shift into more relaxed states before signals are sent to the mind that we are safe in the world and can be present, open and loving.

At times when it is not safe or appropriate to feel our feelings we will tend to repress, meaning we will hold back emotions, thoughts or desires.

Repression will tend to happen either due to trauma or to conditioning, and is primarily unconscious. With trauma such as abuse in childhood, the repression of fear, anger or sadness could be an unconscious coping strategy. With these memories stored in the subconscious, they may be difficult for the individual to access without the help of a trained therapist.

In the case of conditioning, which is primarily unconscious, like the air we breathe without realising it, we often absorb beliefs, patterns and behaviours from our surroundings without questioning them, shaping our responses and perceptions in ways we're not fully aware of. While we might have the capacity to feel and express certain emotions, we often do not because our conditioning shapes our responses without our conscious awareness. In this case, an example could be a child who grows up in a household where emotions are shamed. Consequently, the child unconsciously learns to repress their feelings to fit in with the family, often dissociating from emotions like anger or sadness because they don't feel safe expressing them.

In order to create lasting change in our lives and in our psychology it is paramount that we remove some of this repressed energy from the body. It is our bodies that hold the pain and tension of the feelings we weren't able to feel, and when these feelings are left undigested in the body we will tend to be pulled back into drama and old conflicts or patterns. Again, the shadow becomes the store-house for these unwanted sensations, emotions and memories, and the body then continues to inform the mind that we are not safe in the world. No amount of positive thinking will move us past this state of dysregulation. We've got to come into the body to create safety. We cannot outthink a feeling.

In healing work the concepts of pendulation and titration are important. Pendulation refers to the pattern of moving between experiencing difficult emotions and then coming back to resourc-ing and safety, not getting lost in or overwhelmed by our emotions and instead gradually exploring and releasing suppressed emotion in a safe way. Titration, too, is an important piece of this somatic healing work; it is breaking down overwhelming experiences or emotions into smaller, more manageable parts.

Somatic therapies offer a body-based approach to working with trauma and focus on engaging the body as the vehicle for process-ing trauma rather than (or alongside) traditional talk therapy.

A number of years ago, during a particularly stressful period of my life, I visited a flotation centre and spent an hour and a half in a float tank. For those unfamiliar, a float tank or sensory deprivation tank is a dark and soundproof tank filled with a shallow pool of water that is at skin temperature. The water contains a high con-centration of Epsom salts and so when you lie back you float and experience weightlessness. In the dark and quiet pod with the water at the same temperature as your skin, the usual visual, auditory and tactile sensations are removed, allowing you to shift quickly into deeper states of relaxation and introspection.

I had been in the tank many times before, but during this par-ticularly stressful period of time, after a few minutes of floating and focusing on my breath I felt my body start to gently shake and tremble involuntarily.

Ordinarily I would have consciously stopped my body from moving, but around that time I had been reading about how 'neurogenic tremors' are a natural part of the body's healing process, a way for the body to dislodge an excess of energy trapped in the muscles and nervous system from times of chronic stress or tension. The relief of tension I felt after the floating and tremors far exceeded any relief I had experienced from talking about my stress and overwhelm in the preceding weeks.

After this first-hand experience I went on to spend a year studying Dr David Berceli's TRE – tension and trauma releasing exercises, a set of simple exercises that offer a means of bringing about these 'neurogenic tremors' in a safe and supportive environment that allows for the release of stored tension and trauma from the body. Dr Berceli tells a great story about a time when he was working as a humanitarian aid worker across war-torn countries. When seeking refuge in a bomb shelter in Lebanon in 1979 during a bombing raid, he noticed the children in the shelter trembling with fear, while the adults (who looked to hide their fear from the children) seemed to remain calm. It was here that Berceli first made the link between physical movement and the release of trauma.

Other body-based therapies, such as somatic experiencing, conscious connected breathwork, bioenergetics, deep body work and body-centred psychotherapies, can be incredibly beneficial in working with unresolved trauma and the shadow through the body.

I think of two branches to the body-based practices we might commit to.

First, there are the practices that 'empty the bucket', allowing us to deal with accumulated stress or unresolved trauma from past experiences. In order for us to be emotionally healthy it is important that we create and allow space for ourselves to feel our feelings, including any backlog of suppressed emotion.

If you think of all the challenging, stressful or overwhelming experiences you have had in your life that never had the space to be 'digested' as contributing to a bucket, at some point that bucket will overflow. In other words, if we don't ever take some space to process or digest some of these old experiences we may find ourselves stuck in chronic states of stress or anxiety.

Practices that 'empty the bucket' and help clear out some of this old repressed energy might include the body-based therapies listed above. In the presence of a trained facilitator these types of practice can greatly contribute to the healing journey and support your shadow work. Other regular practices like yoga, dance or movement therapy or massage can also help lessen the load of accumulated stress and tension and 'empty the bucket'. We can think of this work as 'nervous system repair'.

Second, there are the practices that help us to regulate in the moment, to bring immediate signals of safety at times when we feel ourselves losing our sense of ground. It might be that in the early stages of dating a new partner you notice yourself feeling overwhelmed as they get close and, noticing the signs of overwhelm in your body, you do a short breathing practice to bring some immediate calm in the moment. Or perhaps while sitting in the waiting room before a job interview you sense yourself catastrophising and thinking through worst-case scenarios, prompting you to feel your feet firmly on the ground and bum resting on the chair. We can think of this work as 'nervous system regulation'.

Incorporating practices that both empty the bucket of accumulated stress, thus repairing the nervous system, and practices that regulate, or help bring immediate comfort in times where we are triggered, we can promote improved wellbeing, resilience and emotional regulation.

——— Summary: Gold in the Shadow ———

- In the areas of behavioural change, personal growth, coaching or healing work, a focus is often put on the individual's beliefs and thinking. We call this a top-down approach. Working with the body through bottom-up approaches is essential in moving past old patterns, beliefs and behaviours.
- Trauma is any experience that is too much, too soon or too fast for our nervous system to handle and integrate in the moment.
- In overwhelming situations our body's natural response is to shift into a survival state, directing the energy for either fight or flight, and it is paramount that we remove some of this repressed energy from the body.
- The act of working with triggers and integrating shadow materials involves leaning into discomfort rather than away from it.
- When working with the body we can think about practices that repair the nervous system and practices that regulate the nervous system.

Incomplete Sentences

Read the beginning of each sentence aloud and allow yourself to complete the sentence spontaneously in an unfiltered way. After completing all the prompts you can jot down any insights or reflections that stand out to you.

- When I am under stress, I notice tension in my …
- My experience of fight/flight/freeze response manifests as …
- Exploring my triggers has helped me to understand …
- I notice changes in my body when I am experiencing …
- My nervous system feels most regulated when …
- I feel safe in my body when …
- If my body could speak at this moment it would say …
- Listening to my body will allow me to …

Journalling Prompts

1. Describe a recent experience where you noticed a strong connection between your mind and body. How did you become aware of this connection, and what did it teach you about yourself?

2. Explore the role of triggers in your life. What are some common triggers that activate your fight/flight/freeze/fawn response, and how do they show up in your body?

3. In the chapter I shared the idea that 'if you don't use the energy, the energy uses you' in reference to unacknowledged or unprocessed stress and tension. What are some of the disempowering behaviours you turn to when overwhelmed or stressed, and what might be some healthier ways of processing this excess of energy in the body?

4. Write a little about how your caregivers were in the presence of more difficult emotions. Is there any link between how you relate to your difficult emotions and how others related to those emotions when you were younger? How can you best support yourself in the presence of difficult emotions?

5. We get better in life at the things that we consistently practise. How is it you would like to feel in your body and what are the practices that would support that?

The Bow and Arch

The Bow and Arch are exercises first introduced by Alexander Lowen, the founder of bioenergetic therapy, and are designed to release tension and pent-up energy from the body, particularly from the spine and the chest area. These movements help enhance flexibility, opening up the front and back of the body, and supporting the natural flow of energy. Restoration of this flow occurs as we release blocked emotions which we may have been 'armouring' around with chronic muscular tension or holding patterns.

Throughout the exercise look to keep one-third of your awareness on maintaining the stretch, one-third of your awareness on breathing deeply and one-third of your awareness on feeling the sensations in your body.

Start with the bow. Stand with your feet shoulder-width apart, knees slightly bent and heels flat on the floor. Make loose fists with both hands and place them on the small of your lower back, allowing yourself to arch so that your pelvis goes forward and shoulders go back. Lift your chest and arch your back gently, creating a 'bow' shape with your body. Breathe deeply throughout the exercise.

Hold the stretch for one minute, feeling the stretch along the front of your body and the opening of your heart centre. You may begin to feel some vibration happening in the body as the body loosens up.

Now, transition into the arch. Begin with your feet a little closer than shoulder-width apart. Bend forward at the hips, letting your head hang loosely and your fingertips lightly brush off the floor. Bend your knees as much as you need to get your hands to contact the floor (without putting any weight on your hands).

Let your hands hang and try to keep your weight on the balls of your feet and heels on the floor. Now push your hips up by straightening the knees (without locking them). Breathe deeply throughout the exercise and allow any vibrations that occur in the legs. Hold the posture for a minute.

Repeat the bow and arch for three to five rounds of each for a total of 6–10 minutes. With each repetition, allow the body to release physical and emotional tension stored in your body.

I would encourage you to try these exercises at least three to five times in the next week and then make them a regular part of your routine going forward.

CHAPTER FIVE

The Inner Child and Inner Teenager

'Each one of us has a three-year-old child within us, and we often spend most of our time yelling at that kid in ourselves. Then we wonder why our lives don't work.' LOUISE L. HAY

'Vulnerability sounds like truth and feels like courage. Truth and courage aren't always comfortable, but they're never weaknesses.' BRENÉ BROWN

—— The Inner Child and Inner Teenager ——

I sit with Sean, a man in his late seventies, and watch him weep as he relays stories of being sent to boarding school in his early years and a part of him feeling rejected, abandoned and unwanted ever since.

Rather than being able to express or share the sadness and loss he felt when shipped off to boarding school as a young boy, he learned to bottle up his emotions and focus on impressing those around him instead, for fear of them seeing his vulnerability. In other words, his grief and other aspects of his childhood self were pushed into shadow, and his autopilot coping strategy became hard work that yielded praise and validation.

As well as pushing his childhood pain to the side, he had also suppressed his childlike gifts and qualities like playfulness, creativity and spontaneity. As a result, his life had mostly been a rigid routine focused solely on productivity, leaving little room for joy or self-expression. As an adult, he had achieved a great deal both personally and professionally, but always had this lurking part who felt he wasn't enough.

Sean shared with me that this was the first time he had cried in front of someone in years, having always rejected his vulnerability and chosen hard work and busyness instead. Struggling to trust and fully receive the love of the people close to him, he'd always turned to work as a coping strategy for difficult feelings of shame and sadness. His struggles to feel like he was enough sometimes caused further stress as he would unconsciously push away the loving efforts of his partner and kids, who wanted to be close to him. He was beating himself up and struggling to understand why he was pushing away the very thing he had always wanted.

As we looked at in Chapter Four, what is unfamiliar to our system can seem threatening, leading us to retreat to the comfort of our defence mechanisms. This is the nature of the unintegrated shadow. It often creates the very thing we are trying to avoid – in Sean's case, disconnection, isolation and the rejection of love and intimacy.

Over a few months working together Sean took a proactive approach to reparenting his inner child and began to tend to his emotions. He also began to make more space for joy and play in his life and slowly became more comfortable with receiving the love of his family, beginning to see himself as worthy and enough. By recognising and working through his patterns he began to make room in his life for his younger, more vulnerable parts that held not only his shame and sadness, but also his creativity, presence and joy. He approached his inner work with the same energy he had given to his professional life for decades and said he had found ease and comfort in his own skin that he hadn't ever known would be possible.

He said it was the type of work he'd have been dismissive of years ago, but a plea from his daughter to get support had finally inspired him to try a different way. He noted how grateful he was to have done the work of meeting his shadow self and caring for his inner child, allowing him to find the deepest sense of connection he had had in his adult life.

I later sat with Jackie, an American client in her sixties, through a breathwork session, supporting her as she expressed grief and anger connected to her inner child that she later told me she had held for decades.

As a child Jackie watched her parents fight like cats and dogs and waited for the day where one of them would leave, never to return again. Though both of them stayed, she noted that it would have been better if they had just gone their separate ways rather than keeping her in a constant state of fear and uncertainty. Not wanting to add further stress or tension, in those early years she had taken on the role of caring for and wanting the best for her parents, disconnecting from her own emotional needs and laying the roots of codependency.

She shared her sadness that she had had to grow up so quickly and didn't ever get to be cared for and supported in pursuing her own wants and needs. She felt she had become the caretaker for her parents as a child and played out the same role in all her close relationships in the five decades that followed.

In our work together we began to get clear on her values, wants and needs. We also worked with the part of her that rejected support from others. She began to make herself a priority and learned to protect herself and her boundaries with the word 'no', listening to the emotions that had been overlooked for so long and honouring the needs of her inner child.

It was difficult at first, but she stayed with it, carrying a photo of her 10-year-old self with her in her purse and making a daily commitment to showing up for that younger girl who had always needed someone to show up for her.

The relational dynamics in her life began to shift as she found and expressed her voice again. Some people she had considered friends drifted away, while those who remained felt much more connected to her, and appreciated and trusted her more now that she was authentically expressing her true self. Some even commented that being able to support her, and not having it be a one-way relationship with her always being the carer, allowed them to feel much more valued and comfortable in their friendship. The people around her were now meeting a real and authentic person, not a façade.

While these two stories point to how our childhood years and imprints can have a large influence on what we share with and what we hide from others, our teenage years too can influence what we come to value, desire and need in our adult lives to live authentic and fulfilled lives.

In men's groups that I have run for a number of years now, I often encourage the men to make a list of their own needs, identifying what it is they need in their lives to feel fulfilled, inspired and alive. It can be a confronting exercise for many as they recognise how far removed they are from knowing what they need to feel they are living authentically and filling their own cup. For many of the men I work with, they note that since their teens they have learned to prioritise work and the needs of others in order to meet societal expectations and norms. The same, of course, is true for women. The question of 'What do I need?' often isn't as easy to answer as it might seem. This 'teenage' pattern of striving for acceptance and validation is often carried into adulthood, leading to people's lives being run by their inner teenager rather than their authentic selves.

In Chapter Three we began our exploration of 'parts work' and began to recognise some of the many sub-personalities that live within each of us. Most of our shadow self was formed during our childhood and teens, and so the inner child and inner teenager become major parts or sub-personalities within our psyche. In this chapter we will move closer toward these key aspects of ourselves and look to better understand how they show up in our lives and how we can show up for them.

Our inner child often feels the pain of rejection, abandonment, shame or invalidation and so, when neglected, can be triggered by these wounds regardless of our current age. When nurtured, this same inner child can bring the gifts of playfulness, creativity, innocence and spontaneity back into our lives.

Our inner teenager represents a pivotal time in our lives in which we will have had significant growth, exploration and self-discovery. When neglected, the inner teenager can feel the insecurity of peer pressure, body image struggles and the challenge of finding an identity that truly 'fits' us. When connected with and supported, our inner teenager can become the source of authentic self-expression and can bring about the courage to challenge social norms and embrace our individuality.

In this chapter we'll look at moving from neglect of the inner child and teenage parts to nurturing these powerful parts of us.

———— Understanding the Inner Child ————

I grew up in Raheen in Limerick before my family moved to Galway when I was eight. I was a football fanatic, a Liverpool fan who idolised Robbie Fowler. Everyone around me supported Manchester United at the time and, to my shame, I would later go on to jump ship and become a United supporter too.

When we moved to Galway I stayed back a year and repeated second class. I'd already made my Communion and so I watched on as my new classmates made theirs. I'd had some bullying in Limerick and saw myself as a potential target for the cooler kids. I was the new guy, didn't have brand-name clothes or shoes like 'everyone' else and had a head physically far too big for my body!

In that first year in Galway I won an art competition and the local newspaper came in to take my photo. Rather than being proud of my achievement, I was mortified. The class watched as I was brought to the front of the room to have my photo taken. I saw standing out in any way as posing a threat to my safety. I pushed my creativity and artistic abilities into shadow at that time, seeing them as something that might make me shine too brightly and bring unwanted attention to myself. My strategy had become to blend in and be as ordinary as possible.

Around that time I discovered professional wrestling and it became an obsession. The wrestling heroes on the TV, with their exaggerated larger-than-life characteristics, represented qualities of bravery, strength and resilience. Maybe in watching them I was unconsciously trying to bring alive these qualities in my own personality, projecting my disowned strength onto the heroes on the TV screen.

It's funny the things we remember from childhood. The imprints developed during those times are a result of the meanings that we give to our experiences.

Consider: Childhood Memories

Given two minutes to share a little about your own early years, what would you share? Who were you and how and where did you fit in in the world? What first comes to mind about how you came to view yourself and what still feels applicable today?

Our own stories and the stories we connect with are powerful indicators of our unconscious drivers. These stories that we tell ourselves come to be how we make sense of the world around us, giving us a sense of orientation.

A friend once offered me an interesting prompt to explore when he asked me about the story, movie or book that I played on a loop again and again throughout childhood.

What story would you share?

For me, *Harry Potter* was the one that first came to mind … I read the book again and again and got lost in it.

Next, my friend asked me to explain the storyline of *Harry Potter* in simple language as if describing it to a child.

In describing the story I realised why I connected with it so strongly. It was about a little boy who had magic that the people around him didn't recognise. He was weird, an outsider who didn't fit in, but then he found his place in the world and found people who appreciated his magic.

The stories we are drawn to in life, especially those that we come back to time and time again, often reflect the dynamics of our unconscious mind. We see ourselves in the stories we connect with. What story did you connect to in your earliest years?

Your Childhood Story

Think of a story that you loved as a child, one that you could hear or watch again and again, never growing tired of it. It might be a story in the form of a book, or it might have been a film or TV show you watched on repeat.

Describe the plot of the story in simple language and talk a little about the character that you connected with the most. What was it about the character that you connected with?

Now, consider how this story has played or is playing out in your own life and what you saw in the character that you see in yourself too.

Our inner child part represents the aspects of the psyche that carries many of the memories, experiences and emotions from our childhood. When neglected, this aspect can lead us to feeling fearful, insecure, disconnected, hurt and self-conscious. When supported and nurtured, our inner child can be a source of creativity, playfulness, spontaneity, awe and wonder in our lives.

At times in our lives when we lose access to these empowering qualities, we can be reminded of the importance of caring for this vulnerable aspect of ourselves who we may have forgotten about in the busyness of our day-to-day lives. When our adult self is able to show up, our inner child can feel safe. However, when we cannot or do not show up in a grounded and adult way, we are expecting much younger parts of us to take on adult responsibilities.

Ruptures are inevitable in our lives and require repair in order for us to build resilience. A child will experience this sense of repair and will feel safe when it is mirrored to them that it is safe to be who they are. When the child does not receive attunement, that need for safety is not met, and they can be left feeling isolated, hurt and wounded, carrying these unresolved emotions into adulthood. An example of a rupture might be a parent shouting at their child and scaring them in a moment of rage and impatience. If the parent can quickly notice their reactivity and apologise and help the child feel safe, a repair can occur, but without this the child can be left with fear and distrust of the person who is supposed to care for them.

Consider: Relating to Your Vulnerability

- What situations or events usually trigger feelings of vulnerability?
- How do you feel physically when you first notice you're feeling vulnerable (e.g. increased heart rate, butterflies in the stomach, sweating)?
- What do you typically do when you feel vulnerable? Do you embrace it, hide it or distract yourself? Do you tend to seek support and share your vulnerability, or do you keep it to yourself?

- What strategies do you use to cope with vulnerability? Are they healthy (e.g. open communication, self-compassion) or unhealthy (e.g. shutting down, defensiveness)?
- How do you feel about the way you handle vulnerability? Is there anything you would like to change?
- Can you recall a time when you handled vulnerability in a way that you were proud of? What did you do differently?

—————— Healing Childhood Wounds ——————

In podcast interviews I am sometimes asked about my email signature, which for the past few years has included a mission statement that I have as a sort of compass to guide me in life. When I first added it to the end of my emails and to my website, I questioned if it was suitable or would be off-putting to potential corporate or 'professional' clients.

I then reminded myself that it is my north star and is reflective of my truth. If it's off-putting to potential clients or companies, we're not going to be a good fit, and that's OK. Having my mission statement at the end of each email I send ensures it's never too far from my mind and hopefully never too far from how I'm living.

MY MISSION

I created a connected and authentic world,
by allowing the space for myself and others
to live with compassion, curiosity and playfulness.

I am of the belief that 'the wound can become the womb'; in other words, acceptance of and a willingness to lean toward the wounds of our pain, trauma or suffering can enable the womb of possibility for creation, growth and new beginnings in our lives. In contrast, an unwillingness to lean into our wounds stunts the possibility for growth and transformation and keeps us stuck in old defence mechanisms and trauma responses.

My mission statement was born at a men's rite of passage a few years back when I was confronted with one of my own deeply held wounds. Men's 'rites of passage' are about going from 'boy' psychology to 'man' psychology by confronting the parts of ourselves we have tried to run from and turning toward our shadow rather than away from it. In this process we are choosing to finally grow up and to reparent and tend to those younger, more vulnerable parts of ourselves, rather than project our fear or pain outward in destructive ways that abdicate personal responsibility. We were asked to identify a deep-seated belief or fear that we hold, a belief that we took on early in life that we've been playing out ever since.

My belief: 'I'll always be alone ...'

Of course there is a spiritual part of me who wants to bypass that belief with fluffy language or Instagram-worthy quotes of 'if you make peace with yourself you'll never be lonely', but there's also a very human part of me that experiences fear, sadness and shame around my loneliness and a fear of dying with no one close to me. During the rite of passage, we went through processes to confront our deeply held belief. To protect the integrity of the process I won't share the specifics, but a part of the exercise involved identifying what it was that I felt was missing in childhood. I identified connection and authenticity as the missing pieces for me in my youngest years. I didn't feel I fitted in and I didn't feel I could be myself.

These unmet needs or missing pieces pointed to the key aspects of the type of world we might want to create – in my case a world that is 'connected and authentic'.

Next, we were to consider how we might create this type of world in our own unique way. In a way this could be seen as a willingness to reparent ourselves and tend to our younger, more vulnerable part. As a facilitator and guide, I saw the opportunity to create connection and authenticity by creating spaces where I and others can live with compassion, playfulness and curiosity.

Consider completing the exercise yourself, following the instructions below.

The Womb in the Wound

Find a photo of yourself as a child, ideally around the age of seven.

As you look at the picture, ask yourself what did you need at that time that you did not receive?

Next, think about small actions you can take in your current life to support you in meeting these previously unmet needs.

Then complete the following statement:

I bring (what you needed but didn't receive) to the world by (ways that you can fulfil these needs).

Some examples:
- I bring creativity to the world by making beautiful art and music.
- I bring love and presence to the world by being the best father I can be.
- I bring encouragement to the world by supporting others and myself with positive words.
- I bring understanding to the world by actively listening to others.

—————— Reconnecting with Joy and Play ——————

Leading men's retreats has been among the most fulfilling work I have done over the last 10 years. When I moved from the fitness industry toward the personal development space a decade ago and started offering workshops around the country, the vast majority of attendees were women, who every now and then managed to drag along a brother, father, husband or son.

Over a number of years and hundreds of workshops, I slowly watched the demographic in the room shift and more and more men show up of their own accord. Once the rooms started to have an equal split of men and women, I saw the opportunity and need to provide some men-only retreats and workshops to offer a different dynamic and unique space for men to learn more about who they are.

I enjoyed offering the shorter evening or day-long workshops, but nothing beats the magic of a three-day residential retreat where safety and trust can be built, allowing men to let go of the armour and reconnect to their authentic expression. The transformation is visible in real time and the men leave by Sunday looking 100 kilos lighter, with bright eyes that have come alive again and moved past the weariness they had arrived with.

Twenty men show up on Friday, all guarded in their own ways, unsure of what to expect. As we work intensely together for three days and challenge the beliefs we had about who we needed to be in order to be accepted, safety is built among the group and the masks and defence strategies fall away, replaced with authentic and open expression. On Sunday morning a game of soccer usually comes about and I proudly watch on as the group, who only days before were armoured strangers, laugh and play, embracing joy and shedding all stories about who they need to be to be accepted.

We have a 'closing circle' at the end of the three days where each man gets to share the highlights, insights and takeaways from his retreat experience. I would love to think the biggest takeaways were the result of some clever or wise insight I offered or some carefully curated healing process, but in reality, the two biggest things that stand out in every retreat are these:

- 'It's good to know I'm not the only one who struggles and that other people feel the things I feel and think the things I think. It was nice to be able to share what's really going on for me and not have to hide or pretend who I am.'
- 'I need to allow or make more time and space in my life for the things I love. I need more time for play and enjoyment.'

For me, this is inner child work.

'It's safe to be who you are. You are welcome here. Allow yourself to play and just be for a while, without trying to get somewhere or prove yourself'. Sometimes it's about being in environments where we receive these messages and often it's about reminding ourselves of these core messages.

As kids we approach life with a deep sense of curiosity and engage in or pursue activities or experiences for the simple joy of doing them. This allows us to be in the present moment and experience play, adventure and spontaneity. Life can feel big and full, with different environments, different circles of friends and different hobbies or activities.

As adults, these qualities can often get lost. We become fixated on goals and outcomes, on meeting societal expectations, and often see the world through the lens of success or productivity rather than joy, play or pleasure. The novelty of our younger years dwindles.

Our social circles often get smaller and smaller, as do our environments, and life can begin to feel a different, less enjoyable type of full. Perhaps mistakenly, we think that if we cannot see a tangible financial or material return on the time invested in something it is not worthwhile, when in reality the return on investment on activities that bring us joy is immeasurable.

I have coached many clients throughout the years who have come to me saying they needed to change their career as it wasn't giving them what they wanted or needed in life. Many have young families and hefty mortgages and would be taking a huge leap of faith in changing direction or career, potentially putting themselves under unnecessary stress or overwhelm in an effort to reconnect with a sense of aliveness and joy in their lives. Others report that they are ready to leave their relationship.

I will generally ask about the hobbies or interests outside their work or relationship that bring them joy. It can be a bit of a 'chicken and egg' scenario in that they will often report that work leaves them feeling depleted and that every minute outside work is for family time, though the energy they bring to family often feels flat and heavy. It can be easy, when feeling disconnected from ourselves, to project frustration or blame onto our work or our partners. It can be easy, too, to fall into the trap of thinking that all our needs should be met by our career or by our partner. Often these clients find that a complete overhaul within their career or an end to their existing relationship is not what is needed. Instead, what is needed is a commitment to recognising and honouring their own needs, blocking off time for hobbies or passions outside their work and relational commitments, time when they can reconnect to play, wonder, joy and presence. Time where there's nothing to achieve and no one to impress.

Bronnie Ware, a palliative care nurse who sat at the bedsides of people in their final weeks and days, noted some of the most common regrets she saw in those who were faced with their own mortality. She noted, too, that people grow a lot in those final days. The most common regret she noted in the many she sat with was 'I wish I'd had the courage to live a life true to myself, not the life others expected of me.' Another of the common regrets that she wrote about in her international bestseller *Five Regrets of the Dying* was 'I wish I had let myself be happier.' The language is interesting, not 'I wish I had been happier' but 'I wish I had *let* myself be happier.'

How would it be for us to lean progressively more into living a life true to ourselves and allowing ourselves to be happier? With 168 hours in the week, I urge even the busiest of clients to find a minimum of three hours for themselves and watch what happens in all areas of their lives.

At 28, after 10 years away from martial arts, I came to a point of needing somewhere to go that didn't involve work or nights out. Around that time I attended a nine-day retreat in which we were asked to bring an 'introductory item', something that was meaningful to us and would give the group a sense of who we were. It couldn't involve anything related to family or work. I brought with me a Brazilian Jiu-Jitsu medal I had won during my time in America 10 years before.

When asked to share with the group for two minutes what our item represented for us, I spoke about a time in my life in which I was broke but happy, a time when my life revolved around my passions and I felt I didn't need anything outside that. Ten years on, my life looked very different, with a focus on achieving success and approval as opposed to prioritising the things that brought me alive.

Soon after returning home from the retreat, I found a local Brazilian Jiu-Jitsu gym and blocked off the time to go and train. I arrived a few minutes before class, walked to the door and saw the group inside training. Intimidated despite having trained throughout my teens, I got back in my car, turned around and drove home, feeling slightly defeated albeit a little relieved. Knowing I needed something in life to bring back a sense of aliveness and joy, I returned a few days later. I hesitated momentarily before stepping through the door. It's been a hugely important pillar in my life ever since.

I have spoken to others who have metaphorically or literally turned the car around or backed out of appointments or commitments made to themselves, regardless of the activity they have chosen to pursue. There can be a deeply ingrained inner critic who shows up telling us something to the effect of 'grow up, you've got things to get done. You don't have time to play.' If work, family and reaching societal targets have become our primary focus, the idea of engaging in activities just for the fun of it might seem indulgent at first.

I might be stating the obvious here but I think it's a useful reminder:

If you find an activity that allows you to connect to play and presence and you find a community who allows you to feel safe in being yourself, every area of your life will improve.

Finding both the activities and the people who help you feel more alive and reconnect to your childlike sense of joy and wonder may not happen overnight. It isn't the easiest thing in the world to make new friends as an adult, and some of us don't instantly know what hobby or activity might bring us that sense of joy and aliveness. One thing is for sure: we aren't going to find these new friends or new vehicles for joy by staying in our heads or staying in the house. We have got to be willing to leave the comfort of our existing routines and environment.

When I was 20 I was in my second year of an arts degree in Galway, studying geography and economics. Having made it to a grand total of nine lectures in my first year of college, it was a wonder I had made it as far as year two. Now, halfway through second year, my lecture attendance was even worse, and so I wasn't meeting any friends – apart from those I tried to get into nightclubs with after downing bottles of Lidl's cheaper alternative to Buckfast.

An arts degree was at the time a safe bet for someone who had no clue what they wanted to do with their life. In retrospect I knew exactly what I wanted to do with my life, but I didn't have the confidence or belief that I could do it. If I had been honest with myself I would have pursued a fitness career straight out of school, but that didn't seem viable so I put it on hold for a few years. Unsurprisingly a life revolving around skipping lectures, staying in bed and chasing the next night out wasn't very full of joy, hope or optimism.

My dad, wanting to encourage me, suggested I join a few of the clubs or societies in the college to meet some new friends and open my eyes to new possibilities.

'Why don't you join the theatre club?'

'I don't like theatre …'

'Why don't you join the badminton club?'

'I don't like badminton …'

'It's not about liking or not liking badminton or theatre. It's about trying new things and meeting new people outside of a pub or a nightclub …'

He was right. I didn't see it at the time and I didn't join the badminton or theatre club (or improve my lecture attendance), but I now see that we aren't going to find new friends or new passions by continuing to live in the same routines, environments and social circles.

Consider: Time for Play

Do you create or allow space in your life for joy, play and wonder with nothing to achieve and nowhere to 'get'? What would it look like to bring more play into your life and a hobby that allows you to just be, without having to prove yourself or get anywhere?

The Inner Teenager

'He didn't even inhale!'

I am 13 on my lunch break in my earliest days of secondary school, hanging out with some older kids from the year ahead and trying my best not to cough after taking a drag of a joint.

I had gone to a secondary school where I was one of two students in a class of 30 who hadn't attended the same primary school, and so I was the new guy again. The only friend I had at the time was a skateboarder and grunge enthusiast and so I stuck with him and tried to follow his lead. He seemed to have confidence and seemed to know who he was, two things I didn't have. The girls in the class liked him too. I bought a cheap skateboard so I could be like him, learned to play guitar like him and pretended I enjoyed the cool films and alternative music that he liked.

After lunch I would sit in class paranoid, convinced it was a matter of time before a teacher would smell the smoke off my Nirvana or Che Guevara T-shirt and send me to the principal's office. We'd generously spray Lynx Africa to try and mask the smell of Amber Leaf tobacco and somehow almost always got away with it.

My awkward teenage years were a mish-mash of moving in and out of different circles and cliques. I skateboarded and played rugby, played guitar in bands and lifted weights, practised judo, remained a fan of professional wrestling and took an interest in genres of music ranging from hip-hop to traditional Irish to heavy metal. I was friends with most people, including the popular girls in the class, though I assumed my acne-covered face would be a deterrent to any of them seeing me as anything more than a friend.

Looking back now, I see a teenager who had a diverse range of interests and got on well with people from all backgrounds, though at the time I saw myself as an insecure impostor who didn't really fit in anywhere and didn't really know who he was. I still have that judgement of myself sometimes.

In healing, coaching and therapeutic work the concept of the inner child has been spoken about for decades, while the concept of the inner teenager often remains overlooked and unacknowledged. When we consider that the inner child holds the memories, experiences and emotions of childhood it would make sense that there is an aspect of our psyche that similarly holds the memories, experiences and emotions of our pivotal adolescent or teen years.

Consider: Meeting Your Inner Teenager

What immediately stands out to you when you think of who you were in your teen years? What were you most afraid that others might see in you? What did you want them to see instead? How does your inner teenager play out in your adult life today?

In a similar way to how we identified a story we were drawn to in childhood, we can also think back to our adolescent years and consider what movie, book or story captivated us and had us coming back time and time again. What was it for you? What dynamics might it have been pointing to in the unconscious mind of your inner teen?

For me, in those few short years from child to teen I moved from *Harry Potter* to *Fight Club*, a film about a man frustrated with a boring and predictable life meeting a mysterious and charismatic friend called Tyler. Tyler is everything the main character is not, unapologetic, raw and free. Later in the film we find out Tyler is actually a part of the main character, a reflection of his more authentic and primal expression and true feelings and desires.

The story is as good a demonstration of the human shadow self as any.

As a teen I saw myself in the main character, battling between the alternatives of living a predictable and safe life or living authentically and unapologetically.

Consider: Your Teenage Story

What was the story you played on a loop in your teens? Which character did you relate to the most? Can you see yourself in any aspect of that story or character? What do you think drew you to it?

While our formative years lay the foundations for our identity, values and understanding of the world, our teen years bring about a new phase of exploration, self-discovery and possible rebellion in our lives. It is a time of 'finding ourselves', differentiating from our caregivers and figuring out how and where we fit in the world.

It's a time where we often dismiss the more childish aspects of our personality in favour of exploring a more mature, independent sense of self. It is also a time of questioning authority, challenging social norms and trying on different identities to see what fits us best.

Pressures to conform can bring about feelings of insecurity and self-doubt, while changes to our bodies and the awakening of sexual energy can bring about a mixture of curiosity and discomfort. Our inner teenager, then, can carry the unresolved conflicts, unmet needs and unexpressed desires from that crucial time in our life. There is a part living in us all who carries both the pain and potentiality from our adolescence and teen years.

Teen Years

- What was most difficult for me in my teens was …
- What I needed the most that I didn't receive was …
- What I wanted the most during that time was …

Then consider how the spontaneous answers that come to you still impact you.

A teen who doesn't have the chance to authentically express and discover themselves often becomes an adult who struggles to know who they are and what values, goals and interests are important to them. In its extreme we can see the individual who never authentically finds and leans in to their values and interests and then has a massive crisis of identity at midlife – from the outside looking in it looks like they are burning their life to the ground in an act of rebellion. Perhaps becoming aware of the shortness of life and how long they have spent putting the needs and expectations of others ahead of their own feelings or needs, the individual decides to make some changes in their lives. Often drastic changes are not needed and can be destabilising. Instead, sitting with the question of 'What do I need to be happy, fulfilled and energised in life?' and leaning into the answers to that question can allow us to move from showing up in life like insecure teenagers to secure adults who derive our value from within.

Your Soundtrack

It often amazes me how I can remember the lyrics to a song I haven't heard in years, sometimes since childhood, while recalling anything from school feels nearly impossible. Here's a simple exercise using music to reflect on our lives up to this point.

Break your life into 'chapters', each chapter representing a few years on your timeline. Then, for each chapter or time period, look to connect with that time in your life and find a song that represents that time for you.

This could be a song you listened to frequently or one that evokes strong memories. As you listen to each song, write in your journal about the memories and emotions it brings up, paying special attention to any insights or connections to your unconscious. Repeat this process for each stage, allowing the music to guide you deeper into your self-awareness and understanding of your shadow.

Your Timeline

Many of our current belief systems came about as the result of the meanings we gave to the earliest experiences in our lives. Things happened, and we instinctively gave them meaning. It's how we came to make sense of the world and our place within it.

In this exercise you will do a little timeline of the first 18 years of your life, exploring stand-out moments and the meaning you gave to those moments. Then we will look at the beliefs that you formed as a result of the meanings you created and see how those beliefs have impacted or informed you ever since.

Begin by sketching a timeline of your life from 0 to 18 years old. Draw this timeline in whatever way feels inspiring to you. You will have had countless experiences during those 18 years. Which were the most emotionally charged or impactful of those experiences for you?

Your next step is to pick out five to six of the moments that stand out to you the most. Some examples might include your first love interest or heartbreak, the loss of a close family member or friend, experiences of bullying, discovering a passion or talent, exploring your sexuality for the first time or a significant achievement or accomplishment. Some of these experiences that you pinpoint may be memories that you label as more 'positive' and others as more 'negative'. Look to find a few of each, if possible, and to spread them between childhood and teenage experiences.

Next, beside each memory that you have identified, write down what you made that situation mean or what belief you formed as a result. Try to see it through the eyes of your inner child or teen and not the eyes of your current self. It might be easy now to look back on your first heartbreak and dismiss it as teenage lust, but what did your teenage self make that mean at the time? It is likely that most of these experiences are universal in a sense, things that many experience, but in the context of our story we personalise them and make them mean something about ourselves.

For example, when I was a teenager I found judo and quickly excelled in competition, which gave me a great sense of accomplishment. It was something I enjoyed and worked hard at, and the belief that I came to was that 'I can get better at anything I am willing to invest my time and energy in'. In younger years, when my family moved from Limerick to Galway and I moved to a new school, I attached the meaning that 'I'm the new guy who doesn't quite fit in.' One hundred other people might have had these same experiences of winning in judo or moving to a new school and come to different meanings or interpretations as a result.

The final part of the exercise, once you have pinpointed the beliefs that you formed, is to consider how each of these beliefs has impacted or informed your life since. Noticing how often the 'being the new guy' story comes up for me in my life allows me to tend to and care for that part of me who fears standing out or not being accepted. Reminding myself of the belief system that 'I can get better at anything I am willing to invest my time and energy in' helps me to lean into new challenges or opportunities.

On completing the exercise, notice when and where these old beliefs show up in your day-to-day life.

———— **Summary: Gold in the Shadow** ————

- By delving into the past, we can begin to unravel patterns that no longer serve us and to work towards healing.
- By allowing ourselves to engage in activities that bring joy and spontaneity, we can rekindle the essence of who we were before life's challenges weighed us down.
- Our inner teenager often holds the raw, unfiltered emotions and desires that we may have stifled to conform to societal expectations.
- Reparenting ourselves means offering the compassion, guidance and support that we might have missed during our formative years. This involves nurturing our emotional needs, setting healthy boundaries and fostering a positive inner dialogue.

Incomplete Sentences

Read the beginning of each sentence aloud and allow yourself to complete the sentence spontaneously in an unfiltered way. After completing all the prompts you can jot down any insights or reflections that stand out to you.

- Growing up I often felt …
- Exploring memories from my childhood helps me connect with …
- A childhood wound I am ready to heal is …
- I could embrace more playfulness in my life by …
- What my inner teenager needs from me is …
- What I love about my inner child is …
- As I think back to my inner child, I often wonder …
- My inner teenager rebelled against …

Journalling Prompts

1. Reflect on a childhood memory when you felt pure joy or happiness. What were you doing, and what made this experience so special? How can you bring more of that sense of joy into your life today?

2. Think back to your teenage years and identify a moment when you felt misunderstood or unsupported. How did that experience shape your beliefs about yourself and others? What would you tell your teenage self now, with the wisdom you've gained over the years?

3. Imagine being a nurturing parent to your inner child and teenager. What kind of support, love or guidance would they need to heal old wounds and thrive? Write a letter to your inner child or teenager offering this support.

4. Consider a time when you allowed yourself to be vulnerable, whether as a child, teenager or adult. What fears or concerns arose, and how were they received by others? How can embracing vulnerability enhance your relationships and personal growth?

5. What brought you joy as a child or teenager that you've neglected in adulthood? What prevents you from engaging in these activities now? What small steps would help you reintroduce playfulness and creativity into your life?

Dancing the Wild Woman/Wild Man

This week I encourage you to take at least 10 minutes a day for an embodiment exercise we'll call 'Dancing the Wild Woman/ Wild Man'.

Find a space where you can move freely without restrictions and consider making a short playlist with some songs that help you let it all go.

Close your eyes and take a few deep breaths, connecting with your inner wildness. As you start to move, let go of any need to be a 'good boy' or 'good girl'. Allow your body to express itself in a primal, uninhibited way. Allow yourself to get out of the box of conditioning you have lived in.

Dance as if no one is watching, embracing your wild, free and authentic self. Feel the energy and passion within you, letting it flow through your movements. Don't worry about looking graceful or impressing anyone; this is about reclaiming your untamed spirit, breaking the rules and allowing yourself to be messy and free.

Continue for at least 10 minutes or as long as you feel called to, and afterwards, take a moment to reflect on what feels different for you after allowing your true, wild nature some space to emerge. Complete this practice at least five times over the course of the next week.

CHAPTER SIX

Shame and the Inner Critic

'*Shame corrodes the very part of us that believes
we are capable of change.*' BRENÉ BROWN

'*We cannot heal what we cannot feel. So without recovery,
our toxic shame gets carried for generations.
Toxically shamed people tend to become more and more
stagnant as life goes on. They live in a guarded, secretive
and defensive way.*' JOHN BRADSHAW

The Voice of Shame

In 2016 I ended up on *The Late Late Show* to tell the story of how I went from failing with a business and moving back in with my parents to winning entrepreneur awards and running a successful fitness business with thousands of clients all over the world.

At my lowest point, filled with shame and broken both financially and emotionally, a part of me had latched on to the idea that

someday I would make it to the *Late Late Show* to share a story of redemption. I believed that being on the *Late Late Show*, a Friday-night staple in Ireland throughout our childhoods, meant you'd 'made it'. I wanted to give my parents something to be proud of and wanted to prove to the world that I wasn't worthless.

If I had been aware of shadow work back then and ready to do the work, I probably could have saved myself a lot of pain and struggle by tending to my insecure parts rather than running from them and trying to prove myself to the world. Really we're only ever trying to prove ourselves to the part of ourselves that holds a belief of not being enough. Often we go the long way around and run away from the part that feels insecure, pushing that part into shadow, where it unconsciously ends up running our lives from a place of constantly needing to prove ourselves and be in competition with the world around us.

After a TEDx talk I had given telling my story gained some trac-tion and media attention, I got a call from the producers of the *Late Late* saying they wanted to book me in for an interview the follow-ing week. My bubble temporarily burst when they called back a few days later to say Richard Gere was in Ireland and he'd be taking 'my' spot. Nevertheless I was rebooked a few weeks later and something I had held as a dream for a few years now came to fruition.

A part of the story I had shared in the TEDx talk spoke of the shame I felt in having to borrow money from my dad to pay my bus fare home from Dublin on Christmas Eve, finally admitting defeat and facing the reality that I had failed with my efforts to 'make it' in Dublin. I got the bus from Galway to Dublin for the show for what felt like the 'end of the journey' and the completion of that hero's journey from failure to success. Producers of the show tried to push me to walk up into the audience during the interview and give my dad back the €20 I had borrowed a few years before. I am glad I pushed back, knowing both I and my dad would have been mortified at the spectacle.

I was nervous and a little shy, knowing how many people would be tuning in, but overall the interview went well. I turned on my phone after the show and had thousands of notifications and mes-sages from people who had watched. On the way home to Galway I read through as many of the messages as I could. I felt a little hit of dopamine or relief with every supportive message that came through, people saying they appreciated my vulnerability or that they saw a part of themselves in my story.

Then I came to a tweet that stung: 'The Late Late Show gets worse every week. Bottom of the barrel stuff. This guy from Galway doesn't have a drop of charisma.'

I felt my heart sink a little and my inner critic jumped in quickly, overlooking the thousands of supportive tweets and latching on to this and the few other tweets that pointed to the insecure part of me that believed he wasn't enough. 'They're right! Who do you think you are? You might have fooled the people who said nice things about you, but these people see who you really are! A basic and boring nobody without a drop of charisma ...'

Many of us spend our lives trying to achieve things to impress the outside world and overlook the importance of addressing what's driving this need for validation. In my case the shame stories of not being enough led me to chase as many things outside myself as I could to prove my story wrong. When I ran out of places to look externally and turned my attention to my inner world, my shame and my inner critic's narratives, I came to understand the origins of my beliefs, the purpose of maintaining those beliefs and the importance of developing a sense of worth from within.

It is the inner critic who harshly judges and compares our bodies to the beauty standards seen in the media or online. It is the inner critic who berates us for not having reached the markers of success that we have been led to believe are expected of us by a certain age. It is our inner critic that looks to push us back in our box when we dare try something new or commit to making proactive changes in our lives. It is our inner critic who encourages self-sabotage, pushes us toward perfectionism and leaves us feeling like an impostor when we are praised or acknowledged for our success or accomplishments. It is the inner critic that points to the personal development books on the shelf and shames us for not having read them, or bullies us for not having stayed consistent with changes we've tried to make in our day-to-day habits and behaviours.

This list of ways in which the inner critic shows up in our lives could go on and on. Ultimately, though, it is the inner critic who gives voice to our feelings of shame and unworthiness, finding a million and one ways to tell us that we are unlovable or that we aren't enough. With its harsh tone and relentless self-judgement, it isn't surprising that our natural instinct may be to want to get rid of this part of ourselves. As is sometimes said, if a friend spoke to us in the way we sometimes speak to ourselves we probably wouldn't remain friends with them for very long.

While we can create space or separation from a friend or external source who brings us down, we often feel helpless and trapped in the internal prison of our own thoughts played out by the inner critic. Those internal voices and narratives can seem omnipresent and inescapable. You can, however, learn to create separation between your authentic self and the critical voice that seeks to diminish you. The longer you sidestep or resist engaging with your inner critic, the more severe its criticisms will become. Perhaps the most important or impactful work you can do with your shadow self is to address the relationship you have with your inner critic.

You will notice I say 'address the relationship you have with your inner critic', as opposed to suggesting you try to overcome, move past or get rid of that critical voice that so often seems to want to point out all of your flaws, mistakes and shortcomings. Your inner critic is not the enemy. It is a loyal aspect of yourself that doesn't want to see you hurt by the outside world. It is so committed to this mission, in fact, that it will choose to direct criticism toward you and give you back some level of control, rather than be left vulnerable and guessing when and where criticism might pop up externally and unexpectedly from those around you.

If, growing up, I am teased by friends for being too emotional, one of my inner critic's roles may well become policing my emotions, constantly judging or criticising myself to ensure that I suppress or hide those emotions from future ridicule. This self-imposed criticism becomes a self-protective mechanism. Judging myself first stops me from doing the behaviour that might be judged by others.

The tricky nature of the inner critic, though, is that it serves as both a protector and a saboteur. As such, it is important that we learn to work skilfully with it without trying to avoid it or destroy it. As long as we try to remove, delete or deny any aspect of ourselves we will experience the effects of an internal war, with one part of ourselves fighting with another. Instead, as with all aspects of the shadow self, we must get curious and move toward our shame and inner critic in an effort to understand its origins, its purpose and its drivers. Any part of ourselves that we have rejected and pushed into shadow was at one point shamed, and so to integrate those aspects and become unconditionally loving of ourselves we must meet the previously shamed parts with openness, self-compassion and curiosity.

With greater understanding and awareness of this part of ourselves, we have the opportunity to change how we relate to our shame and to the critical voice within. As we gain a greater understanding of when, how and why our inner critic and shame show up, we can create separation from that part of ourselves rather than fusing with it and taking its judgements as gospel. Working skilfully with the inner critic involves discerning between when its voice is being helpful and when it is being harmful.

We can also develop and awaken our sometimes dormant 'inner ally', who like a nurturing parent or trusted friend provides support, encouragement and unconditional acceptance. Developing this inner ally and practices for self-compassion can provide a counterbalance to the relentless attacks of the inner critic and wounds of shame by offering both reassurance in times of doubt and frequent reminders of our worthiness.

———— Origins of the Inner Critic ————

Like most of our conditioning, the beliefs held by our inner critic are largely developed in our formative years when we are like sponges in our environment, picking up implicit and explicit messages from all around us that shape how we see ourselves, others and the world.

Explicit messages are the clear-cut and direct messages we hear: 'Boys don't cry' or 'Getting angry isn't very ladylike.' Implicit messages, meanwhile, are those messages that are implied without being explicitly stated. A child might see their parents prioritising work over everything else and come to the belief that their own self-worth is tied to their work ethic and productivity. Countless early experiences with parents, primary caregivers, siblings, teachers and other figures of authority begin to shape our perception of self while forming an internal dialogue of self-evaluation. 'Am I living up to what is expected of me?' 'Am I a good boy or girl?', 'Am I enough?' In efforts to maintain love, acceptance and approval our inner critic speaks up any time we dare to step outside the expectations that were placed upon us in younger years.

It isn't just our home life that shapes the inner critic's beliefs of how we need to show up in the world. Some of the self-criticism that later plagues us is the result of societal norms and cultural

expectations that build unrealistic standards of beauty and success that we carry into life. In the '80s and '90s supermodels and
action movie heroes influenced the perception of beauty standards
and body image for men and women, while a rise in marketing
and advertising campaigns pushed luxury brands, materialism and
consumerism as the path to success, worthiness and happiness. In
the early 2000s reality TV shows and talent competitions painted
pictures of plucking people from their 'horrible', 'mundane' ordinary lives to superstardom, with the implicit message that in order
to be happy and successful, you must ensure you are more than
'just' an ordinary person with an ordinary life. I have to remind
myself (and clients) of the freedom that comes with allowing ourselves to be ordinary. This permission to be ordinary can alleviate
the pressure felt from years spent trying to live up to impossible
standards set by media and advertising.

This pressure has magnified further in more recent years. With
the explosion of social media highlight reels many kids, teens and
adults feel a pressure to portray a picture-perfect, filtered and
blemish-free life. While in pre-social media days, many will have
been competitive with others, in some ways social media has led
to individuals comparing every day to their best day. A person
might share a photo that gets 100 likes or comments, but then this
becomes the new expectation or standard for every time they post.
When that new standard is not met, the inner critic is quick to let
the person know.

Of course the household, the school system and the media are
not the only sources that create standards for our inner critic to
uphold. Religion often brings with it a rigid set of expectations
and sometimes feelings of shame, guilt or unworthiness when our

authentic expression is in contrast or conflict with the values and code of conduct of the religion in which we were raised. And so our inner critic, influenced by our family, friends and culture, constantly compares us to the impossible standards of beauty, success, moral integrity and happiness seen in other people's lives.

—— Toxic Shame, Guilt and Healthy Shame ——

Shame

Shame is a universal emotion experienced by everyone, though in the midst of the experience of shame we can feel isolated, alone and like the only person in the world who feels the way we feel. The feeling of shame will generally be triggered by the sense of not meeting internal or external standards, resulting in us experiencing self-doubt and feelings of inadequacy and unworthiness.

Shame, then, is the energy and emotion behind the voice of our inner critic. Shame in itself is important, though what we do with that shame and how we relate to it is key. We are tribal beings, and shame ensures we respect and remain conscious of the feelings, needs and values of others. Those without shame demonstrate traits of sociopathy.

The roots of shame lie in early childhood experiences in which a child's behaviours were met with criticism, judgement or rejection. As we become socialised and learn what behaviour is appropriate and what is not, we are met with experiences where we break the rules, make mistakes or act in a way deemed unacceptable in the given context. Shame arises when we are scolded, outright rejected or simply receive a more subtle glance of disapproval.

Cultural expectations, too, can result in feelings of shame around certain behaviours, desires or emotions. For example, in cultures where heterosexuality is the expectation, those who have a different sexual orientation may face discrimination, ridicule or even violence, resulting in feelings of shame around expressing themselves authentically.

With these reactions from those around us, we internalise the belief that certain aspects of ourselves are unlovable or unacceptable. Shame becomes the protective mechanism hiding these 'unlovable parts' to avoid further pain, fear or discomfort.

Guilt and Healthy Shame

While shame can bring about a sense of being inherently flawed or unworthy, guilt can often point us to areas where we lack integrity or have violated our moral compass. Guilt tends to be focused on specific behaviours or actions, while shame often extends beyond actions to reflect upon our entire sense of self-worth and identity.

How those who surrounded us reacted or responded to our mistakes in childhood can have a large bearing on how shame manifests for us in adulthood. If our mistakes or 'bad' behaviours were met with compassion and guidance in childhood, we are more likely to have a healthy relationship with shame in adulthood. If, however, our mistakes were met with rejection, ridicule and harsh judgement we may have internalised a more toxic form of shame with a sense of unworthiness and inadequacy.

While toxic shame can eat away at our self-esteem and self-worth, guilt or healthy shame serves as a recognition of mistakes or wrongdoings, allowing for a change of behaviour going forward.

Toxic shame says: 'You are inherently bad or wrong and do not deserve love or acceptance.'

Healthy shame, meanwhile, says: 'Your mistakes do not define your worth. They do, however, offer an opportunity to learn and grow.'

The feeling of shame, like all other feelings, brings with it a somatic, body-based experience. We may notice physical sensations like a sinking feeling in the stomach or a flushing in the face. We might also notice a change in our posture or a feeling of inward collapse. Maybe we notice tension, tightness or holding in our chest, fists or jaw. Our breathing might be shallow as we feel this temporary discomfort or emotional distress. These physical manifestations point back to the mind–body connection that we spoke about earlier in the book. In reaction to this emotional distress or physical discomfort we will often unconsciously move to patterns of behaviour to get away from the discomfort.

As we move closer to our inner critic and our shame, in efforts to meet these parts of ourselves from a place of curiosity and openness, I would encourage you to consider what physical sensations you tend to experience when shame is present. Consider too, what your default reaction is when you look to move away from these uncomfortable feelings.

Consider: How Do You Relate to Your Shame?

- What situations or events usually trigger feelings of shame?
- How do you feel physically when you first notice you're feeling shame (e.g. flushed face, sinking stomach, urge to hide)?

- What do you typically do when you feel shame? Do you express it, hide it or distract yourself? Do you tend to apologise excessively, withdraw, or become defensive?
- What strategies do you use to cope with shame? Are they healthy (e.g. self-compassion, seeking support) or unhealthy (e.g. self-criticism, denial)?
- How do you feel about the way you handle shame? Is there anything you would like to change?
- Can you recall a time when you handled shame in a way that you were proud of? What did you do differently?

The Inner Critic's Purpose

The critical voice within is so often an internalised voice based on external feedback or criticism from others. When exposed to repeated criticism, judgement or neglect as children, we begin to adopt the external voices as our own.

When I was working with a client recently and asked her to share some of the dialogue of her inner critic, she responded with 'He says ...' I was struck by her inner critic being a 'he' and would later come to learn that her inner critic reminded her strongly of her harsh father, who had always pointed out her shortcomings. Others internalise the voices of their bullies and carry the energy and content of their judgements for decades.

While sometimes our attention is on the content of our inner critic's dialogue, it is useful, too, to be curious about the tone and energy you feel from that part of yourself. We can think of shame and the inner critic's narratives as anger turned inwards. In times when we were met with criticism, ridicule or judgement, when we would have liked to have expressed anger in order to protect or defend ourselves, we perhaps had to direct that anger toward ourselves and internalise it to stay safe.

'The bullies were right. You always mess things up,' your inner critic might tell you after slipping over your words in a work presentation and turning red in front of a room full of colleagues. 'You're disgusting,' a harsh inner critic might tell you as you stand naked in front of a mirror, judging yourself for not looking like the models or celebrities you grew up seeing on television or in magazines.

What could this cruel inner aspect of ourselves want for us? Put simply, our inner critic wants us to be OK and acts as a self-protective mechanism for us. At the core of our existence we are tribal and social beings who crave belonging and acceptance. Wanting us to survive and stay safe within the social hierarchy, our inner critic carries the memories of past hurt or pain.

The inner critic looks to maintain the societal standards that were placed upon you in youth and looks to keep you compliant to the way of living that made you a good boy or good girl. It wants you to reach the standards of success that have been outlined by your culture. Living authentically, breaking the rules, taking risks or deviating from the norm can seem terrifying to the inner critic and so they remind us to get back in our box. In order to do that it'll often chime in to interrupt your authentic expression and remind you to morph back into the adapted self who needed to show up in a certain way to maintain safety and love.

Remembering times in your past when you felt hurt or vulnerable, it looks to protect you from judgement, rejection or failure going forward. The critic who tells you, 'Don't join the gym, everyone will stare at you,' remembers a time in the past when you were hurt and does not want you to experience more of the same. And so, beyond the initial harshness you might hear in the words of your inner critic, with the understanding of its purpose and driver, you may be able to find an element of compassion and empathy. When worked with and neutralised, this inner critic can actually become an important part of your internal support system.

A refusal to change how we relate to the inner critic can result in us living within the confines of our childhood conditioning for the rest of our lives, rather than living a life inspired by our own authentic values and aspirations. I recently worked with a man who had put himself under huge pressure by taking on his father's business, but not because he wanted to – in fact, it was the last thing in the world he wanted to do. As we worked together it became clear that despite being in his fifties now, his early conditioning and belief that 'good boys do what their fathers expect' still had him stuck in cycles of self-abandonment. The problem with overlooking our own needs in order to meet the expectations we think others have of us is that we internalise the anger and direct it toward ourselves. We also often end up resenting the other person in the long run.

We can sometimes judge ourselves for doing the opposite to what we say we do in life and fall into a shame spiral, seeing ourselves as inconsistent or lacking integrity. If instead we can bring a real sense of curiosity to our behaviours we can become more empowered. In the case of harsh judgements from the inner critic it is important to check in with ourselves and look to figure out what value or need it is looking to protect.

The Inner Ally

In the presence of our inner critic and the emotion of shame we can often feel ourselves collapse and regress to younger versions of ourselves, forgetting that we are capable, grown adults and not helpless children controlled by fear, shame and self-doubt. The inner child craves love, acceptance, connection and support, and understandably can feel threatened or overwhelmed by the judgements of the harsh inner critic. Like a fearful child seeking protection from a scary or harsh world, we may find ourselves reverting to old familiar coping mechanisms or defence strategies in efforts to shield our vulnerable inner child from further pain when our inner critic looks to bully or ridicule them.

Robert Masters, an incredible shadow worker and a mentor of mine, talks about the importance of getting between the inner critic and inner child when we are exploring the shadow. I experienced this first hand in a group therapy process a number of years ago. In some of the group therapy processes I have taken part in and facilitated over the years, we bring out a circular carpet which is rolled out on the floor. The group stand around the perimeter of the carpet as a facilitator and participants step on the middle of the carpet to do their 'carpet work'.

At this point, after explaining their current challenge or situation, the participant (guided by the facilitator) will choose different members of the group to represent the different aspects of their psyche. This type of psychodrama work involves embodying and exploring our many inner voices through role-play, with the carpet being the overall landscape and the individuals playing different characters in the person's life, or different parts of themselves. In a similar way to a journalling practice taking our internal world onto paper, this type of psychodrama allows us to create a visual 3D representation of what is going on for us internally, offering us a bit of space from the situation for perspective and understanding.

In this particular session, one person was chosen to represent my inner child. I had them hunch down to embody the energy of this vulnerable part of me and gave them some lines to say aloud that represented the feelings of fear and longing for support that that part of me felt. 'I'm scared and I just want people to like me.'

Next, someone else was brought in to represent my inner critic. I placed them next to the child and had them towering over that part, hurling criticism and abuse. 'You're a weirdo and no one's ever going to like the real you!'

The person playing my inner critic, towering over the person hunkered down playing my inner child, accurately captured the energy of what I would feel internally when shame, self-doubt or feelings of unworthiness were present for me in my life. It was difficult to watch and even more so to realise that this was the dynamic playing out within my psyche on a near-daily basis.

The piece of work concluded with me bringing an additional character out onto the carpet to protect the fearful inner child. I placed the person who played this supportive character between the critic and child, had them assume a posture of assertiveness and confidence, and gave them lines of support for the child and lines of interruption for the critic.

We called this part the inner ally.

'STOP! You won't talk to him like that!' my inner ally told the person playing my inner critic, before turning to the person playing my inner child. 'When you show up authentically and trust yourself by being yourself, you'll meet the most amazing people who appreciate you for being you.'

Difficult as it was to watch my inner critic attack my inner child, it was equally empowering to watch this 'inner ally' character step in and intervene.

Critic, Child and Ally

Consider how this dynamic plays out for you. What is a harsh judgement your inner critic often directs at you?

In my case the judgement was 'You're a weirdo and no one's ever going to like the real you!'

Next, connecting with the younger part of you who experienced the wounding, what belief do they hold? For me the belief was 'I'm scared and I just want people to like me.'

Can you see the interplay between your inner critic and inner child?

Next, consider some supportive messages you could share from your inner ally. 'When you show up authentically and trust yourself by being yourself, you'll meet the most amazing people who appreciate you for being you.'

Developing the Inner Ally

Our inner ally is akin to a healthy parent, there to support and encourage us. Our confidence in life is built through keeping commitment to ourselves, and so part of the inner ally's role is to take stock of and acknowledge our progress, no matter how small.

That being said, the role of the healthy parent or inner ally is not to blindly praise every action of the individual but instead to do what is needed to support the healthy development of their self-esteem. That might involve constructive feedback, setting in place new boundaries, providing guidance or allowing space for mistakes to be made.

In beginning to connect with and relate to this inner ally or healthy inner parent part, it can be useful to think of the traits or characteristics of an ideal mother and father supporting you. You might think of two supportive figures who embody the qualities that you would most like to have in a mentor or ally. Perhaps one of the inner parents encourages you to take chances, to practise courage and stretch your comfort zone, while the other is more nurturing and patient with you.

A part of the role of the inner ally is to create boundaries to support health, self-respect and self-care. The inner ally remains unconditional in their love and support of us, while creating conditional boundaries that support our development. Take the example of an individual fuelled by her inner critic who finds herself stuck in workaholism, constantly pushing herself to the brink of exhaustion. Recognising the effects of this relentless drive, the inner ally may step in and create a boundary of finishing work by a certain time and turning off the work phone and laptop. When the critic creeps back in with reminders that 'without your work you're nothing', it is the inner ally who can provide support and hold the boundary, allowing for much-needed downtime and recovery.

Alongside putting in place healthy boundaries, consistent practice of empowering habits or behaviours that demonstrate a care and respect for ourselves is a key aspect of developing our self-esteem. Every action we take, no matter how big or small, contributes to how we perceive ourselves. Honouring our desires and needs, surrounding ourselves with people who are supportive, living in line with our values and making space for the empowering voice of our inner ally all play a role in the development of our self-esteem.

In the past I have offered clients the practice of keeping an 'inner ally journal' as a conscious means of cultivating self-esteem and self-compassion. The journal could take any form that helps document the client's experiences, taking note of their wins, lessons and inherent worth and value. A simple starting point with the inner ally journal would be to take five minutes in the morning to write a note of encouragement to yourself from the inner ally or allies, taking into account all that you have coming up in the day ahead. The evening practice then could be to take another five minutes to write an acknowledgment to yourself capturing how you navigated the day.

———— Interrupting the Inner Critic ————

All change starts with awareness, and so taking some time to reflect on the role your inner critic currently plays in your life is a great start in beginning to work with it.

Consider: Getting Close to Your Inner Critic

- When and where does your inner critic show up most often? What tone or energy do you feel from their voice? Does it remind you of anyone from your past?
- What is it that your inner critic tells you? How are you impacted when you believe its judgements?

You can also run a little experiment for a few days where you keep a small notepad close to hand and write down any of the judgements you hear from your inner critic, from the time you wake up in the morning to the time you get to bed. The conscious act of writing down these critical messages can be illuminating and show how much space the critical part of you takes up, pointing to your mistakes, your shortcomings and your perceived inadequacies. Writing down these judgements can also point to the underlying beliefs and fear of your inner critic. As you begin to get clearer on the voice, tone and content of your inner critic, allow yourself to create some space when it emerges.

Regardless of the content being spewed by the inner critic, you will most likely notice its tone is assertive and sure of itself, speaking in statements and not asking questions. There isn't any sense of curiosity or openness from the critic within. So when the inner critic takes over and we become fused with it, we take all of its judgements as truth, forgetting that it is just a part of who we are and is not our whole being.

This is a fatal mistake. The inner critic is just an aspect of ourselves that is looking to keep us safe based on its memories of our childhood. As kids we will have most likely learned to be passive when shamed or criticised, and so now as adults we often recreate this passivity and fold in the presence of our inner critic. It is important that we instead become assertive in meeting our inner critic.

One great step in creating space from this part of yourself is to give your inner critic a name. Naming this part of ourselves creates a little distance between us and the voice, externalising it without discrediting its presence. From here we can reclaim some agency over our thoughts and emotions and foster a healthier relationship with this part.

Another useful step in interrupting the inner critic is to verbally or mentally assert the word 'stop'. This simple but powerful command can consciously interrupt a cycle of negative thoughts and give us back some control of our thoughts and emotions.

You might even visualise your inner ally stepping up, squaring up to your inner critic and confidently and assertively commanding them to stop. This interruption can empower us to move toward a more compassionate and constructive self-dialogue.

After interrupting the critic, we might give space for our inner ally to consciously speak to ourselves in the way we would speak to a close friend who is being hard on themselves and losing sight of their gifts and inherent value. The inner ally, akin to a nurturing parent, isn't there to lie to us and make airy-fairy affirmations that deny the truth, but instead to provide support and encouragement.

Black, White and Grey

A useful exercise for finding the voice of your inner ally is to create three columns on a piece of blank paper and to label the columns critic, neutral and ally.

In the critic column you can write down the harsh words of your inner critic. For example, 'Look at how fat you are. You're disgusting!'

In the second column, you can write down a 'neutral' or objective statement, not based on judgement but on facts. Based on the above example I might write, 'You are seven kilos heavier than you were a year ago.'

The third column is where you find the voice of your inner ally. Sticking with this same example the inner ally might say, 'You have lost weight in the past and you know what you need to do. Trust yourself and track your progress.'

While we can interrupt our inner critic by naming it, commanding it to stop and challenging its disempowering narratives with the support of our inner ally, we can also seek external support in efforts to stop the cycle of negative thoughts, beliefs and emotions.

One of the features of shame is that it creates a sense of isolation and a belief that we are bad, wrong or unlovable. In efforts to hide our 'badness' we may withdraw from social connection, instead turning to addictions in an effort to feel some form of connection, but as the old adage says, 'Our secrets make us sick.'

Unacknowledged toxic shame can often be the trigger for cycles of addiction. I believe one of the key elements of 12-step recovery groups that proves successful for many who attend is the process of showing up consistently and sharing the wounds that were previously hidden out of sight. At the same time participants hear the stories of others, removing the sense of isolation that toxic shame has given them. There is a tremendous effort required to hide our secrets and mask our truths. Great healing can happen and toxic shame can dissolve when secrets are shared in safe spaces.

Meeting Your Inner Critic

Sit comfortably in a place where you won't be disturbed. Take a few deep breaths, close your eyes if it's comfortable for you and visualise a safe and inviting space.

As you settle in and breathe deeply, imagine a chair directly opposite you. When you feel ready, invite your inner critic to sit in that chair. Do not try to force an image of the inner critic. Instead see what emerges and allow the image of your inner critic to materialise in whatever way feels right for you.

When you feel ready you can begin to ask your inner critic some open-ended questions. Do not look for specific answers, but instead listen attentively while allowing space for any emotions that you may experience. As the dialogue unfolds, look to understand the origins, purpose and drivers of your inner critic. Some questions:

- Do you have a name you would like me to call you?
- What is your reason for being here?
- What are the situations in which you feel the most fear?
- How are you helping me?
- When were you born and what first hurt you?
- What do you really want for me?

To bring the exercise to a close, thank your inner critic for revealing themselves to you.

Open your eyes when you feel ready and jot down any useful insights gained during the dialogue. Look to reflect on how you can work with, rather than against, this part of yourself in order to bring about greater self-understanding and acceptance.

Sitting with Shame

Begin by closing your eyes and taking a few grounding breaths.

Then connect with a time in which you felt shame. Notice what happens in your body, connecting it with the sensations of shame.

Continue to breathe and feel the sensations in the body. The mind may want to go to stories about why you're feeling shame or what you need to do to get away from the discomfort of feeling your shame, but look to stay with the sensations.

Now see if you have a sense of what lies behind the shame. What is this shame looking to reveal? Perhaps it is tied to feelings of inadequacy, rejection or past mistakes. What is underneath the shame?

Finally, see if you have a sense of how you could address this shame in a healthy way that acknowledges and honours your worth and humanity.

———— **Summary: Gold in the Shadow** ————

- When we receive criticism or are shamed, we internalise the voice, creating an internal narrative that judges our actions and self-worth.
- Though it might seem counterintuitive, our inner critic is trying to help us and keep us safe.
- Calling on the support of our 'inner ally' is a proactive step to get between the inner critic and inner child.
- Consider naming your inner critic, assertively stating, 'Stop!' when they show up, and then channel a more supportive voice from within.

Incomplete Sentences

Read the beginning of each sentence aloud and allow yourself to complete the sentence spontaneously in an unfiltered way. After completing all the prompts you can jot down any insights or reflections that stand out to you.

- When my inner critic speaks, I often feel …
- One thing my inner critic frequently tells me is …
- If I could challenge my inner critic, I would say …
- My inner critic reminds me of …

- My inner critic is most present when …
- I struggle with self-compassion when …
- The societal standards I feel pressure to meet include …
- When I experience self-doubt I tend to believe …

Journalling Prompts

1. Think about a recent time in which your inner critic was particularly vocal. Write about the thoughts and emotions you experienced in that time and explore the potential origins or societal expectations that drove these thoughts and emotions.

2. Write about a time in your life when you experienced deep feelings of shame. What triggered this feeling of shame and what impact did this feeling have on your behaviours, thoughts and relationships? How might you offer yourself self-compassion in the future when feelings of shame or unworthiness appear?

3. Take some time to write about the type of supportive inner ally you would like to develop. This ally is like a trusted friend or nurturing parent who shows encouragement, support and unconditional acceptance. What qualities does your inner ally possess? What could you do to develop a stronger connection to this supportive part of yourself?

4. Reflect on some of the criticism or judgements you received in your formative years and how you may have internalised some of those judgements via your inner critic. Now consider the concept of reparenting your inner child. What are some of the practices you could implement to care for the vulnerable inner child who still experiences wounds of shame or self-criticism?

5. Write a little about your beliefs and attitude around self-compassion. How would it feel to extend the same love and kindness

you give others toward yourself? What barriers or resistance do you encounter when practising self-compassion? How might you foster more self-compassion going forward to combat shame?

Mirror Work

This week I encourage you to try out a 'mirror work' practice, designed to support you in developing self-acceptance and self-compassion by directly confronting and transforming some of the negative self-perceptions of your inner critic.

Find a quiet space and stand in front of a mirror where you can see your reflection clearly. Look into your own eyes and take a few deep breaths, grounding yourself in the present moment. Notice how you feel and what sensations are present for you as you look into your own eyes.

Gently speak to yourself with words of care, support and appreciation coming from your inner ally. As you say these words, try to genuinely feel their truth while allowing any emotions to surface without judgement. If your inner critic voices negative thoughts, acknowledge them without giving them power, and then return to the affirmations of your inner ally.

Spend at least five minutes with this practice, maintaining eye contact with your reflection, and notice the shift in your inner dialogue as you consistently reinforce self-compassion and kindness.

Look to complete this practice at least five times over the next week.

CHAPTER SEVEN

Anger, Boundaries and Needs

'Bitterness is like cancer. It eats upon the host. But anger is like fire. It burns it all clean.' MAYA ANGELOU

'I sat with my anger long enough until she told me her real name was grief.' C.S. LEWIS

———— Boundary Violations ————

'He really likes you, you know …'

I don't believe her. 'He' is the dog she and her ex bought a few years before, who is making it clear he doesn't want me in the picture.

I've been dating her for five months now and every time I arrive at her place and leave my backpack down, it's a matter of time before he pisses on it when we're not looking.

'He' isn't the only challenge we're experiencing.

It's early days and already it's an unpredictable rollercoaster of emotion, but I'm closing my eyes to every red flag that presents itself. I am mistaking intensity for chemistry, mistaking emotional charge for connection and repeatedly abandoning myself in the hope of connection with her. She is unpredictable and slow to make even the smallest commitments or plans together, which puts me on edge.

I chalk that down to me being anxious, though.

I also can't drop a nagging feeling she is in contact with her ex and I am serving as some kind of backup plan or distraction, but there's something keeping me in it. She says she's not in contact with her ex and they won't ever be getting back together. So I persevere, keep trying to make it work, adapting to her needs and denying my own in an effort to win her over.

David Deida, a well-known spiritual teacher, once said, 'Choose a partner who chooses you.' I'm ignoring his advice and I'm suffering as a result. My healthy adult self has left the building and the insecure inner teenager has been forced to take charge. Friends start to notice my loss of mojo in a way only friends would. They can see my confidence dropping and me losing my centre. I am not the grounded and secure person I was only a few months before.

After a few years of practice, I was generally getting better at listening to my body, my gut, my intuition, but in this case I was ignoring every signal I was being sent and going to my head, justifying and playing mental gymnastics to make sense of the whole scenario. My body is shouting 'no' at me loud and clear in the form of anxiety telling me to run a mile. It's telling me this isn't a healthy dynamic and something is off, but she's telling me there's nothing to worry about and I need to relax. I take her word for it, put myself down and feel shame around the anxiety I've been experiencing.

Maybe I just don't know how to be in a relationship any more?

A part of me is seeing my ability to stay in the chaos as a sign of my resilience, though a friend challenges that by saying, 'Just because you have the capacity to be with chaos doesn't mean you should stay in the chaos.'

Makes sense …

Eventually it all becomes too much for me and I call an end to things.

Within days she is back with her ex and I find out they've been in contact and seeing one another behind my back the whole time. Fuck, I feel stupid. Stupid and angry for the months spent abandoning myself and prioritising someone I didn't even know, making a four-hour round trip every weekend to spend time together, only to find out it was all a lie. I'm at that stage of life where all my friends are getting married and starting families, and I've just wasted a few months of my life trying to win over a moody dog who enjoys pissing on my stuff – and the dog's owner, who seems to respect me even less.

At least the dog was honest.

I was angry at her for lying and making me think I was crazy for feeling anxious, but even more angry at myself for ignoring my gut and letting it happen. Friends tell me it isn't my fault, I shouldn't beat myself up: 'She's the one that lied.' But friends are always going to take your side in situations like this and I had to take responsibility for putting myself in the dynamic and staying in as long as I did. This wasn't the first time I had felt these types of feelings. A part of me was choosing this. A part of me felt I deserved this.

I text her to say I'm hurt.

She responds by saying she's sorry and I didn't deserve any of it.

It doesn't help.

The anger, resentment and beating myself up go on for months. The experience was painful, but my response feels disproportionate. When the response feels bigger than the situation there's always a shadow at play, something deeper that requires attention and healing.

My relationship to anger and finding my voice was being highlighted in the intensity of this whole scenario. Yet again I'd allowed myself to lose myself in order to stay in connection with someone else. Yet again I had lost my voice, abandoned my boundaries and devalued my self-worth. Around the same time I'm working with a client who breaks down in a session and tells me, 'I'm just so tired of having to re-earn my own trust again and again.'

I felt that one.

That client had repeated a cycle of overworking and burning out and is recognising a continuous pattern of working themselves into the ground, afraid to put boundaries in place with their boss and thus sacrificing their health to keep someone else happy. I feel their pain. I'd built a great life for myself and invested heavily in my emotional and mental wellbeing for years now, after years of struggle, only to completely self-abandon for a stranger.

Consider: Boundary Violations

- Where in your life or for whom have you abandoned yourself, overlooked your own boundaries and put yourself last?
- Who or what do you resent for not appreciating you or seeing your worth?
- How is that bitterness or resentment impacting you?

First I blame her for not seeing all that I had to offer, then I recognise it was myself who couldn't see all I had to offer and instead chose to settle. I recognise, too, that I wasn't being me. I was showing a filtered and people-pleasing façade, afraid that if I presented my true self she'd walk away. In essence I was trading authenticity for acceptance – again. I was so set on being a nice guy that I was willing to be inauthentic to do so. I feel like the rug, along with my slowly acquired confidence, has been pulled from under me.

I go to my mentor for a therapy session and tell him, 'It's been months now and I can't let this anger and resentment go. It's tormenting me and robbing me of all joy. I hate her for lying to me, I hate myself for not walking away a hundred times and I hate myself even more for not being able to just leave all this in the past and move on.'

He tells me to count myself lucky that I'm addressing it now, that he's worked with people who have taken decades to get over ex-partners and the pain caused as a result of lies, betrayal or self-abandonment. He's wise and patient. I'm grateful to have him in my life. He asks me what I think I should do.

'Maybe I should do some loving kindness meditation and direct love and forgiveness toward myself and toward her.' I'm full of shit. He knows it and I know it. I am not going to get away with this effort to spiritually bypass this with 'love and light'.

It is time to step into the shadow and move past this recurring pattern …

Over a few sessions we work with the anger, the self-abandon- ment and the parts of me that stayed in the dynamic. We also explore the part of me that's mistaking intensity for chemistry. I come to understand how this unexpressed anger (and efforts to bypass it) only lead to a heavy, cold, debilitating resentment. Rather than con- tinue to bypass the fiery energy of frustration and anger, I step fully into it for the first time in my life and allow it to become supportive fuel rather than something to fear or get past. Once I got past the victim stage of being owned by this anger and resentment, I stepped into a bit of warrior energy: 'I'm done with this and I'm not gonna take it any more. I'm fed up with having to re-earn my trust again and again. I'm done abandoning myself and settling for less than. I am ready to start really honouring myself and protecting myself.'

This relationship had been a tipping point, igniting a mound of suppressed anger that had been bubbling close to the surface as a result of the countless big and small violations of my own boundaries on a near-daily basis for years. All the times I would move, deny or swallow my own preferences, boundaries, wants or needs in order to keep others comfortable, all the times I would play the nice guy and disconnect from my internal world in place of managing the people in the environment around me.

I'd had enough.

Many of us learned early on that anger is bad, destructive or wrong and so pushed it into shadow, choosing instead to be 'nice' or 'agreeable' or 'easygoing'. We learned to live a life dictated by appeasing what's going on around us rather than honouring what's going on within us. We learned to keep the peace, to settle, to keep our heads down.

The challenge with pushing anger into shadow is that like all other shadow material it doesn't go away, but instead takes life in the form of sarcasm, passive aggression, gossip, silent resentment and self-sabotage. Anger turned inwards also results in debilitating shame and a relentless inner critic. The individual disconnected from their anger becomes like Play-Doh, adapting to whatever environment they occupy and not having any strong sense of self. They also become disconnected from their passion and their fire and lose touch with their inner drive and boundaries, often leading to feelings of powerlessness and a lack of authenticity in their interactions and decisions.

While some learn to deny their anger, others learn to default to anger to stay safe. Individuals overtaken and controlled by their anger project pain and hurt onto others, leaving a path of destruction. Some swing between these two extremes like Jekyll and Hyde, playing the nice guy or girl at work and meeting everyone else's needs, then coming home and exploding at their partner or kids.

The integration of clean anger, meanwhile, provides a healthy and natural protective energy rather than a destructive energy and can actually be something that supports our development of self-esteem as well as connection and intimacy with others.

——— Clean Anger ———

David Hawkins, a renowned spiritual teacher and psychiatrist, developed a 'scale of consciousness' which can help us to understand how various emotions impact our spiritual growth and experience of life. At the bottom of the scale are states such as shame, guilt and apathy, while toward the top of the scale are states such as love, joy, peace and enlightenment. Anger plays a critical role on this scale. While seen as 'negative' by many, it is also a powerful catalyst for change and positive action.

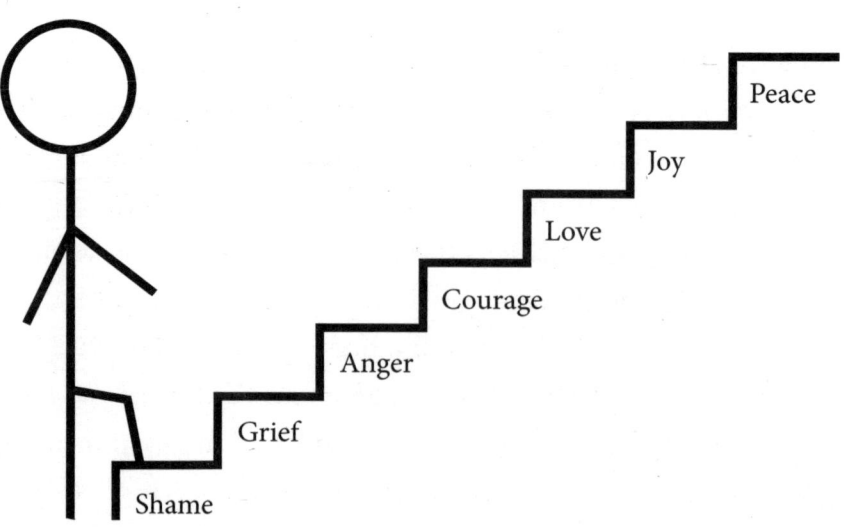

In lower states like shame, guilt and apathy we might find our-selves stuck in blame, hopelessness, humiliation and low self-worth. We are victims of our experience and feel powerless to change. Shifting into anger can indicate a more active state than these lower levels on the scale and can be an indication of moving more toward empowering action or change. In simple language, you might think of it as those times in which we can become 'fed up with our own BS' or we refuse to settle for what we're currently experiencing anymore.

After putting up with toxic behaviour from a partner for months or years due to fear of being alone, an awakening of anger might finally allow someone to find their voice again and set some firm boundar-ies in their relationship. For someone else, the energy of anger might be the push toward a healthier lifestyle and provide an initial moti-vation to join a gym after years of neglecting their wellbeing. After years of being overworked and underappreciated in a dead-end job, anger could be the catalyst for someone else to finally update their CV or look into further education to make changes in their career.

On a collective level we see the critical role anger plays in people taking a stand against unjust systems and practices, fuelling movements for social and political change. This shift from passive suffering to active resistance can be a significant turning point in our individual and collective stories. Becoming aware of and wel-coming our anger rather than making it bad or wrong can allow us to work with it skilfully and not be unconsciously manipulated by it.

Embracing Clean Anger

The unconscious expression of anger tends to appear in the extremes of underexpression or overexpression.

With underexpression, we see the people-pleaser who never finds their voice or speaks up for themselves. Completely disconnected from their anger, they say yes when they want to say no, neglect their own feelings, need to appease those around them and are like chameleons, adapting to whatever environment they are placed in to avoid conflict and gain approval. This strategy often begins early in life when certain needs are not met, leading to feelings of pain. This pain generates anger, yet there is an even stronger fear of expressing this anger. As a result, the individual defaults to saying yes to requests and going along with others to avoid conflict and maintain harmony.

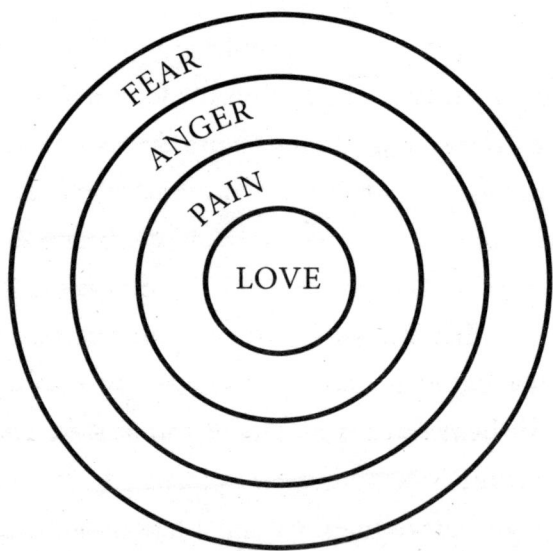

To move beyond this pattern, it is crucial for the individual to confront and process their layers of fear and anger. In stepping into the fear of feeling and expressing their anger, they can work through the pain and ultimately rediscover a sense of self-love and internal validation.

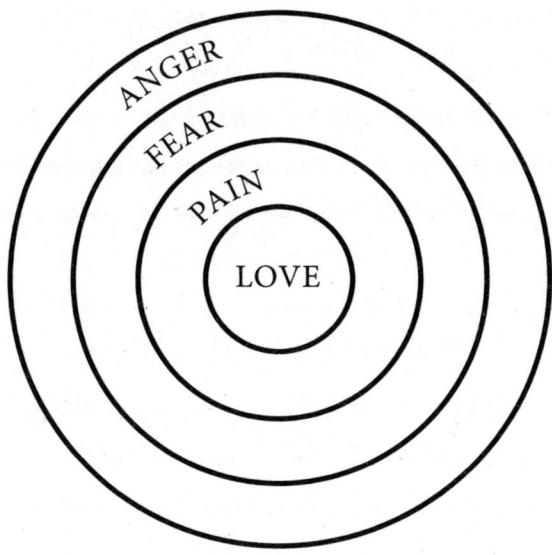

For those who lean toward bullying tendencies, the opposite pattern emerges. These individuals often prioritise expressing anger over fear as a way to protect their vulnerability. Early in life, they may have also experienced periods when their needs were not met, resulting in pain. However, instead of internalising this pain and fearing conflict, they externalise it through aggression and dominance. By placing anger above fear, they seek to assert control and safeguard themselves from feeling vulnerable. This aggressive behaviour becomes a shield, allowing them to avoid confronting deeper emotions of fear and hurt.

To truly heal, these individuals need to recognise and address their underlying vulnerability, learning to express their emotions in healthier, more constructive ways. It isn't as black and white as to say the 'bully' is bad for acting in the way they do. In the same way some learn to appease and stay safe by becoming people-pleasers, others learned that their only way of staying safe in the world was to overpower others and rely on their anger to protect their vulnerability.

Often, when we have not got to know or understand our anger we will move between these two extremes. The people-pleaser at work may morph into the bully when they get home or vice versa.

Consider: Polarities of Anger

- Where and with whom do you find yourself people-pleasing, placing the needs of others above your own?
- Where and with whom do you ignore the needs of others and allow anger to take you over, leading to bullying behaviour? This might even include bullying yourself. Anger turned inward often becomes shame voiced by the inner critic.

When we move past unconscious patterns and expressions and begin to work skilfully with our anger, we can begin to protect ourselves and all that we value, moving toward a more honest and aligned life, while staying open to others and being authentic in our expression.

Things happen in our lives that warrant our anger: betrayal by a friend; disrespect from a partner; unfair treatment at work; witnessing injustice in the world; the loss of a loved one due to negligence. There is plenty in our individual experience of life and plenty to see in the collective that warrants our anger.

For many, fearing our anger led us to numb, to distract, to settle or to turn the anger inward toward ourselves through toxic shame and the inner critic. In settling and disconnecting from our inner voice we lose our passion, our wildness, our authenticity, and over time we can become depressed as we become completely discon-nected from ourselves and struggle to find meaning in life. We are all unique individuals and in order to show up authentically in our lives we must have a healthy relationship with anger, being able to connect to our 'no' and hold boundaries that protect what is mean-ingful and important to us.

When I chose to work with and become intimate with the anger I'd experienced in the relationship dynamic mentioned earlier, it became the catalyst for a new-found sense of clarity and a commit-ment to recognising my worth and the need to protect that with non-negotiables and healthy boundaries. I'll share a little more on that later.

Consider: Triggers

- What triggers your anger?
- What or who pisses or has pissed you off?
- Where have you been betrayed, rejected or shamed?

Sometimes it is a myriad of subtle aggressions or minor offences over time that build to a boiling point. Small actions that bring about mild frustrations which, left unchecked, begin to compound and create tension within us. At first these frustrations may cause some irritation or mild annoyance, though over time they can easily intensify to anger. The unintegrated anger and resentment from these experiences can be destructive energies that eat us alive, leave us feeling like victims and rob us of our capacity to move forward and find peace in our lives.

However, when integrated, this same anger can be a source of protection and a powerful catalyst for positive change in our lives, allowing us to recognise and protect our inherent value. Taking clean anger out of the shadow offers us the chance to safeguard our emotional wellbeing and integrity, allowing us to maintain connection to our authentic selves and not get lost in the demands or expectations placed upon us.

From 'Nice' to Authentic

I go to my therapist to explore the relationship dynamic that has unearthed decades of repressed anger. We explore the pattern that's recurring for me not only in intimate relationships but often in work and personal friendships too: a people-pleasing part. There's a clear pattern playing out where a fear of rejection, judgement or isolation leads me to prioritising the other person's feelings and needs and overlooking my own. Sometimes it's buckling to the pressure of a corporate client asking me to offer a workshop at a fraction of my usual fee, other times something as simple as saying yes to lunch with a friend when I have promised myself I am going to stay home and recharge my social batteries.

Irrespective of the situation or scenario, the general theme is doing everything within my control to keep the peace and maintain the approval of the other person or people. The harder I fight to maintain the love or acceptance of others, the further I become disconnected from myself. Rather than express my own wants, feelings, needs and desires, I suppress them and try to convince myself that if the other person is happy it'll all be OK. Over time, resentment begins to build and build. I people-please, present the nice guy, and in the process offer an inauthentic expression of myself for fear of the real me being rejected. Then I blame the other person for 'hurting me' or 'not appreciating me', but really they aren't experiencing me, but instead a façade of who I think they want me to be.

That's the problem with being the nice guy or nice girl. It's not authentic.

I wasn't being authentic in that relationship or in many of my other relationship dynamics. I looked back on the previous few months and tried to figure out where things went wrong. It's a painful thing to wake up and realise how much you've abandoned yourself in the pursuit of someone or something else. All relationships require compromise, of course, but to compromise yourself in efforts to win over someone you barely know can be a painful wake-up call. I had to own my part in it all, face up to where I had been inauthentic and look at the ways I lied by omission by withholding my true feelings, wants and needs. I was living completely from the outside in rather than inside out.

People-pleasers often believe they're afraid of speaking the truth, but at the core, it's the fear of what they might lose – approval, connection or harmony – that holds them back. In those moments of fear, they lose sight of the potential for greater freedom, authenticity, and deeper relationships that could be gained by honouring their truth.

I had judged this woman for betraying me and pulling me into her world of confusion, though when I turned the mirror back on myself I could see how my being disconnected from anger had led me to betray *myself* and pull myself and others into *my* world of confusion.

I have often found gold in the simple act of noticing my judgement or frustration toward someone else, turning it back toward how I am treating myself and then seeing where there might be some truth. In this example I judged her for 'pulling me into a world of confusion'. I then turned the mirror on myself and asked, 'How have I been pulling myself into a world of confusion?' and was able to find examples of how I was contributing to the whole dynamic and, in essence, how a part of me was choosing this.

I call this the 'sacred mirror', noticing that what irritates about how others are mistreating us can often bring us closer to understanding the ways in which we may be mistreating ourselves.

Why People-Please?

It is useful to explore the beliefs or fears that lie behind people-pleasing tendencies. Consider times when you withhold your truth, overlook your own feelings or needs, or say yes when you want to say no.

Then consider the prompt: what do I believe would happen if I spoke my truth?

Some of the fears might include being rejected, being judged as being too much, being met with aggression or making the other person feel uncomfortable.

Knowing Your Values and Needs

I am not suggesting you go from being a nice guy or nice girl to being an asshole!

I am instead suggesting that we trade a default of nice for a choice of authentic. An authentic life is one lived with a commitment to honouring and protecting our values and needs. Values are deeply held beliefs that guide our decisions and direction in life. There are cultural values shared by a community or group, and personal values unique to us, derived from our own experiences and reflections.

Awareness of and commitment to a values-led life is crucial for the process of individuation – the development of the authentic self. Our values become evident when we reflect on who we are when we're at our best, or look to what we admire the most in others.

In addition to our values, it can be useful to consider our 'shadow values', the opposite traits to those things we say we value. If you value connection, your shadow value might be disconnection. Although you may know consciously that you desire connection, acknowledging the shadow value shines light on the potential for distancing yourself from others due to fear, past experiences or unresolved emotions. Thus, for you to live an aligned and authentic life, it is important to commit to connection, and to keep an eye on the times when autopilot living leads to the shadow value of disconnection playing out in your life. That might be the disconnection of withholding your truth and silently resenting the other person rather than taking the chance of sharing your truth and staying in connection.

If you value honesty, your shadow value might be manipulation. Again, to be authentic it will be important that you prioritise being honest. Being nice rather than authentic might again mean you don't share how you really feel for fear of hurting the other person, though this is a subtle form of manipulation – telling the other person what they want to hear so that *you* don't feel uncomfortable.

Values and Shadow Values

What are some of the values that are most important to you? Consider what traits you value in other people, the traits you would like others to use to describe you and the traits that describe you when you are your best.

Next, list your 'shadow values', the opposites of these values, and consider how these shadow values sometimes play out unconsciously in your life.

Explore some of the ways that you act out these shadow values.

Alongside our values, as human beings we all have needs. We have basic human needs such as shelter, food and connection. We also have individual needs that might include things like adventure, creative outlets or learning new skills. Some have come to the false belief that to have needs makes them needy, when in fact the opposite is true.

Denying or neglecting our needs leads us to play out our neediness through the shadow, where it often manifests as silent resentment, frustration, stress or irritability. Unacknowledged frustrations often build into anger, and denied anger can escalate to rage. By examining the situations, behaviours, environments or relationships that cause frustration, agitation or anger, we often uncover violations of our values and needs.

Our values and needs contribute to our unique recipe for a well-lived life. When we actively live according to our values and honour our needs, we tend to experience positive emotional well-being, a sense of meaning, connection, alignment and fulfilment.

Conversely, unmet needs can lead to a sense of being out of alignment, lacking integrity, or disconnected from purpose and meaning.

So, what is your unique recipe of values and needs for a good life?

What are Your Needs?

Consider what your personal needs are in life beyond the fundamental needs of food, shelter and safety. What do you need in order to feel grounded, safe, inspired and fulfilled? This is sometimes referred to as your 'when life works' list.

For me, I know that I need work that I find fulfilling, and connection with people who allow me to express myself honestly. I need a creative outlet that supports self-expression, and regular travel and adventure to help inspire me. I need to always be studying or learning new things, I need regular time in nature and away from technology and I need to train Brazilian Jiu-Jitsu regularly. When I am meeting, prioritising and protecting these needs I feel I am at my best. When I am not, I often feel disconnected from myself.

What needs are most important for you to meet, prioritise and protect?

What is your unique recipe for a fulfilling life?

Better Boundaries

As we become clearer in our values, needs and non-negotiables and we connect to our clean anger, we can begin to create boundaries, both with ourselves and with others, to protect those aspects of ourselves that are so precious. This awareness of what matters most for us, and a commitment to protecting that which matters most, shifts anger from a potentially destructive energy to a protective and empowering act of self-care and self-love.

If I outline health as a key value of mine, I may need to place a boundary for myself around my alcohol or sugar intake. If I outline authenticity as a value of mine, I may need to place a boundary with a close friend or loved one who ridicules or mocks me when I express myself authentically. Every time we choose not to act in line with our values or needs, we are effectively abandoning ourselves. Doing that repeatedly over time is a surefire way of feeling disconnected from ourselves.

It is important to note that to create a boundary with someone is not to try and control them. The idea of boundaries has often been weaponised, with people using the word 'boundary' to mask what is often avoidance, manipulation or an attempt to dominate the other person's experience. In sharing a boundary, we can make a request for a behavioural change, as opposed to a demand. A demand is a forceful expectation for them to comply with your expectations, while a request is an expression of your need or desire, with a respect for the other person's autonomy and willingness to respond.

Finding our voice again and stating a boundary is a courageous and empowering act that can be hugely challenging if we have grown used to placing the feelings and needs of others ahead of our own. It can be easy and comforting, when met with uncertainty, resistance or pushback, to collapse and revert to our old way of being. When we are not used to expressing our feelings and needs honestly, it can be messy at first and our delivery can be clunky or awkward.

It takes practice to articulate ourselves clearly and confidently.

Based on a style of communication called 'non-violent communication', I find the following structure useful for sharing feelings, needs or boundaries with others, owning what is ours and not reverting to blaming or shaming the other person. Effectively this framework is allowing us to shine light on our shadow and reveal our hidden feelings and needs, rather than express them in indirect and unhealthy ways which often involve pointing the finger.

Step One: Assume best intent

To begin, it's important to remember that the other person may be completely unaware of how their actions are affecting us. Assuming best intent can reduce any defensiveness you might be met with and increase empathy. You might say something like 'I'm sure it wasn't your intent,' or 'I know that you probably didn't mean to upset me.'

Step Two: Make an observation

Rather than going to generalisations such as 'you always' or 'you never', share a specific observation. 'Yesterday we had arranged to meet at 1 pm and you did not show up until 1.40 pm.' Sticking to facts rather than generalisations puts the focus on the behaviour and not the person's character.

Step Three: State your feelings

Using 'I' statements, share how you feel as a result of this behaviour. It isn't 'you upset me' or 'you made me feel'; instead, we fully own that the feeling comes from us. 'I feel frustrated' or 'I feel sad.' This can feel vulnerable, of course, but is us owning what is ours, not putting it on the other person.

Step Four: State your needs

Here you can share the need that is not being met as a result of the behaviour. What is it that you need when you experience the afore-mentioned feeling? For example, if I identified that I felt frustrated that my friend was 40 minutes late, what I may have needed was some communication or an acknowledgment of them running late.

Step Five: Make a request

This is a clear request for a behavioural change that can help to meet your needs. Remember, this is a request, not a demand, so it is important that you are simply sharing what you need and the consequences of this need not being met. You're providing them with a choice and explaining how their actions affect you.

'If we arrange to meet again and you get caught in traffic, can I ask that you text me to let me know you are running late? If not, I will have to choose to leave and assume you are not coming'.

Practise Communicating a Boundary

Here is a template based on the above. Consider taking the current frustration you have and placing it in the template below. You don't have to share it with the person in question; you can just use it to practise being able to see the feelings and needs below your frustration.

Assume best intent
'I understand that you might not be aware of this …'
Make an observation
'I've noticed that [specific behaviour] …'

State your feeling

'I feel [emotion] …'

State your need

'Because I need [specific need] …'

Make a request

'Could you please [specific request]?'

Putting together the above steps you might share something like this:

'Hey Jack, I understand that you might not be aware of this. I've noticed that you usually contact me when you need help with something specific. I feel our friendship is one-sided because I value mutual support and connection in friendships. Because I value this, could we also spend time catching up or chatting about things other than when you need assistance?'

———— People-Pleaser Challenges ————

If you identify as falling on the people-pleasing and underexpression side of the anger scale, here are a couple of steps or 'mini challenges' you may find useful.

Do not allow yourself to say YES to anything in the moment for the next seven days

People-pleasers tend to make commitments without checking in with themselves first. I have often felt myself react to requests with the word 'yes' coming out of my mouth, while an accompanying tension and discomfort in my body informs me that I have just committed to something I do not want to do.

For the next seven days, consider pausing and taking time before committing to anything, no matter how big or small. Whether it's a friend asking if you'd like to grab lunch tomorrow or a colleague asking for help with a work project, let them know that you can't confirm right now but will come back to them by the end of the day. This allows you some space to be honest with yourself about what you do or do not want to commit to without the pressure of having to make decisions on the spot.

Create some stock responses in advance

'Hey Pat, I have been following your work for a while and I'd love to pick your brain for an hour. When are you free?'

The people-pleasing part of me is humbled by this frequent request from strangers, and it fears that saying no might cause them to go from appreciating my work to thinking I have got too big for my boots. The other parts of me can think of nothing worse than having my brain picked. The language alone of 'brain-picking' makes it feel like an uncomfortable, one-sided exchange.

Either personally or professionally, we can often find ourselves repeatedly facing the same request or demand for our time, energy or expertise. It's important to honour our boundaries and prioritise our own wellbeing while still maintaining positive relationships and professional courtesy. If you've struggled to say no or respond to a consistent or repeated request personally or professionally, it is likely you will come up against this same request again, and without a plan you may find yourself repeating the same people-pleasing tendencies.

Blocking off some time to craft responses for future frequent requests that you receive can be a useful practice. In response to the request for an hour of 'brain-picking', I will often let the requester know that I am tight on time but can send through some suggestions if they pass on specific questions that they have. I often don't hear back, though when I do I can honour my own need for boundaries while also offering guidance or support based on the specific question or request.

Practice decisiveness

'Would you like to book your next appointment?' asks my therapist.

'Hmmm, maybe …'

'STOP!' he cuts me off. 'Breathe into your balls …' (Needless to say, he isn't your conventional therapist.) 'Breathe deeper and get clear. It's time to get out of the land of maybe and move into the land of yes or no …'

People-pleasers often live in the land of maybe.

In some ways it is a convenient cop-out, when not feeling confident to give a solid answer that they will stick to. We might know that we are a no but fear letting the other person down, and so choose to alleviate the short-term tension by half committing with a maybe. People-pleasers can be slow to make decisions, to commit or to assert their own preferences or needs. If this is the case for you it can be useful to commit to a period of time in which you embody more decisiveness and commit to living in the land of yes or no, rather than living in the world of maybe.

A friend once told me a story of a guy he went to college with, who was blunt in response to the weekly question of 'Are you going out tonight?'

This guy would respond with a simple 'yes' or 'no'. When it was a no he did not feel the need to justify or explain himself. 'No' was enough.

Although his directness seemed a little blunt, maybe even rude at first, my friend noted over the four years they spent together in college that he learned how reliable this man was. While others would always say 'yes' but only sometimes follow through, this man stuck to his 'yes' or his 'no' and was reliable and trustworthy.

Trust in others and trust in ourselves is built through keeping commitments to ourselves and others. Consider challenging yourself for a given time to getting out of the land of maybe and practising decisiveness with a clear yes or no, without feeling the need to justify yourself or your response.

Keep a truth diary

People-pleasers often withhold their truth in order to keep others comfortable. They say what they think others want to hear, swallow the words they don't think others want to hear and prioritise the needs and desires of others over their own. This behaviour stems from a deep-seated fear of rejection or conflict, leading them to suppress their authentic selves.

Beyond withholding their truth with others, people-pleasers may also deny their own feelings, desires and opinions to themselves, creating an internal disconnect that further distances them from their true selves. This self-neglect not only harms their sense of identity but also perpetuates a cycle of inauthenticity in their relationships, meaning no one really meets them, but instead only the façade they present.

Keeping a 'truth diary' for a number of months can be a really useful practice for better recognising and understanding where you might be withholding your authentic expression.

At the end of each day simply reflect on these prompts:

- Did I speak my truth today?
- Where did I not speak my truth?
- What would it have looked like if I had spoken my truth?

This helps us recognise where we may be withholding our truth and then consider what it would have looked like if we had spoken our truth.

Consider: How do You Relate to Your Anger?

- What do you typically do when you feel angry?
- Do you express it outwardly, turn it back toward yourself, or distract yourself from it?
- Do you tend to confront the source of your anger directly, or do you avoid the confrontation?
- How do you communicate your anger?
- What strategies do you use to calm yourself down?
- Are they healthy (e.g. deep breathing, taking a walk) or unhealthy (e.g. overeating, drinking)?

Embodying Clean Anger

Owning and working with our anger in a genuine way cannot be confined to an intellectual understanding and must include the body if it is to be truly felt and understood.

Every time we experience frustration, anger or rage our bodies respond with a surge of energy that more often than not goes unexpressed and effectively sits in our system. We then go about our day trying to keep it together and remain civilised. It is no wonder we

often go to unhealthy habits or addictive tendencies to try to numb or distract ourselves from the intensity of these unexpressed feelings.

I once attended a retreat in which we did a lot of work on expressing and giving space to our anger. There was a lot of shouting, smashing pillows against the ground and punching punch bags held by the facilitators. I can only imagine what the staff at the retreat centre would have thought had they walked in on a room of 60 people unloading years or decades of suppressed anger and rage, with an accompanying soundtrack that would satisfy even the most pissed-off of teenagers blaring out over the speakers.

On this retreat, it was common for many, myself included, to move from anger to grief, the anger having acted almost as a protector to the sadness that lay behind. I have seen this in particular with men I have worked with over the years who received the message that 'boys don't cry' while perhaps also learning that a willingness to tap into aggression might offer a way of staying safe when threatened, intimidated or vulnerable in some other way. Thus anger for many becomes easier to initially access than grief, which perhaps feels more vulnerable.

There can also be sadness that comes when we connect to our anger and recognise all the ways we have betrayed ourselves or been betrayed. In my case my anger toward myself or others who had hurt me was a layer above the sadness for the part of me that just wanted to fit in and be accepted for who I was, and so once I had exhausted myself with shouting and punching the tears soon followed.

Others at the retreat seemed to grow six inches taller and come alive with energy that had been dormant for years. After overcoming the initial self-consciousness of saying (or more likely shouting) the things they wanted to say to the person or people who hurt them in the exact way they wanted to say it, there was a real sense of reclaiming power and sovereignty in the room.

'We've become civilised to death!' roared the facilitator over a microphone. 'Trained to be good boys and good girls, compliant boys and compliant girls … This is your chance to let go. So give it everything and let that fiery energy burn … Allow yourself to be real. You don't need to be nice or appropriate here. You need to be real and you need to be you.'

This ritual at the retreat was a chance to bring a sense of completion to all of the things we had wanted to say when our boundaries were violated or overstepped, when we were betrayed or shamed or unappreciated for being ourselves. It was an opportunity to find our voice again and to alchemise the energy that had been suppressed.

Consider: Your Withheld Anger

- How many times have you bitten your tongue to keep the peace? How many times have people overstepped your boundaries, overlooked your needs, bullied or tried to dominate you? How many times have you wanted to say no but chosen to say yes to maintain connection or avoid rejection?
- Are you open to the possibility that there may be some dormant energy sitting in your body, ready to come alive and bring new levels of passion and inner fire into your life?

Embodiment is essential in integrating and being more intimate with our anger.

One attendee at that retreat insisted that she 'didn't need to go there' and had read plenty of books about anger and done lots of work on anger with her talk therapist a few years earlier. Despite all the work she had done she felt stuck in life, tied to her past and to the people who had let her down or hurt her. With a lot of encouragement from the skilled facilitators, she eventually allowed herself to dip into the deep well of anger that she had buried below her intellectual understandings and rationalisations.

She allowed herself to feel the sensations in her body – the tightness in her chest, the energy running to her limbs and the heat in her face. Then with the support of the facilitators she began to voice her suppressed emotions, letting out the words and movements she had held back for so long. As the facilitators mirrored back to her that it was safe to express, her voice grew louder and she allowed herself to take up space, to be seen and express her truth with confidence.

She later shared how scary the thought of touching her anger had been before and how empowered she felt after. She looked like a different person – lighter, more open, more alive and unburdened from the weight of previously suppressed emotions.

Sitting with Anger

Begin by closing your eyes and taking a few grounding breaths.

Then connect with a time in which you felt angry. Notice what happens in your body, connecting it with the sensations of anger.

Continue to breathe and feel the sensations in the body. The mind may want to go to stories about why you're angry or what you need to do to get away from the discomfort of feeling your anger, but look to stay with the sensations.

Now see if you have a sense of what lies behind the anger. What is this anger looking to protect? Perhaps it is standing in front of shame, or sadness, fear or vulnerability. What is underneath the anger?

Finally see if you have a sense of how you could express this anger in a healthy way that protects what is important for you.

Summary: Gold in the Shadow

- Clean anger allows us to find and share our voice, protect all that matters to us, connect to our passion and lean into positive changes in our lives.
- Anger often arises when our values are violated or when our fundamental needs – such as the need for respect, safety or autonomy – are not met. By identifying these underlying values

and needs, we can see where frustrations, resentment or anger may be pointing to our values or needs being threatened.

- Boundaries define what is acceptable for us and what is not in terms of behaviour, actions and interactions, and allow us to be clear with others and with ourselves as to how we wish to be treated.

- Dance, vocal expression, working out or taking it out on punch bags are a few ways in which you can move energy and connect to the roots and origins of your anger. Allow yourself some space to be uncivilised and remember, if you don't use the energy the energy will use you!

Incomplete Sentences

Read the beginning of each sentence aloud and allow yourself to complete the sentence spontaneously in an unfiltered way. After completing all the prompts you can jot down any insights or reflections that stand out to you.

- When I feel angry, I …
- I tend to deny my anger because …
- If I were to fully express my anger, I fear that …
- I feel my boundaries are often violated when …
- The last time I felt overtaken by anger, I …
- My anger is protecting my …
- When I deny my anger, my body feels …
- The biggest challenge I face with anger is …

Journalling Prompts

1. Reflect on how your upbringing and past experiences have shaped your relationship with anger. What did you learn about anger growing up and how does that influence your current behaviours?

2. Make a list of common triggers that provoke your anger. For each trigger, write about why it elicits such a strong emotional response. How are these triggers connected to past experiences, unmet needs or unresolved issues? What strategies can you develop to manage these triggers more effectively?

3. Recall a time when you denied or suppressed your anger. Write about the specific circumstances and why you chose to deny your anger. What physical sensations or emotional signals did you experience? What were the short-term and long-term consequences of denying your anger for yourself and others involved?

4. Identify the core values and needs that are most important to you. How do these values and needs influence your emotional responses, especially anger? Write about how being in alignment or out of alignment with these values and needs affects your overall wellbeing and interactions with others.

5. Think about a significant boundary violation that left a lasting impact on you. Write about the steps you took or wish you had taken to heal from this experience. How did this event shape your understanding of boundaries and self-respect? What can you do moving forward to protect and honour your boundaries?

Conscious Anger

This week we have an embodiment exercise designed to consciously work with our anger in a safe way. I encourage you to practise this at least three times in the coming week. It can also be useful to create a 'conscious anger' playlist with music that allows you to feel more comfortable tuning into your anger during this practice. We all have good reasons to have anger and so anger is not the problem; it is what happens when we deny our anger that becomes the problem. This is a safe and healthy way for you to express yourself.

Find a private space where you can move and make noise without feeling self-conscious. Stand with your feet shoulder width apart, close your eyes and take a few deep breaths. Begin by tensing all the muscles in your body, holding the tension for a few moments, and then release it with a loud, primal scream, shout or vocal expression. You may need to do this into a pillow if you have others living with you or close by.

Feel the energy that comes with this vocal release and allow your body to move instinctively – stamp your feet, punch the air, shake your limbs or follow any other natural impulses that the body has to move – letting the anger flow out through your movement, breath and voice. You can also use a hand towel, gripping it tightly and wringing it out, or grab a pillow and beat the floor with it, channelling your anger into these physical objects. Give yourself full permission to express whatever needs to come out, without judgement or restraint.

Continue to 'let go' for 10–15 minutes, using your voice, breath and movement to express the fiery energy of anger in this safe and contained way.

Afterward, sit or lie down in a comfortable position, close your eyes, and breathe deeply, feeling the aliveness and freedom in your body following this short practice. Reflect on any insights that emerge from allowing anger to move through your body.

CHAPTER EIGHT

Change, Loss and Grief

'Grief is alive, wild, untamed and cannot be domesticated. It resists the demands to remain passive and still. It is truly an emotion that rises from the soul.' Francis Weller

'The degree to which you are willing to be hurt, not wanting to be hurt but willing to be hurt, is the degree to which you are willing to love, be loved, and be taught by love.' Gangaji

Grief

A flamboyant Italian man arrives at the dinner table in a long fur coat.

'We're going to the beach to breathe!'

It's the second evening of a three-day conference in Costa Rica in 2016 that's been advertised as TEDx meets Burning Man. Two hundred entrepreneurs who are being called 'change makers' from all over the world have gathered for a weekend of inspirational talks, experiential workshops and extravagant parties. I am one of the 200, excited to be in the company of so many interesting people. It's a chance to learn, to connect with like-minded souls and to go back home to my own business and everyday life feeling inspired and rejuvenated.

Unlike at a 'normal' business event or retreat, this dinner interruption and invitation from the tall, energetic Italian man isn't seen as anything out of the ordinary. I blindly follow everyone to the beach, where we lie down and begin to breathe in a deep, rhythmic and circular way. I've got some resistance and scepticism at first, but soon I begin to feel my mind quiet and feel myself drop into my body.

This is an unfamiliar feeling, but everything at this festival feels weird and unfamiliar so I go with it. At this time I have tried meditation for a number of years and always struggled to quiet my mind,

and so any time I sit with a group in meditation I generally fidget throughout the session and am the first to open my eyes at the end. After what seems like just a few minutes, I hear the charismatic Italian leader tell us that when we feel ready we can slowly open our eyes and begin to bring some movement back into our bodies.

It turns out we have been breathing together on the beach for close to an hour, not just a few minutes as I had thought. I am surprised to see I wasn't the first to open my eyes and everyone else has already left the beach by the time I come back round. I don't know it at the time but this is my introduction to conscious connected breathwork. By the time I open my eyes the flamboyant Italian man has left, never to be seen again.

I have no idea what has just happened but I need to learn more.

A year later, in 2017, I went to Poland and spent a week with 'The Iceman' Wim Hof at his home near Przesieka. A week of daily breathwork and cold immersion began a journey of deepening my understanding of the mind–body connection and helped me understand that in order for us to reawaken to our feelings and bodies, we must breathe deeply. In the time since then, I've studied many forms of breathwork and now offer my own teacher training in a style of conscious connected breathwork that I call 'Journey The Breath'.

Conscious connected breathwork involves breathing deeply in a connected way where there is no pause between the inhale and exhale. The inhale is deep and full, the exhale completely relaxed.

After a few minutes of breathing in this way, the conscious mind begins to quieten and the breather generally starts to become much more aware of the physical sensations in their body. The breather will often experience something called 'transient hypofrontality', where the everyday thinking mind (the neocortex) becomes less active and the limbic emotional brain comes more 'online'. As a result, many of the usual defence mechanisms of the ego fall away, and memories and repressed emotions often come to the surface. In other words, the persona drops and shadow material can make an appearance. Unconscious material is brought to consciousness through the body and the breath.

During a breathwork session one day, in my mind's eye I see an envelope fall through the letterbox in slow motion and hit the floor. I open the envelope to find a set of keys that the sender is returning along with a note:

'I hope you find your happiness, *amore mio.*'

As I continue to breathe deeply, the tears come. The unexpressed grief that I had bottled up five years before when I had broken up with a girlfriend of three years and she had moved out.

We'd actually broken up 30 minutes before I stepped on stage to deliver a keynote speech at a wellness conference for a room of a few hundred people, and so I bottled up the feelings, told myself I would come back to them at a 'more appropriate time' and presented from stage with a smile that masked the numbness and confusion I was feeling. A few weeks later, when she moved out and dropped her keys through the letterbox along with the note, I quickly read the note with a lump in my throat, ripped it up and binned it, pushing it out of my conscious awareness and maybe again convincing myself I'd come back and make space at a more appropriate time.

I avoided finding an appropriate time, though, burying myself in work and alcohol-fuelled nights out for distraction instead, finding any way possible to avoid feeling the pain of the loss of the relationship. As a boy I had always taken on the message that men were not supposed to feel, and at the time I don't think I even knew how to access my emotions. I'm sure a part of me worried, too, that if I made space for my tears I might fall into my grief and never re-emerge. I had cried when my first mentor in fitness took his own life when he was 28 and I was 18, cried when other friends had passed away in my late teens and early twenties and cried when I hit my lowest point after a business failure at 24. These all felt like reasons to cry, but to cry for any of the other heartbreaks, losses or challenges I had had in my adult life felt indulgent and self-pitying.

Again, what is pushed into shadow does not go away, but takes on a life of its own, playing out in unconscious ways. The body remembers what the mind tries to forget and now, five years later on a random Tuesday in the midst of a breathwork journey at home, it seemed the time had come and my body was remembering what my mind had wanted to forget.

She had been my first love, a beautiful Italian woman who I'd lived with the majority of the three years we spent together. We'd travelled around the world together, shared memories and adventures, triggered one another's wounds and supported one another's healing. She would cook beautiful Italian dinners and I would cook questionable Irish breakfast fries. I would convince her to come and try Jiu-Jitsu, while she would drag me along to salsa classes. I let her get closer to me than I had ever let anyone and she did the same for me.

A part of me believed we'd be together forever, but now she was gone.

My conscious mind may have wanted to push the three years to the side, but my body had held onto the unexpressed pain which was now ready to be felt. I cried for what could have been, cried for what I had lost, cried for all the ways I couldn't show up for her and cried for all the things I wish I had done differently.

When the tears finally slowed there came a sense of completion and gratitude. Not gratitude in a happy-clappy superficial way, but a genuine sense of appreciation for the relationship, the lessons and the journey we had been on together. I felt complete, ready to move on with appreciation, acceptance and eyes opened to the felt understanding that in order to heal, we've got to be willing to feel.

When we do not allow ourselves to grieve what we have lost, we miss the process of healing, which can leave us feeling stuck, numb and disconnected from our true selves. Without bringing that relationship to completion in this way, I would have no doubt carried old unacknowledged triggers, patterns and wounds into all future relationships and would have held back my love for fear of another relationship not working out. In Chapter Ten, where we talk about shadow in relationships, we'll look at how we can identify the lessons from previous relationships and not carry them forward.

The nature of life is that we are in a constant state of change, loss, death and rebirth, and so grief is an essential and healthy expression proportional to the depth of love we felt for someone or something. Everything and everyone in our lives right now will at some point be gone. When we do not learn to surrender to change and allow ourselves to grieve what we have lost, we keep ourselves stuck in a state of fear, unable to open our hearts to life.

Grief and love are two sides of the one coin, with neither able to exist without the other. There is much that we love and so there is much to grieve in life.

Consider: Taking Space to Remember

Take a moment to consider the following aspects of loss in your life, how much or how little space you allowed to feel those losses and how they have shaped your journey.

- Loved ones you have lost.
- Relationships that have ended.
- Loss of identities as you transitioned through different phases of life.
- Grief related to the parts of yourself you have denied or pushed away.
- Grief for the pain, hardships and injustice you see in the world.
- Grief for the life you hoped for that didn't manifest.
- Grief inherited from your ancestors passed down through generations.

With so much there to trigger our grief, we can be fearful of it and may instead choose to numb ourselves to it and just get on with things instead. The challenge in this is that we numb all other emotions as well. It may seem paradoxical, but when we allow space for our grief, our hearts break open and we become much more connected to aliveness.

Suppressing our grief or sadness robs us of our vitality and life force and hinders our ability to find joy in our present life. When we open up to our grief we reconnect to the whole spectrum of human emotions, and allow ourselves to move from a constant state of doing in distraction to a grounded sense of being in presence. We come alive again and into connection with both ourselves and others.

Teacher Francis Weller has a beautiful quote: 'Grief keeps the heart fluid and soft, which helps make compassion possible.' He also notes that the emotionally mature person must carry grief in one hand and gratitude in the other. Without being able to hold grief, he says, we will lose our capacity to feel compassion for the suffering of others. Without being able to hold gratitude, we'll find ourselves lost in cynicism and despair.

The Importance of Grief

Grief, which often includes numbness and intense feelings of sadness, anger and denial, among others, is the appropriate response to the loss of something or someone who was meaningful to us.

While initially we might solely associate grief with the death of someone we love, it actually encompasses a wide range of losses. This can include the loss of a relationship, a job, a sense of identity, or the loss of a dream or future we had envisioned for ourselves. We might also have grief around the life we hoped for that didn't happen, ageing and the passing of time, changes to our bodies, or shifts in our understanding of the world.

It's important to recognise and honour these different forms of grief and their significance, not to downplay them or shame ourselves for the difficult feelings we might experience around change and loss. In many ways we live in a grief-phobic and death-phobic culture that does not want to acknowledge the reality of death, loss and change or to feel the feelings that come with those losses. Thus they are often pushed into the background of our consciousness, hidden in the shadows, out of sight and out of mind. In efforts to mask our vulnerabilities our mind often has a tendency to deny the reality of loss and the pain of separation that comes with it.

Years or decades spent in our heads and disconnected from our emotional bodies has many of us struggling to feel the feelings required to let go.

When we don't fully release our pain and feel the associated feeling through grieving, the separation from what we have lost remains unfinished, and our sense of self remains tied to the loss, preventing us from forming new connections or stepping forward in life with full presence and aliveness. When we have not culti-vated the capacity to sit with our grief and allow space for it, we will find ourselves reacting to it in ways that diminish our wellbeing and vitality. An unwillingness to feel our grief and the associated emotions might result in numbness, depression or a chronic sense of emptiness, while becoming lost or overtaken by our grief over a long period of time can lead to prolonged sadness, anger or diffi-culty moving forward.

Conscious grief and mourning, meanwhile, enable us to reclaim the energy we had invested in what we lost, freeing it up for new relationships and experiences. By fully engaging with our grief and its associated feelings, we can heal more completely, open ourselves to new connections and experiences and regain access to the full spectrum of human emotion.

Consider: How do You Relate to Your Grief or Sadness?

- What situations or events usually trigger feelings of grief or sadness in you?
- How do you feel physically when you first notice you're grieving or feeling sad (e.g. heavy heart, tears, fatigue)?

- What do you typically do when you feel grief or sadness? Do you express it openly, keep it inside or distract yourself?
- What strategies do you use to cope with grief or sadness? Are they healthy (e.g. talking to a friend, journalling) or unhealthy (e.g. isolating yourself, substance use)? Do you engage in any behaviours to numb or escape the feeling of grief or sadness?
- How do you feel about the way you handle grief or sadness? Is there anything you would like to change?
- Can you recall a time when you handled grief or sadness in a way that you were proud of? What did you do differently?

Comfortably Numb

I visited my local doctor as I approached the tail end of my twenties, hoping he could provide me with some guidance as to why I couldn't seem to lift out of the depressive state I had found myself in for a number of months now.

On paper my life was great. I had spent my twenties relentlessly chasing goals and targets and had achieved most of what I had set out to achieve. My life looked completely different from how it had looked only a few years before.

Despite all I had achieved in the latter half of my twenties and the complete 180 I had done in terms of how my life looked from the outside in, I had reached a point of having lost all enthusiasm for my work, my health and my relationships, and for months now had felt like I was dragging my feet and just going through the motions. I had some guilt and shame about how I was feeling too: 'I should be grateful', 'I should be happy', 'I should be content'.

But I wasn't …

A part of me hoped the doctor would take bloods and find some kind of imbalance to explain what was 'wrong' with me and why my mood remained so low, though I was equally relieved when my bloods came back normal.

Sometimes doctors or the medical field get a bad rap for throwing tablets or prescriptions at every patient who comes through the door without first addressing their lifestyle factors or digging a little deeper to gain an understanding of the patient's life circumstances. My experience with this doctor couldn't have been any more different.

He took an interest in what I was feeling, where I was struggling, and listened intently. Then after asking for permission to share, he offered some 'off-the-record' non-medical advice or perspective.

'I felt similar when I was around thirty. I was no longer the young hungry alpha in his early twenties trying to take on the world, and equally I hadn't yet reached a stage of having kids or starting a family. In some ways, it felt like a weird middle ground and I felt quite lost not knowing my place in the world.'

What he shared resonated and made me feel understood. It may not have been his intent at the time, but his reflections shone light on how much of my life I was wishing away at the time by living in the memories and nostalgia of my past or regrets of things I could have done differently, longing to be 10 years younger and get to live life differently. With so much of my energy still bound to my past while simultaneously building fantasies in my head of a future where things would all fall into place, I was in a sense placing my life on hold, living in my head and disconnecting from my body.

When we're stuck in our heads in the future or past, or caught up in stories of how things 'should' be rather than accepting things as they are, we are often staying in the head to avoid the feelings that are being experienced below that noise in the body.

The relentless pace and intensity at which I worked and chased goals in my twenties left no time for feeling or emotion. It became clear that I needed to slow down and reconnect with myself in a different way. Pushing down feelings for an extended period and prioritising thinking and doing over feeling and being was beginning to take its toll, and the depressive state I felt stuck in was the result.

I had lived most of my adult life in my head, using thoughts and actions to avoid feeling and being. Many of us learned early on to disconnect from our bodies – cutting off from the present moment in doing so. Our feelings are experiences in the body, and so in order to address how we feel we must go beyond thinking. Reconnecting to the body again and going from comfortably numb to fully alive is a key step in the healing journey. This involves moving from stories in our heads to sensations in our bodies. Connecting to our authentic feelings allows us to be more present and truly engaged with life.

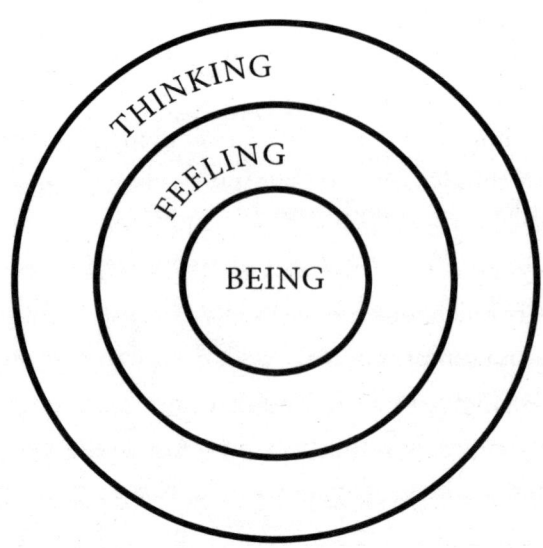

In reconnecting with my body through a number of plant medicine journeys in my late twenties and developing regular practices like conscious connected breathwork, TRE and bioenergetics, the direction of my life has shifted to a more authentic way of being that trusts the wisdom of my feelings and my body, rather than being confined to judgements of the thinking mind.

In order to avoid the vulnerability of feeling or showing the feelings that have been deemed unwelcome, many of us learn from an early age to stay in the head with a myriad of defence mechanisms including projection, denial, repression and rationalisation. This thick layer of conditioning can keep us from connecting to our authentic feelings and lead to a sense of being emotionally shut down. Restoring a natural flow of energy and expression requires moving beyond the noise of the mind and allowing space for the unfelt feelings.

Consider: Feelings and the Body

- Reflect on your current relationship with your body and your feelings.
- Consider how often you find yourself living in your head, driven by thoughts and actions, rather than being present in your body and experiencing your emotions.
- How might you begin to shift this balance? What practices or changes could you introduce to reconnect with your authentic feelings and sensations? Take a moment to imagine what it would feel like to move from a state of numbness to one of full aliveness. How could this transformation impact your sense of self and your engagement with the world around you?

Containing Our Grief

Breathwork and other body-based practices that reconnected me with my emotional body had opened the door to feeling again, but now I was getting drowned in grief at times and almost 'looping' and getting lost in it. There was an important lesson in it for me – coming to understand the importance of getting into the right relationship with grief or any other emotion, not being detached or removed from it, not being drowned out and overtaken by it, but allowing a space for it in my life. Space in which I show up for myself in a grounded and adult way, not expecting my younger parts like the inner child or inner teen to hold the intensity of grief, but consciously choosing to sit with and allow space for it so that I do not pass that pain forward by acting in shadowy ways.

A teacher of mine has spoken about the 'grief tending' he did after the death of his daughter. He would take an hour each day and allow himself to fall apart, to cry, get angry, to be numb and to let whatever feelings wanted to come, come. This contained time was honouring his need to feel without deferring it or avoiding it. He had his remaining family and a business which he wanted and needed to continue to show up for, but taking this hour for himself each day to grieve meant he could continue to show up fully in life without the consequences of repressed emotions seeping uncontrollably into every aspect of his life.

We all have wounded parts and it can be easy to get lost in them or have them run our lives, though we also all have healthy parts that care deeply for us. I have worked with clients over the years who have been at their lowest point, and often remind them of the fact that as low as they are feeling and as bad as things have got, there was a part of them that chose to show up to our session in the hope of healing.

Sitting with Grief

Begin by closing your eyes and taking a few grounding breaths.

Then connect with a time when you felt grief. Notice what happens in your body, connecting it with the sensations of grief.

Continue to breathe and feel the sensations in the body. The mind may want to go to stories about why you're grieving or what you need to do to get away from the discomfort of feeling your grief, but look to stay with the sensations.

Now see if you have a sense of what lies behind the grief. What is this grief looking to reveal? Perhaps it is intertwined with love, loss, longing or regret. What is underneath the grief?

Finally, see if you have a sense of how you could express this grief in a healthy way that acknowledges and honours what you have lost or what you miss.

Grief Tending and the Village

A mentor of mine once told me that animals who end up in the zoo become sick and depressed, not through any fault of their own, but due to the unnatural environment they have been placed in. Similar could be said for many of the current challenges we see in physical and mental health for us as humans. Technologically we are at our most advanced, though the further we continue to move from nature and our natural way of being, the sicker we are becoming in body, mind and spirit.

We have seen drastic changes over the years to our diet, our lifestyle, our work environment and our relationship with technology. We have seen big changes, too, to the ways our communities are structured. In many parts of the Western world we see a strong lean toward individualism, and in this we are seeing an epidemic of loneliness, addiction and numbing.

Humans were never the fastest or strongest in the animal kingdom. It was our teamwork and collaboration that supported us in our development. In previous generations, it was essential that communities came together and supported one another through hard times. With smaller communities, everyone within the village would have had a role or profession that contributed to the overall health of the village. This would have brought a sense of meaning and purpose to each individual's life, knowing they were contributing to and were connected to something bigger than themselves. The individual's concern will have been on the health of the community, then the health of their own family, and then on their own health.

Now, this hierarchy of priorities has flipped on its head, with individualism becoming the dominant ethos. Modern society often prioritises and rewards personal success, self-care and individual wellbeing over communal health. This shift has contributed to a sense of isolation and disconnection for many, weakening the communal bonds that once provided a strong support network during challenging times.

One of the gifts lost with the shift is collective support in times of personal challenge or grief. In the past, grieving was a shared experience, with community members coming together to mourn, provide comfort and help each other heal. Today, many people are forced to face grief, loss, confusion and change in isolation. Traditional grief-tending ceremonies seen in indigenous cultures offer powerful lessons and insights into the universal human experience of loss. These rituals honour the deceased while also facilitating the emotional and spiritual healing of the living.

In Ireland, 'keening' was a traditional form of mourning the dead and was an integral part of funeral rituals. Keeners were professional mourners brought in to lead the lament at wakes or funerals. These women would wail, cry and sing, expressing profound grief through their vocalisations. The keening would start as a quiet or gentle moan or cry that would build into chaotic screams and wailing. Keening offered both a communal and a spiritual function. Spiritually it was seen as a support in guiding the dead to the afterlife. Communally the keening fostered a sense of solidarity and gave an outlet to the community to connect with and express their collective grief.

With songs, cries and wails lamenting the person who had died, the community would also lament and commemorate the pain of loved ones lost in earlier years. The keeners often also served as midwives in the community, offering them a unique closeness to life and death. Their keening gave the community a chance to fall apart and be brought to their knees in the depth of their sorrow, allowing them to fully experience and process their grief.

I believe there is an unspoken grief for the loss of community that we experience, not only in times of hardship but across all times. Carl Jung once said, 'Loneliness does not come from having no people about one, but from being unable to communicate the things that seem important to oneself, or from holding certain views which others find inadmissible.'

Consider: The Role of Community

Reflect on a time when you felt a strong sense of community and how it impacted your wellbeing. Consider the feelings of loss or grief you've experienced with the absence of such connections. Contemplate what an ideal community would look like for you, including its values and the role you would play in it. Finally, think about small actions you can take to build or strengthen meaningful connections in your life, recognising the importance of true community for your physical, mental and emotional wellness.

Finding Closure

In the world of social media, friending or unfriending people happens with the simple click of a button, while in the 'real' world the process of finding true connection or real emotional closure requires a much deeper journey. This is especially true when dealing with loss due to betrayal or profound disappointment. The loss of a significant relationship is not as simple as just unfriending and forgetting. To move on from someone with whom we have fallen out or experienced a painful ending requires emotional processing and confronting the feeling of loss or betrayal held. We must grieve and feel the loss of this relationship if we are to heal and truly open ourselves up to new connections.

One of my teachers, Caroline Myss, talks about the dungeon, a place deep within our psyche where we keep prisoners in dark and cold cells, those prisoners being the people in our lives whom we have refused to forgive or those we wish harm or towards whom we harbour ill will. It might be an ex-partner who betrayed us, a former colleague who bullied us or a family member whose actions deeply hurt us. Sometimes we've left people down in the dark dungeon so long we've forgotten they are even there. It is a sobering thought, too, to consider who might have us in their dungeon. It is likely we are a hero in some people's stories and a villain in others'. Finding true emotional closure requires confronting the shadow aspects of ourselves related to those we've put in our dungeon.

By better understanding the wounds and grievances that keep us bound to those we resent, we can heal, integrate and move forward with new-found energy, no longer held back by resentment.

Finding Closure

Try the following exercise for finding closure.

Step 1: Identify the Relationship

Identify a person who is in your dungeon with whom you wish to seek closure. It might be an ex-partner, a family member, a former friend, a childhood bully or anyone else with whom you feel unresolved or incomplete.

Step 2: Reflect on the Triggers

Take some time to reflect on the emotional triggers that are alive for you and associated with this person or relationship. What feelings are unresolved for you? Write down any of these feelings or any judgements that are a source of suffering for you.

Step 3: Ready to Let Go?

Looking at the person you have identified and the feelings and judgements you have outlined, ask yourself honestly, are you ready to let go of your resentments?

What is it costing you to keep them in your dungeon? What are the potential benefits, or what parts of yourself do you get to avoid by keeping them in your dungeon?

If you feel genuinely ready to let go, continue to the next step.

If you are not ready at this time, know that the steps you've taken so far are a great start.

You cannot force yourself to let go before you are ready.

Step 4: Write the Transformational Letters

Next, write a letter to this person (which you will not send). Include anything you need to say, such as your perspective, emotions and reflections on the relationship dynamics. Allow yourself to express fully without editing or filtering. This is a chance for you to bring some of your shadow into the light, to express some of the anger, grief, vulnerability or shame you may have suppressed or swallowed.

Next, write a response from the other person's perspective: imagine stepping into their shoes and consider what they might say to provide closure for you. Write down their understanding, apologies or acknowledgements that you need to hear to feel complete.

Step 5: Symbolic Letting Go

To complete the exercise, consider some symbolic way of bringing it to completion, perhaps tearing up or burning the letter. As we let go of resentments we reclaim our emotional freedom and become unstuck from our past.

—————————— **Moving Forward** ——————————

At 18 I took a flight to California with $500 in my pocket to spend three months working and training at a cage-fighting gym in San Diego. Excited, but equally scared about my first long trip away from home and stepping into the unknown, I wanted to hug my dad at the airport. I think he was nervous too, seeing me leave for America on my own without too much of a plan. We weren't huggers, though, and so we settled on a handshake and a 'take care of yourself out there'.

Back then in 2007, mixed martial arts, more commonly referred to as cage-fighting at the time, wasn't the mainstream phenomenon that it is today. It was still somewhat of a niche activity that many refused to see as a sport, claiming it was too brutal. I had spent my teens boxing, training in judo and lifting weights at home in Ireland, and now fancied my chances of going to California and becoming a mixed martial arts fighter.

I told my parents I was going to America to train in judo. I knew this would be met with more enthusiasm than sharing the truth: that I would be training in a cage during the week in San Diego, California, and crossing the border to Tijuana, Mexico, on the weekends for fights or competitions. A month in, I got a call from my mother, who informed me someone in the village had told her what I was really up to in America!

Over those two summers I would train two to three times a day and work in the gym, cleaning or offering inductions to new members looking to sign up for training. During one of these gym inductions I asked a man in his mid-forties who was a few stone overweight, 'Do you have much training experience?'

'Yup' he responded confidently. 'I wrestled in high school.'

'And do you have a training goal in mind?'

'I wrestled at a hundred and seventy pounds so I'd like to get back there ...'

Mid-forties seemed old to me at the time. In my head I quickly calculated that the man in front of me would have left high school over 20 years before and was a long way away from the 170 lb he had been in his wrestling days. Yet a part of him seemed attached to that time, perhaps in denial about his current chapter of life. He had a confidence bordering on arrogance during the gym induction, perhaps still seeing himself as the teenage athlete he once was. Sometimes this type of self-belief or confidence can be useful, though in this man's case, after more than two decades away from a gym, jumping back in too quickly and trying to pick back up where he had left off meant he was injured within weeks, and another hiatus from his training commenced. In comparing himself to a past version of himself as a teenager who had no commitments other than school or training, he had overlooked the fact that he was now a father, a busy business owner and a man 20 years older than the version of himself he was trying to impress.

In what felt like the blink of an eye, I woke up in my early thirties seeing a part of myself in that man: still clinging to past versions of me rather than reinventing myself, evolving and fully embracing the current chapter I was in. I saw similar versions of this story in my years working in the fitness industry. A client would come in, we would talk about their goals and they would often reference getting back to the weight they were a few years before, or meeting the fitness level they had attained in their last chapter of life. This clinging on to the past offers a metaphor for how many of us end up living: yearning for what once was, rather than embracing what is.

We hold on to memories of our former selves, sometimes idealising them or fixating on what could have been, and in doing so we resist the inevitable changes that life brings.

While it is natural to look back on our past achievements with a sense of nostalgia, it is equally important to respect the chapter we are in now to cultivate a vision for the future. Holding on too tightly to past versions of ourselves prevents us from fully engaging with the present and future. Instead, having a clear and inspiring vision can provide direction and motivation, helping us appreciate and acknowledge our past without staying stuck in it. Developing a vision for the future can support us in transforming our pain into purpose. It shifts our focus from what we have lost to what we can still accomplish, fostering resilience and hope.

In the context of grief and loss, having a vision for the future doesn't mean forgetting or disregarding the past. Instead, it means integrating our experiences and lessons into a new narrative that can bring us into the present with the wisdom of our past experiences.

Embracing Each Chapter of Your Story

Reflect on your past by thinking about specific experiences or achievements that you often find yourself longing for or comparing your current self to.

Write down these memories, noting their significance to you and how they influence your present thoughts and actions.

Next, acknowledge the emotions tied to these past events, whether they are pride, regret, joy or sadness. Consider how these feelings impact your current mindset and behaviour.

Now, gently shift your focus to the present and the chapter of life you are in. Assess your current situation, recognising areas where you might be holding on to outdated self-images or goals. Write about what aspects of your past you are clinging to and how this affects your ability to embrace the present.

Finally, envision your future. Imagine where you want to be in the next few years. Visualise new goals and aspirations that excite and inspire you. Write down this vision in detail, including specific steps you can take to move towards it. Consider what new skills, habits or changes in mindset are necessary to achieve this future.

Conclude by reflecting on how letting go of past attachments can open up space for new opportunities and growth, allowing you to fully embrace the journey ahead.

——— Summary: Gold in the Shadow ———

- Death, loss and change are often pushed into the background of our consciousness, but a denial or repression of our grief robs us of our vitality and life force, keeping us stuck in the past.
- Numbing ourselves to grief often leads to us becoming emotionally disconnected across the whole emotional spectrum and thus we dull our capacity for joy, love and connection.
- By allowing ourselves to grieve what we have lost we reawaken to our capacity for love, joy, presence and connection. Rather than avoiding or becoming overwhelmed by certain emotions, allowing space for them ensures that we can process and integrate life's experiences in a healthy way.
- By better understanding the wounds and grievances that keep us bound to those we resent, we can heal, integrate and move forward with new-found energy, no longer held back by resentment.

- Having a vision for the future is crucial in this healing process, as it provides direction, purpose and hope. It supports us in seeing that with all endings comes room for new beginnings.

Incomplete Sentences

Read the beginning of each sentence aloud and allow yourself to complete the sentence spontaneously in an unfiltered way. After completing all the prompts you can jot down any insights or reflections that stand out to you.

- The hardest part about change is …
- One thing I wish I could say to someone I've lost is …
- Grief has taught me that …
- Gratitude during times of change feels …
- Change often makes me feel …
- One way I cope with grief is by …
- Change has taught me that …
- I find peace in …

Journalling Prompts

1. Consider how grief and gratitude coexist in your life. Write about a situation where you felt both emotions simultaneously. How did each emotion shape your understanding of the other?
2. Reflect on the coping mechanisms you use to avoid grief. How do these mechanisms affect your relationships, work, and overall sense of self?
3. Write about your relationship with change. Do you embrace it, fear it, resist it or a combination of these? How has this relationship evolved over time?

4. Consider the role of forgiveness in finding closure. Who or what do you need to forgive, and how can this act of forgiveness help you let go and move forward?

5. Envision your life six months from now, having moved forward from your current challenges. What changes do you see in yourself and your circumstances? What steps can you take today to start this journey of progress and growth?

Conscious Connected Breath

When we do not want to feel our feelings, we will typically armour with muscular tension in the body while holding our breath, or breathing in a more shallow way. Deep breathing is essential for restoring feeling to our bodies. 'Conscious connected' or 'circular' breathing is a powerful practice for helping us become more connected to our emotions and 'felt sense'.

Sit comfortably with the back upright and the chin slightly tucked to elongate the spine. Inhale deeply through the nose, filling the lungs, and as soon as the lungs are full exhale, again through the nose. Allow your inhale to be active and your exhale to be relaxed; by that I mean encourage your inhale to be full and allow your exhale to just 'fall' out of the body without force.

Once the lungs are empty, come to your next inhale, connecting the breath so that there are no gaps or pauses between each inhale and exhale. Some people like to visualise drawing a circle with their breath, the inhale being the first half of the circle and the exhale the second half.

Continue to breathe in this way for 10–20 minutes with an active inhale, a relaxed exhale and no gaps or pauses between each part of the breath.

You may experience some mental resistance in the early stages of this practice, but stay with the breath and follow the sensations in the body. As you stay with the practice you will become more aware of these sensations, perhaps tingles, tension or changes in temperature.

As you connect more to sensation you may also feel yourself moving closer toward your emotions, which are simply a collection of sensations in your body. Look to allow yourself to be with your emotions without reacting to them or feeling the need to do anything with them.

You will find a 10-minute accompanying audio track for this practice, as well as a full 1-hour conscious connected breathwork practice, at patdivilly.com/shadow.

CHAPTER NINE

Facing Fear

'Your mind would rather manage old familiar anxieties than confront new and unknown ones.' ROBERT GLOVER

'We fear only what we haven't understood.' BYRON KATIE

Fear

When I was a child, my family and I often travelled from Limerick to Galway on weekends to visit my grandmother in Salthill. Frequently, my cousins would join us, and we'd spend our days watching VHS tapes of the previous year's *Late Late Toy Show* that my grandmother had recorded for us at Christmas, or playing football in the back garden until it got dark in the evenings.

One end of the garden was lined with a row of hedges. I remember very early on in life my cousin telling me there was an evil fox living in those hedges. From that moment on, I was terrified of going near them. I avoided the area where the evil fox lived,

choosing to stay on the other side of the garden instead. As I grew older, I of course learned from others that there was no evil fox in the hedge. With this new-found knowledge, my fear vanished, and the whole garden opened up to me again.

I think our fears in life work in a similar way.

Often, our fears are illusory, not based on any reality but instead created by our imagination or inherited from others. These imaginary fears constrict us and make our world smaller. Instead of being able to enjoy the whole garden, or the whole experience of life, we stay in the small part that feels safe. Unbeknownst to ourselves, to cope with the sense of helplessness or anxiety we feel around our fears, we set our entire lives up to control and avoid the part of the garden where the evil fox lives. We build boundaries and limit our experiences based on perceptions that have never been questioned or challenged.

Fear has been an essential part of human evolution, a primal response designed to protect us from danger and ensure our survival. It triggers the fight-or-flight mechanism, heightening our senses and preparing our bodies to react swiftly to threats. Yet, despite its evolutionary necessity, fear can also reduce us to a child-like state, paralysing us and inhibiting our ability to navigate life's challenges. This dual nature of fear – both helpful and harmful – depends on how we respond to it.

Any change we have consistently struggled to make in our life will have a fear threshold that we have not yet stepped over. Taking fear out of the shadow and learning to feel, be with and experience our fear is an essential step in creating lasting transformation in our lives.

Can you think of something you have wanted to achieve but always struggled with? What fear might be holding you back?

When the subject of fear comes up, people will sometimes reference things like the fear of heights, the fear of spiders or the fear of flying. I would suggest, however, it is fears such as the fear of change, fear of intimacy, fear of failure, fear of judgement or the fear of feeling that can be the most limiting for us.

When we fear change, for example, we cling to the safe and familiar, missing out on opportunities for growth or new adventures and connections. Fearing intimacy can lead to isolation and prevent us from forming deep connections and meaningful relationships. Fearing failure can keep us from pursuing dreams and taking risks that lead to fulfilment. The fear of judgement makes us conform, suppressing our true selves to fit into societal moulds. The fear of feeling can numb our emotions, depriving us of the full spectrum of human experience.

Our unwillingness to confront these and other shadow fears confines us to a narrow existence, overshadowed by the potential of what could be if we dared to face them. If we are willing to take these fears out of the shadows and allow ourselves to face them, our world expands exponentially, and new opportunities and the possibility of real transformation become available to us.

We cannot step into a bigger life unless we are willing to face and embrace our fears and lean on our courage and faith.

—— The Safety Officer and Origins of Fear ——

I served as an altar boy in primary school, not to get closer to God but closer to the pretty girls in my class. When the local priest came into the school to ask who would be interested in being an altar boy or altar girl, I had no intention of raising my hand, until I saw who else had raised theirs. Some of the coolest in the class were expressing interest and so I knew it was a way of getting closer to them.

It worked.

A few weeks later, after serving Mass, a few of us sat around waiting for a lift back to the school.

'Let's play a game where we name who we fancy from the most to the least …'

I didn't like this plan …

Each of the girls proceeded to name me last on their list of who was most attractive.

I wanted to run away, or for the ground to swallow me, anything to get away from the sinking feeling of shame around being deemed the least attractive by all of the girls I had fancied. I tried to hide my embarrassment by cracking a sarcastic joke, which was met with some laughter, temporarily deflecting away from my shame. One of the lads later told me that my sense of humour reminded him of Chandler from *Friends*. I hadn't ever watched *Friends* but took it as a good thing, and learned that day that humour was something I could hide behind.

Now, almost 30 years later, that sarcasm or humour can still be quick to jump in when I feel shame in my system. Only a few weeks ago, at a deep personal growth retreat that I attended in the UK, I wrote down and made a commitment to myself on the first day: 'I will not hide behind humour when I am scared or feel shame.' Throughout the week, as fears or shame crept in in the group therapy sessions, I felt that old defence wanting to kick in frequently, but kept that promise to myself. I got to move a little closer to my shame and fear and come to a greater understanding of myself.

As the inner critic tries to keep us in the good boy/good girl box with outdated narratives and strategies, another part of us called the 'safety officer' looks to keep us from perceived threats and vulnerabilities, driven by a deep-seated need for control and security.

The safety officer gets to work in our younger years when we experience disconnect or emotional pain. Wanting to avoid future pain and keep us safe, it develops strategies of protection and hides the parts that we are afraid to show. When left unexplored, the safety officer can later turn into a type of prison officer, keeping us stuck in a prison of old patterns as it constantly scans our environment for potential dangers, both physical and emotional, and reverts to old protective means of avoiding these perceived dangers.

Any time that part of ourselves we felt the need to hide comes close to the surface, the safety/prison officer jumps in with its protective strategy.

It can be easy later in life to beat ourselves up for some of our patterns or judge certain parts of ourselves, but it is important to understand how much this protective part, the safety officer, has done to keep us safe when we did not have any other means of protection.

Safety Officer Strategies

Think back to a moment when you felt fear or shame and observe your immediate reactions. What did you do to cope with these emotions? Did you, for instance, use humour to divert attention, or did you withdraw or become defensive?

Reflect on how these behaviours served you at the time and trace their origins to your past experiences.

Consider how these patterns appear in your life today and identify triggers that bring them to the surface.

Finally, write down one commitment to yourself to address these reactions more directly in the future, recognising that while these strategies once protected you, they may now limit your growth.

This exercise helps reveal the protective strategies you rely on and encourages deeper self-awareness and change.

Consider: How do You Relate to Your Fear?

- What situations or events usually trigger feelings of fear in you?
- How do you feel physically when you first notice you're feeling fear (e.g. increased heart rate, sweaty palms, trembling)?
- What do you typically do when you feel fear? Do you face it, avoid it or distract yourself?
- What strategies do you use to cope with fear? Are they healthy (e.g. deep breathing, grounding techniques) or unhealthy (e.g. avoidance, substance use)?
- How do you feel about the way you handle fear?
- Is there anything you would like to change?
- Can you recall a time when you handled fear in a way that you were proud of? What did you do differently?

Control and Surrender

Joseph Campbell, in his work on the hero's journey, often referred to the 'dragon's cave', symbolising a place where great treasures are hidden but guarded by a fearsome dragon. Entering the dragon's cave is a metaphor for embracing our deepest fears and the shadow aspects of our personality.

At 24, after my fitness business failed, I went home to Galway with my tail between my legs and moved back in with my parents. I felt completely lost, ashamed of having failed and emotionally broken. I got some work in a pizza shop and spent the rest of my time walking up and down the local beach for hours each day, contemplating what a failure I was and what I was going to do with my life.

I would wipe back tears when bumping into people on my daily walks and dreaded bumping into my parents' friends, knowing the inevitable question of 'What are you doing with your life?' would come up. I felt like life had brought me to my knees and I had no choice but to 'surrender', let go of my grandiose ambitions about how my life should be and deal with the fact that my reality looked nothing like my expectations, and my thinking it should was causing me to suffer.

I finally surrendered to the fact that I had no idea how to run a business and began reading books and studying people who did. I came to realise how much of a fear I had around being seen, and so I put myself out there on social media and began teaching fitness classes again. The fears I confronted slowly began to open me up to opportunities that would have otherwise been unavailable to me, and over a few years I went on an incredible journey both inwardly and outwardly.

A few years later the business had grown exponentially, far beyond what I could ever have expected. I was acknowledged as one of Ireland's best young entrepreneurs, had just been interviewed on the *Late Late Show* about my 'success story' and the next day flown to Necker Island to spend a few days with a small group of entrepreneurs and one of my business heroes, Richard Branson. I had gone from a lost and insecure 24-year-old to a successful and well-known fitness entrepreneur in a few short years. I had found my place in the world, or so I thought.

A part of me wanted to cling to that identity that gave me a sense of 'being somebody' and the false sense of control and safety that came with that. Another part of me knew, though, that that chapter of my life was done, that there was something else waiting for me if I was willing to step into the unknown.

I am of the belief that we come into the world with certain lessons to learn, experiences to have and people to meet, all for the purpose of better understanding ourselves and embracing our unique expression of life. To honour this process we've got to learn to surrender. The ego latches on to ideas about how our lives 'should' look and how our five-year plan needs to unfold for us to be happy or successful, but when we go from the head to the heart, we might realise that we're meant for something different.

The first step in 12-step recovery programmes is the individual admitting to powerlessness over alcohol (or whatever the addiction) and recognising that their life has become unmanageable. This isn't with a sense of self-defeat, but instead with a recognition that they do not have control over their relationship to the substance or addiction. This admission involves dismantling the protective façade of control and self-reliance that the ego clings to, making space for a new, more authentic identity. Paradoxically for many, surrendering the illusion of control leads to them accepting help from others and finding freedom and empowerment in the process.

A similar surrender is often needed by us as we step into the fear of the unknown, an acceptance that we do not have the level of control in life that we perhaps previously thought we had. I had fought tooth and claw for four years to fulfil my ego's desires to become successful and well-known. I had leaned into my fears of judgement, of success, of failure and of being seen.

I had built a business that was lucrative and would continue to be if I just kept it going. The fearful part of me wanted to cling to this identity and life I had worked so hard to create, but despite all this, a part of me knew my time in that phase of life was done. And so I left the fitness business behind and again stepped into the unknown, surrendering control without a plan, but knowing there was something waiting for me on the other side of the fear of letting go of control.

Our identity, how we are seen by others and how we see ourselves, is perhaps one of the greatest addictions we have in life, and the idea of letting our current identity go can trigger our deep primal fears. I believe, however, this willingness to let go of how we are seen and how we see ourselves plays an essential role in leaning into an authentic and fulfilling life. Our lives have been built around this identity or persona we have formed, which has helped us to feel safe in the world, and so the thought of letting go, surrendering or loosening our grip on how we see ourselves, letting old identities fall away, is an essential part of the journey that can trigger feelings of grief, fear and even anger. Some call it an 'ego death'.

The person who embraces sobriety must grieve the loss of their old identity and embrace the fear of not knowing who they are without their addiction. Someone who has hidden their sexual orientation must lean into the fear of potential rejection or discrimination if they are to stop hiding this significant part of who they are and live a life true to themselves. Becoming a parent creates a profound shift in identity and may lead the individual to experience fears around inadequacy or the loss of freedom that comes with their new role and identity.

As we have spoken about earlier in the book, we project both our 'dark' and our 'gold' onto others, in seeing things in others that are difficult for us to see in ourselves. Many of us are inspired by people in life who have the courage to reinvent themselves, mirroring back something that lives somewhere in us too.

Consider: Admiration for Reinvention

- Think about someone you admire who has reinvented themselves.
- What did you notice about how they navigated their own identity shifts, and what lessons can you apply to your own journey?
- From the outside looking in, their reinvention may have looked smoothed or effortless, but try to imagine what parts of themselves they may have needed to have let go of or what fears they may have had to lean in to.

The Dragon's Cave

Find a quiet, comfortable place where you can sit undisturbed for a few minutes. Close your eyes and take a few deep, calming breaths.

Imagine standing at the entrance of a dark cave.

Inside, you sense the presence of a dragon guarding something valuable.

As you approach the cave, ask yourself, 'What fear or obstacle does this dragon represent in my life?' Allow whatever thoughts, feelings or images arise to come to the surface without judgement. Reflect on what treasure or hidden potential might lie beyond this fear, waiting to be discovered.

When you're ready, open your eyes and write down any insights that came to you during the exercise.

Holding Our Fear

Growing up, I'm sure many of us felt fear as we stepped into new environments or unknown situations. There might have been worry or dread with the thought of our parents dropping us off for our first day of school, or overwhelm and insecurity in going from being one of the oldest and biggest kids in the primary school to one of the youngest and smallest in secondary school. Maybe there was fear of going on our first date, or taking our first driving lesson, fear of showing up on our first day of work or standing up in front of a group for the first time to present something.

We have all had many firsts throughout our younger years, initiations in which we stepped into the unknown, left behind the life we knew before and opened up to a different life. Back then, though, it felt somewhat 'normal' and an obvious part of the process of growing up. Parents or grownups hopefully encouraged us and supported us, and it was possible to look around us and see our peers going through similar changes or situations, making it easier for us to navigate the change and uncertainty of it all.

As we get older, maybe we go on to find a partner, a job and a small circle of friends, a routine that works well for us, and settle into a way of living that feels comfortable, safe and predictable. After a while something inside us nudges us to make a change. We are called to our own unique hero's journey and invited to step away from the familiarity of the life we know so we can step into the life that is waiting for us.

That call might be to have a difficult conversation with our partner, to hand in our notice at work and pursue work that feels more meaningful, or to take up a new hobby. That voice inside us is nudging us to step into a bigger life and leave the safety we have grown accustomed to. It's different from childhood now, though. It's different from the changes we made as kids. We won't have a 'grownup' parental figure reminding us that we'll be OK when we make the change, or a circle of friends around us going through the same changes in life, making it seem more normal and par for the course.

To embrace our own unique path and journey, we must learn to support ourselves and encourage ourselves as we leave the familiarity of the life that we currently know. We have built our lives in a way that offers us a sense of safety and control, and the thought of bringing any change to that sense of safety can awaken our fears and anxieties.

When the fear creeps in we may find ourselves reverting to a childlike state, experiencing an inward collapse and perhaps an attack from the inner critic, who shames us for our lack of courage. In essence it is our inner child who is experiencing fear when we leave the safety of our familiar known world. When we realise this we can step in and care for ourselves. The reparenting idea we spoke about in Chapter Five becomes a key piece in leaving the comfort zone and stepping into something new.

In working a number of years ago with a client who had piled on weight in her teens and never been able to lose it in the 20 years since, we uncovered the hidden belief and shadow fear that losing weight would mean she would get unwanted attention. (You'll find an exercise later in the chapter to support you in shining light on hidden fears.)

Tracing back her story and belief, she spoke about the unwanted attention she got from older men in her early teens. Her safety officer decided that if she put on weight she would be able to avoid this unwanted attention and not have to feel that discomfort anymore. Now, almost 20 years later, her shadow fear and the strategy of her safety officer were continuing to play out. She would consistently begin training or diet plans, but 'fall off the wagon' after a few weeks and find herself back at square one, with her inner critic reinforcing a belief that 'I never stay consistent'.

In our work together we made a connection with the younger part of her who had experienced the unwanted attention of older men. She expressed the anger she felt and the sadness she felt that no one was there to protect her.

She then began to reparent and work with this part, keeping this shadow fear at the front of her mind and building her confidence to know that as a grown woman she could now speak up for the part of her who did not want this attention. Within weeks she began to shift more weight than she had in 20 years and over months got to the best shape of her life, tending to her inner child and teenager in the process, asserting her boundaries and finding her voice again.

The first step in tending to our inner child in times of fear is to name what we are experiencing. Rather than identifying with the fear by saying, 'I'm afraid,' we can say, 'I am experiencing some fear.'

In our beautiful mother tongue of Irish, we would say, *'Tá eagla orm'* (I have fear on me). This way of speaking reminds us that emotions are experiences we encounter rather than defining characteristics of who we are. This allows us to approach our feelings with greater compassion, perspective and understanding. Then we can relate to our emotions rather than from them, can notice and acknowledge the fear that we are experiencing without pushing it away or allowing it to overtake our system.

Next, we can check in with the part of ourselves that is feeling some fear. How old is that part and what belief are they holding about what might happen if you surrender control and step toward your fear? What is the current situation reminding them of that was painful in the past? What did that younger version of you need in that situation in the past and how can you offer that to yourself now as you lean into the discomfort of change?

Tending to this younger part and allowing self-compassion and understanding will be an important part of your self-care as you step away from your 'ordinary world'.

Sitting with Fear

Begin by closing your eyes and taking a few grounding breaths.

Then connect with a time when you felt fear.

Notice what happens in your body, connecting it with the sensations of fear. Continue to breathe and feel the sensations in the body. The mind may want to go to stories about why you're afraid or what you need to do to get away from the discomfort of feeling your fear, but look to stay with the sensations.

Now see if you have a sense of what lies behind the fear.

What is this fear looking to reveal? Perhaps it is protecting you from a perceived threat, or it is intertwined with uncertainty, vulnerability or past trauma. What is underneath the fear?

Finally, see if you have a sense of how you could address this fear in a healthy way that acknowledges and respects your need for safety and security without keeping you stuck or small.

Collective Fear

Alongside the fears that we experience on an individual level related to our story and place in the world, we are also influenced by collective fear. Collective fear is a case of a group of people, perhaps a community, a country or even a global population, experiencing fears simultaneously as a result of a common threat of perceived danger. When large groups face similar threats, their shared experiences can intensify feelings of fear and uncertainty. At times this can lead to a sense of solidarity, but it can also lead to widespread anxiety.

Different people respond to fear in different ways, all seeking a sense of security and certainty when things are uncertain. Some seek out more information or lean on the opinions of people they trust, others lean against the mainstream narrative by default and find ways to distract themselves. Generally, the more fearful we are, the more black and white the world seems as we cling to our existing belief systems and defence strategies. In relating 'from' our fear we see the world through a fearful lens and lose perspective. In relating 'to' our fear, we can notice the part of ourselves that sees the threat or danger, but can also hold a bigger perspective beyond the fear.

Much of the marketing and advertising we see in the world is fear-based, tapping into the deep-seated fears and anxieties that are inherent in our psychology and pushing on our subconscious primal instincts. This can be pushed on us from childhood. I remember growing up how much I wanted brand-name shoes or the newest Manchester United football jersey, already influenced at that young age to associate those things with my own self-worth. Marketers and advertisers, knowing that people crave a sense of security and reassurance, will often aim to create a sense of necessity around their products or services by pushing on people's fears and insecurities. Some will create perceived threats of what will happen to the consumer if they don't buy the product. Others will instil a fear of missing out or a sense that we don't fit in with the tribe if we haven't got the latest product on offer. It is common for marketing to push on common insecurities like the fear of ageing, financial instability, being single or 'alone' or experiencing social rejection.

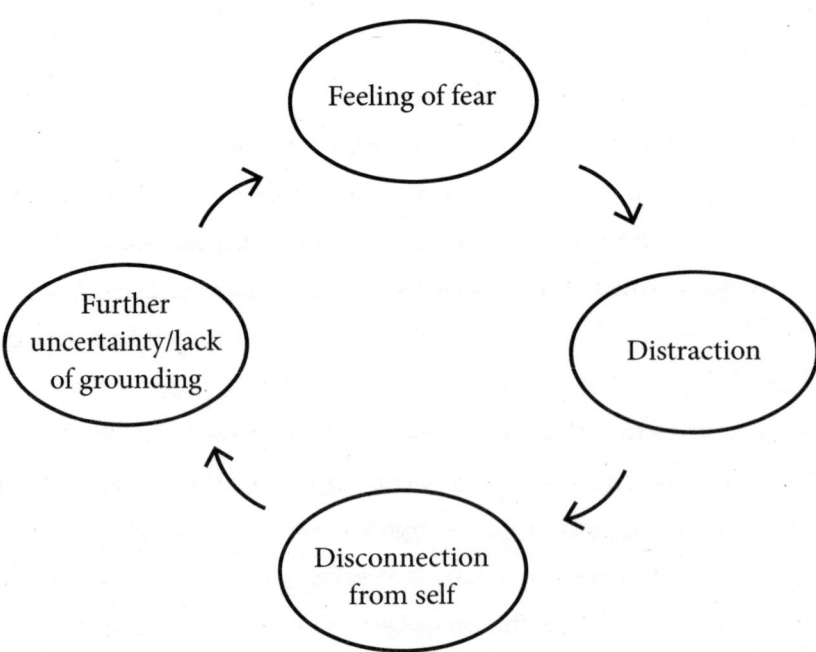

Learning to be with our fear and tend to ourselves makes us much less susceptible to fear-based marketing. Rather than looking for a solution 'out there', we can allow space to be with and understand our feelings before going to impulsive or reactive behaviours based on anxieties, fear or insecurities.

It isn't just marketing and advertising that can prey on our unmet fears; the news and social media can also lead us to stray further from ourselves. There is a phrase relating to the media that dates back to the end of the 1890s: 'If it bleeds it leads.' This was said by William Randolph Hearst, who noticed that it was the news stories that were most horrific that captured the public's attention.

When we experience fear, our brain releases stress hormones such as cortisol and adrenaline. These hormones trigger a fight-or-flight response, preparing us to respond to the perceived threats. Over time, frequent exposure to fear-inducing stimuli can lead to a heightened sensitivity to these reactions, potentially reinforcing the neural pathways associated with fear. Managing our exposure to fear-inducing media through selective consumption and mindful practices is an important step in maintaining emotional wellbeing and having a balanced perspective on the world around us. In much the same way that our bodies digest the foods that we consume, our psyches 'digest' the media that we consume. You may notice that after watching a horror movie you are more prone to nightmares.

Social media and its algorithms significantly contribute to the spread and amplification of collective fear, too. The internet and social media came about as a tool for us to use, but have quickly shifted to something using us. By prioritising emotionally charged content and creating echo chambers, the social media platforms distort perceptions of danger and escalate societal anxieties, impacting both individual wellbeing and broader social dynamics.

The internet can also become a hiding place for those who become fearful of being present or taking part in the 'real world'. The problem is that the true needs are never met and these outlets act only as pseudo-means, leaving the individual feeling unfulfilled and disconnected. I have definitely found myself hiding on the internet at times. One of the most important commitments we can make to ourselves if we want to live a self-led life is to become committed to take back our attention by setting firm boundaries around our phone and media usage and not becoming slaves to the algorithm.

Consider: Fear and Consumption

What role does fear play in your consumption habits? What insecurities are easiest for marketers to push on for you? What is your internet usage like?

Embracing the Unknown

People often reference 'public speaking' as one of the most common fears, though really it isn't about the speaking – we speak in public all the time. The fear that comes with public speaking is the fear of judgement. What if I say the wrong thing? What if I can't find the words and don't have anything to say? What if I am rejected by the group?

For the last 10 years a lot of my work has been around speaking, presenting and facilitating, though prior to that I would have been one of those who would list public speaking as my biggest fear. I dreaded being asked to read in secondary school, skipped any lectures in college that required me to present to the group and avoided any situation where I might have to speak in front of others in public.

At 25, after seeing some success with a fitness business I had set up, I was asked to give a 10-minute talk at a local business group. Despite the fear, I said yes and prepared a slideshow with 10 slides, one for each minute of my talk in case I ran out of things to say. I survived, and after that first 10-minute talk made a commitment to myself to getting comfortable with public speaking.

I set the intention of doing 100 free talks over the next year to gain experience and confidence. I would speak anywhere people would have me – primary schools, secondary schools, gyms, big and small businesses, sports clubs. I once turned up to a talk expecting to be presenting in a gym and instead was presenting for a woman and her friends in her garage. Another time I ended up presenting a nutrition seminar in a fast-food takeaway shop in the midlands. By the end of the year I hadn't quite hit my target of 100 free talks, but I had got close, with 88 talks around the country. There had been plenty of train wrecks and times when I felt completely exposed and vulnerable, though I recognised that as much as this was about becoming comfortable with public speaking, the more important practice was in leaning toward and being with the feelings of fear, changing how I related to it and allowing it to guide the way rather than keep me stuck.

Leading on from the year of free talks, I advertised my first three-day retreat in Galway, and as the retreat came close felt the reemergence of that familiar feeling of fear. I had given plenty of

1–2-hour workshops at that point, but now I would be delivering sessions for eight hours a day, three days in a row.

How could I possibly fill the time?

In any case, I had committed, had 15 people signed up and had to come out of the shadows and embrace any fears head on. In this case the accountability of having to show up for others supported me in leaning into fears I probably would have otherwise avoided. Sometimes we've got to jump and grow wings on the way down, though this capacity to trust ourselves in the unknown can be scary at first.

Within minutes of starting the three-day retreat I realised my initial structure and plan weren't going to work and I would have to throw the plan out the window. A year of delivering talks around the country and rarely knowing what type or group of people I would be presenting to, or what type of venue I would be at, had supported my capacity to embrace the spontaneity of the moment. Removing the plan and letting the retreat unfold naturally allowed me to connect more deeply with the attendees, respond to their immediate needs, and create a much more dynamic and engaging experience. That retreat proved another reminder of the magic that can unfold with a willingness to surrender and to let go of control, replacing expectations of what should happen with a trust in what could happen.

At the end of the three days we headed to Blackrock, a 10-metre diving tower at the beach in Salthill. It was a nice way of symbolically ending what had been an incredible three days and taking the leap into the next chapter of life. One by one each of the retreat participants jumped from the diving tower, some filled with confidence, having jumped off diving towers many times before, and others terrified, taking a jump like this for the first time. After a few minutes everyone had jumped, bar one of the participants, who stood nervously at the top of the diving tower. It was a beautiful day and the beach was packed with people. Slowly people started to notice him pacing back and forth on the top of the diving board, almost jumping, then retreating in fear. The longer he spent walking back and forth, the more attention he drew from the growing crowd, who began to cheer him in support. The longer he stood atop the diving board, the more stories he built in his head about what could go wrong. This is a key characteristic of fear: the more time we give it, the more it grows and the more it can paralyse us, feeding off our imagination and escalating our anxiety.

The rest of the group began to grow cold in the water waiting for him to jump and join us. I shouted, 'Jump in the next 10 seconds and I'll give a hundred euro to charity.' Often when we make it about more than ourselves we'll push beyond our own self-imposed limitations.

He quickly jumped ... and the crowd went wild!

A few weeks later, the group from the retreat got together for dinner and a few drinks in Galway. Our friend from the diving tower spotted a lady in the bar and commented, 'She's beautiful,' to one of the other attendees. Those weren't his exact words, but that was the sentiment.

'You should go and talk to her.'

'I can't,' he responded. Much like on the diving board a few weeks before, he began to battle internally with the part of him that wanted to go and say hello and the part that feared rejection. The longer he stayed in his head, the more horror stories he began to build about how she might reject him.

After a few minutes of deliberation he finally walked over and spat the word out: 'Hi.'

She responded to his greeting with a smile, looked him in the eye and announced, 'I recognise you! You are the guy that stood on the diving board for a half-hour a few weeks ago!'

Because the nature of fear is that it contracts us and makes us small, being with and stepping into courage to meet our fear reawakens us to a natural flow of energy. As Fritz Perls once said, 'Fear is excitement without the breath,' and often after meeting our fear we feel this energy of excitement and aliveness.

In both the cases of the diving board and chatting to the lady in the bar, the man experienced a huge surge of energy after stepping through the threshold, and his world opened up to bigger possibilities than existed when he kept himself imprisoned by his fear.

Similarly for me, leaning into the fear of giving that first 10-minute talk to a small group of business owners and later the fear of offering a three-day retreat opened my world to new possibilities and provided me with evidence that on the other side of fear lie growth, opportunity, and a self-trust that can only come from choosing to walk into the unknown.

Revealing Shadow Fears

This exercise is designed to help you uncover and address the hidden shadow fears that may be holding you back from pursuing your deepest desires. By bringing these shadow fears to light, you can begin to meet and transform them and move forward with greater clarity and courage.

Think of something you deeply desire in your life. It could be related to your career, relationships, personal growth or any other area. Write at the top of a page, 'I hold back from going after [your true aspiration] because, deep down, I'm so afraid that ...'

An example might be 'I hold back from going after a loving relationship because, deep down, I'm so afraid that …'

Set a timer for 10 minutes. Start writing, allowing your thoughts to flow without judgement or editing. Keep the pen moving, and don't worry about grammar or spelling. Explore all the reasons why you might be hesitant or afraid to pursue your desire. Let your subconscious fears and beliefs surface.

Here are a few prompts that might support the exercise:

- 'I fear that if I pursue this, I will …'
- 'Deep down, I believe that having this will make me …'
- 'I'm worried that achieving this will cause …'
- 'If I go after this, others will think …'
- 'Part of me thinks that I don't deserve this because …'
- 'What scares me most about getting this is …'

After the 10 minutes are up, take a moment to read over what you've written. Reflect on the fears and beliefs that have emerged. Then ask yourself these questions to help integrate your insights:

Which fears surprised you the most?

How have these fears been influencing your behaviour and decisions?

What steps can you take to address and transform these fears?

How can you support yourself in moving past these fears to pursue what you truly want?

— Summary: Gold in The Shadow —

The more we look to deny or avoid our fears, the more of a grip fear will hold on our lives, making our world small and limited, pushing us into a smaller and smaller comfort zone. Taking fear out of the shadow and learning to be with our fear is an essential step in creating lasting transformation in our lives.

- In times of stress or uncertainty we tend to cling to control in order to ease the intensity or tension we feel. It is important that we distinguish between genuine threats to our physical safety and fears triggered by threats to our ego.
- Collective fear occurs when a group of people, community, nation or global population experience pain simultaneously, often intensifying the anxieties or worries of the individual. News media and social media contribute to this effect.
- To be with fear in a grounded way we must tend to the younger, more scared parts by allowing space for the sensations we are feeling in the body, and noticing what this fear reminds us of, before giving ourselves what that younger part of us needed in the past.

Incomplete Sentences

Read the beginning of each sentence aloud and allow yourself to complete the sentence spontaneously in an unfiltered way. After completing all the prompts you can jot down any insights or reflections that stand out to you.

- The thing I avoid the most because of fear is …
- I often hold myself back because I'm scared that …
- One fear that keeps me from pursuing my dreams is …
- Deep down, I fear that others will think I am …
- I worry that if I take a risk, I will …
- A hidden fear that influences my decisions is …
- If I wasn't afraid, I would …
- My fear of being judged causes me to …

Journalling Prompts

1. Reflect on a fear or anxiety that you have been avoiding. What are the ways in which avoiding this fear has affected your life, decisions, and relationships? Consider how facing this fear might lead to growth or positive change.

2. Think about a recent experience where you faced a fear or entered a situation that made you anxious. Describe the emotions and physical sensations you felt before, during and after crossing this threshold. How did confronting this fear affect your perception of yourself and your capabilities?

3. Recall a time when you transitioned from feeling scared or anxious to experiencing full-fledged fear or anxiety. What triggered this shift? How did your body react physically (e.g. changes in breathing, muscle tension)? Reflect on the differences between being scared and experiencing fear, and what you learned from this experience.

4. Consider a fear or anxiety that seems to be influenced by collective attitudes or societal expectations. How does this fear manifest in your life, and how might it be connected to broader cultural or social influences? Reflect on ways to navigate and understand collective fears while maintaining individual autonomy and authenticity.

5. Explore the physiological aspects of fear in your own experience. Describe how your body responds when you feel afraid or anxious (e.g. changes in heart rate, sweating, tension). How does understanding the physiological reactions to fear help you manage or cope with these emotions effectively?

Gibberish Practice

Fear often keeps us caught in our heads, disconnected from our bodies and living in stories of worst-case scenarios. To deal with the anxieties we are experiencing, we try to make sense of things and use our rational thinking to bring a sense of certainty to what feels uncertain. In Chapter Three, I introduced a shaking practice as a short dynamic meditation to go beyond the busy thinking mind and connect with the body. I encourage you to try another active practice, a 15-minute gibberish meditation. In this practice, you'll be letting go of control, quieting the rational mind, and allowing yourself to ease emotional tension, break through mental blocks, and invite play and spontaneity.

Find a comfortable place to sit or stand, close your eyes, and take a few deep breaths. Begin speaking in gibberish – nonsensical sounds and words that have no meaning. Let your voice flow freely, allowing any emotions, especially fear, to express themselves through this chaotic language.

Don't hold back; let go of any need to make sense or be understood. Allow the gibberish to act as a cathartic release, freeing your mind from the constraints of rationality and the hold of fear. Allow yourself to lose control.

After 10 minutes, gradually slow down, letting the gibberish fade into silence. Sit quietly for the remaining five minutes, observing the calm and clarity that follow this energetic release.

Look to complete this short 'gibberish' meditation at least five times in the next week. You will find an accompanying audio track with gibberish background noise and further explanation at patdivilly.com/shadow.

CHAPTER TEN

Shadow in Relationship

'We are born in relationship, we are wounded in relationship, and we can be healed in relationship.' HARVILLE HENDRIX

'Vulnerability is the only bridge to build connection.' BRENÉ BROWN

———— Completing Childhood ————

'Your intimate relationship offers an opportunity to complete childhood ...'

It's a strange thought to start an eight-week clinical training programme in Imago couples therapy. I scan the names on screen and notice I'm the only attendee who doesn't have a PhD after their name or a Dr before it. A touch of impostor syndrome kicks in and I wonder if I have signed up to the right course or if it's a matter of time before I'm politely asked to leave. I momentarily consider sticking the letters 'MSc' after my name in an effort to blend in with

the group of academics and clinical psychologists on screen. It was an MSc in Exercise and Nutrition Science that I'd earned 13 years earlier, but they won't know that.

After transitioning from the physical fitness space toward coaching and the exploration of mental and emotional wellness in my mid-twenties, I had spent close to a decade deeply immersed in inner work and self-inquiry in efforts to better understand my thoughts, emotions and behaviours while helping my clients do the same. I continued to add tools to the toolbox as I studied modalities that would support shadow integration and improved physical, mental and emotional wellness.

It had become evident to me, though, how pivotal a role relationships, conflict and communication play in better understanding ourselves and growing up psychologically. I noted in my own life and in the lives of many of my clients that those powerful emotions that were so often the driving force behind outbursts, reactivity or addiction were triggered in the relational realm.

Spiritual teacher Ram Dass tells a great story of reaching incredible states in his meditations while with his guru in India and perhaps thinking he had reached enlightenment, then coming back to his childhood home in America for his holidays and concluding, 'If you think you're enlightened go spend a week with your family.'

Most of us do not choose to live a monk-like existence meditating peacefully on the side of a mountain, isolated and at a distance from people who might potentially trigger us or throw us off our centre. We live in the 'real world', as social and tribal beings wired for connection. We experience an early sense of safety in life in our connections with our primary caregivers, but also experience our first emotional wounds in relation to other people when we experience a sense of disconnection or separation. Our early emotional wounds and shame-based stories or beliefs occur in relationships and so too can our emotional healing, if we wake up to our patterns and defence strategies. Real shadow work happens in relationships and in being seen by others in all our messiness and glory. Real shadow work cannot be done in isolation.

Reflections on the journey that's brought me from push-ups and broccoli to training with a group of relational therapists and psychologists are interrupted as the lead facilitator sends us to breakout rooms to practise some of the fundamental communication skills that will support our time in the training. I am not found out and I go on to complete the clinical training module in Imago therapy, gaining a new perspective and new techniques on how skilfully working with triggers and shadow can move us from conflict to deeper connection and how our relationships can be a vehicle for deep healing, growth and understanding.

Carl Rogers, an American psychologist known for his person-centred approach to psychotherapy, once said, 'The curious paradox is that when I accept myself just as I am, then I can change.' Sometimes, of course, it doesn't seem so easy to accept ourselves as we are, let alone love ourselves as we are.

A friend recently asked me, 'How many people in your life love and accept you just as you are, without feeling the need to fix or change you?' It made me pause and reflect. We're so often told that we need to love ourselves – it's a common mantra in personal growth circles. But my friend's simple question reminded me of the transformative power of being loved by others. While self-love is essential, the truth is we don't always know how to love ourselves – especially if we've grown up in environments where love was conditional. Sometimes we need to experience love from others to learn what it feels like. It's as if they hold up a mirror, showing us the parts of our shadow we haven't yet learned to embrace. When someone sees us fully and loves us in our messiness, our imperfection and our humanity, it gives us permission to soften towards ourselves.

Sometimes in others accepting our flaws, we can learn to accept our own. In feeling the kindness of others, we can practise being kinder to ourselves. And in their presence, we can start showing up for ourselves in ways we never thought possible. Love, both given and received, has the power to heal.

Transference is where we bring old psychological energy from the past into the present moment and unconsciously redirect feelings, desires and expectations from one person to another. We will often choose intimate partners who mirror the best and worst traits of our parents or primary caregivers, because those traits feel so familiar and thus safe – we seek out more of the same. This ties to the idea of our intimate relationships being a vehicle for completing childhood. If I grew up with a very critical parent who was domineering or bullying, I would not have had any power to challenge them as a kid, but an unconscious part of me might later choose a partner with similar traits for the purpose of healing that part of myself and bringing the repressed aspects out of shadow and into the light.

Without an awareness of our wounds and shadows, adult relationships can become a game of projection ping-pong, where neither person takes responsibility for their internal struggles, each instead projecting blame onto the other. With an awareness of our wounds and shadows, adult relationships can transform into opportunities for growth and healing, where both people take responsibility for their inner experiences and work together to create a deeper, more authentic connection. This is true of all relationships, not just intimate or romantic relationships, though typically the more intimate the relationship, the more primal our wounding and projections will tend to be.

Conscious Love

The aforementioned Imago couples therapy works on the premise that we often choose partners who reflect both the positive and negative traits of our parents or primary caregivers, though we may not recognise this at first. Thus when we feel a strong attraction toward a partner we are often picking the perfect person to support us in working through and healing emotional or psychic wounds from childhood. Our attraction is driven from shadow material and unconscious patterns. This is maybe why a potential partner looks great on paper but we just don't feel drawn to them, while we may feel a magnetic pull to another partner even though it doesn't make sense or we can't quite explain why.

While I may have had to repress my authenticity and overlook my needs as a child to keep a parent happy, as an adult, noticing myself overlooking my own needs to stay in connection to another person offers a chance to reconnect with my true self and express my needs in an intimate relationship.

While we may have previously found ourselves shadow boxing with a partner and blaming them for our stress or triggers, learning to work with challenging material and old wounds can shift us into shadow dancing and becoming allies rather than adversaries.

Imago therapy outlines three stages of relationship:

Stage 1: Romantic Love

The first stage, romantic love, is a time characterised by intense passion, emotional bonding and idealisation. We meet and fall head over heels for the person, seeing them as a 'missing piece' in our puzzle. Attraction is at its most intense and flaws or differences are typically overlooked.

Blinded by love, we may find ourselves in a state of denial, magnifying the person's positive traits and minimising or denying any of their negative traits or shortcomings. There is a sense of excitement, hope, optimism and maybe even an infatuation with one another. The other person can do no wrong and we may feel sure we've met the 'one'.

This phase typically lasts 3–12 months, sometimes a little less, sometimes longer, depending on our childhood wounds and relationship history. As we get older and go through a number of relationships, we may notice this phase of infatuation being shorter.

Stage 2: Power Struggle

As the initial euphoria fades, couples shift into a more rounded understanding of one another and differences and flaws become apparent. In this phase we often shift to magnifying the person's negatives and minimising their positives as we begin to feel ourselves triggered by many of the little things they do. Misunderstandings or disappointments may begin to manifest and disillusionment may appear as the idealised vision we had of this person fades. We might feel we have been duped as it becomes apparent this person is a unique sovereign being with their own wounds, needs, fears and dreams. They were not sent here to complete us!

We may begin trying to change one another in order to get our needs met. Typically couples will go to one of four options once they hit the 'power struggle' stage:

Option One: End of Relationship

Some couples, when met with the power struggle, may choose to break up, go their separate ways and conclude that they are not suited to one another.

Option Two: Cold Relationship

These couples instead choose to stay together for convenience, for practical reasons or to avoid the discomfort of a break-up, living parallel lives with emotional distance. In this case an unspoken agreement is made to settle for a relationship void of intimacy or connection.

Option Three: Hot Relationship

This couple chooses to stay together and play out patterns and cycles of repetitive fiery conflict.

Option Four: Conscious Love

Finally there are those who choose to commit to 'conscious love' and to actively work on transforming their relationship with a commitment to personal and relational growth.

Stage 3: Conscious Love

Stepping into conscious love is a commitment to 'growing up' in a relationship, understanding one another's needs and supporting one another's growth and healing. There is a recognition in this stage that the conflicts and arguments that emerge have little to do with what is happening in the present moment and are instead reactions to old childhood experiences and defence strategies.

'The thing is not the thing' – in other words, the content of an argument or trigger is pointing to something deeper. Rather than being seen as a reason to leave, react defensively or walk away, conflict can be seen as an invitation to step in and inquire further. As each person owns their own history, projections and part in the relational drama, deeper connection, intimacy and safety can be found.

In this stage couples can go from adversaries to allies.

I have seen this sequence play out in the dynamics of many clients I have worked with over the years. (Of course, I have seen it in my own life too.)

A couple who recently came to me described how they had fallen head over heels for one another and had a blissful first 12 months together. After getting engaged quickly, a few cracks started to appear, though they put that down to the stress of their upcoming wedding.

When the cracks seemed to only get bigger after the wedding, they became worried and committed to seeking out help, showing a strong commitment and desire to work through their issues.

The couple were quick to tell me that they didn't ever fight or get hostile with one another like other couples they knew, though they felt they were quickly becoming more and more distant from one another. The connection they had had in their first 12 months was a distant memory and they feared for the direction they were going if they continued to live these parallel lives, staying together only out of expectation or convenience.

Entrenched in the power struggle stage, their unmet needs and unresolved childhood wounds were being triggered, leading to feelings of disconnection and dissatisfaction. In the work we began to do together they came to recognise how their past experiences and unmet needs were influencing their behaviour.

The husband had grown up with a very critical father and had internalised his father's voice, now living with an inner critic who constantly pointed out his flaws and shortcomings. When his wife would gently share her feelings, frustrations or needs he would immediately jump to a belief that he had messed everything up, couldn't get anything right and wouldn't ever be enough. The resulting shame he would feel would lead to him getting defensive and distant.

The wife had grown up with emotionally absent parents and carried a deep-seated fear of being abandoned. When she had first met her husband she thrived on the safety, support and consistency she felt in his presence. Now she was confused, hurt and fearful of the disconnection she felt when he would become distant and defensive. Even more confusing to her, sometimes the frustrations, feelings or needs she shared with him were nothing to do with him, but he would take things personally and assume he was coming up short.

Taking ownership and prioritising conscious love, they began to work towards a more connected and fulfilling relationship.

She came to realise how she was projecting her fear of abandonment onto him, interpreting his defensiveness and distance as a sign that he would eventually leave her, just as she felt emotionally abandoned by her parents. This projection amplified her feelings of insecurity and desperation for connection, leading her to unknowingly place unrealistic expectations on him to fill the emotional void left by her parents. When he would withdraw after a disagreement, she would panic and feel an overwhelming fear that he would abandon her, mirroring her childhood experience with emotionally unavailable parents. She might accuse him of not caring about her or their relationship, projecting her unresolved feelings of neglect and abandonment onto him, even when his withdrawal was more about his own feelings of inadequacy and not about a lack of love or commitment to her.

He projected his internalised criticism onto her, interpreting her sharing of feelings or needs as pointing to his inadequacy. This projection made him believe that her requests or expressions of dissatisfaction were criticisms of his character, similar to the criticism he received from his father. This belief triggered feelings of shame and a sense of failure, leading him to become defensive and distant as a way to protect himself from further perceived criticism. When she would express a need for more emotional connection, he might hear, 'You're failing me,' reminding him of the critical voice of his father, now his inner critic. This would lead to him feeling overwhelmed and shutting down emotionally, thinking he could never meet her expectations, and thus distancing himself to avoid the pain of perceived failure.

One of the first steps in the work we did together was in recognising and owning projections. Projection is common with aspects of our shadow that are difficult for us to accept or acknowledge. For him, it was easier to point the finger at her being critical than to accept that it was his own inner critic that was causing him to feel inadequate and defensive. For her, it was easier to see him as distant and uncaring than to recognise that her deep-seated fear of abandonment was causing her to misinterpret his actions and react with panic and insecurity.

Someone who feels insecure about their own attractiveness or self-worth might project their insecurity onto their partner by constantly accusing them of being interested in others or being unfaithful, without any evidence to suggest that is the case. A person who struggles with their own perfectionism might project this onto their partner by placing impossibly high standards on them and becoming frustrated when these standards are not met, without recognising their own internal pressures.

James Hollis, a well-known Jungian psychologist, notes that 'to clear our projections is an act of love'. Clearing our projections involves first recognising and acknowledging the unconscious assumptions and expectations we place on others.

Recognising Our Projections

These prompts can be useful in acknowledging and recognising some of our common projections in relationships.

Note moments of tension or conflict that are common for you in a relationship. What is it that happens to trigger you and how do you typically react?

> Identify the feelings that are most common for you in these situations. These might include feelings like sadness, anger, jealousy, anxiety or shame.
>
> Ask yourself, does this situation remind me of any past experiences or relationships?
>
> You can also ask, am I attributing my own unresolved feelings or past wounds to my partner's actions?

Protect or Connect?

The only thing we can ever know for sure in times of conflict or disconnection is what is going on in our internal world. We can never know for sure what is going on in the other person's inner world and the intentions or emotions they are experiencing. We can only know how we feel and what story we are telling ourselves to make sense of the situation. Despite this, in efforts to defend our vulnerable state, we often project, defend or blame in order to soothe the anxieties we may be feeling around the relationship. Revealing what is going on in our internal world, rather than making assumptions about what is going on in the other person's world, can be incredibly vulnerable and is the fastest way to coming into authentic connection.

The couple I mentioned earlier began to recognise and name their projections. He would share when he noticed he was jumping to judgements of himself and stories of not being enough when she would share her feelings and unmet needs. In response, she was able to acknowledge his feelings and reassure him that her sharing was not a criticism of him but a way to express her own needs and desires. She would share the feelings of fear that were emerging for her when she felt emotional distance. This allowed him to respond by acknowledging her fears and providing reassurance: 'I want you to know that I am committed to you and our relationship. When I withdraw, it's not because I want to leave you; it's because I'm dealing with my own feelings of inadequacy.'

Revealing ourselves in this way can feel edgy and scary, though this type of vulnerability is an essential part of deepening connection and intimacy. Recognising when we are playing out patterns of the past or viewing our current reality through a historical lens can allow us to heal old wounds and show up in the present.

Revealing Ourselves in Relationships

For true connection to occur we must be willing to reveal rather than conceal, choosing to share what is happening in our inner world without making assumptions about the other person, their experience and their inner world.

When triggered, look to take a little space to check in with yourself, identifying the feelings and thoughts you are experiencing.

You can share these insights with your partner by expressing: 'I feel [emotion] because I'm telling myself [story].'

Encourage your partner to do the same, and listen without judgement. This is a practice of vulnerability and authentic connection, allowing both of you to understand and support each other more deeply.

———— Owning Our Experience ————

When I used to run three-day men's personal growth retreats I would often offer some ice-breaking exercises as part of the opening session. These were designed not only to get the attendees acquainted but also to introduce some communication principles that would prove useful throughout the weekend.

One of the exercises I would sometimes share involved meeting someone new and for five minutes going back and forth making statements that began with 'I'. This exercise meant they had to share something they were experiencing rather than staying on the surface with small talk or questions about the other person. The men had all taken three days of their lives and spent their hard-earned money to be there, so it was important for me to give them the best chance of having a transformative experience. This exercise would set the tone in moving from small talk to something a bit deeper.

Using 'I' at the start of each sentence meant they were 'owning' their statement. As an example, feeling awkward in this type of exercise might lead someone to saying, 'This is weird,' but having to begin with 'I' would shift that statement to 'I find this weird.' This phrasing meant the person was taking responsibility for their experience and also not making assumptions about how the exercise was for the other person. Maybe for the other person this experience didn't feel weird at all, and so 'I find this weird' would be more accurate than projecting their feelings onto the other person.

Toward the end of the retreat there were some incredible breakthroughs among the group and it was beautiful to watch men who had been guarded strangers just two days before being so open and supportive of one another. On the final day we sat in a circle and each man shared how his weekend had been and what he was taking home with him. It was particularly inspiring to see some of the younger guys in their twenties sharing how comfortable they had felt opening up and being vulnerable with a group of men for the first time.

When we got to an older man who had been sent along by his wife, he announced, 'It is nice to see you guys sharing your emotions but it's important you know that real men don't talk like this in the real world.'

I was disappointed to hear his statement.

The man had spent the previous three days deflecting away from any questions about himself, choosing to give advice instead from a position of being above it all. He had been sarcastic and mocked some of the exercises, and had sat out for parts that he had decided he 'wouldn't get anything from'. None of that bothered me. I understood there were defence mechanisms playing out to mask fears, that he might have felt triggered that his wife had sent him there and might have had judgements about me thinking I knew it all. I had done what I could to put him at ease, assuring him I had plenty to work on in my own life and wasn't telling anyone how they should live, but instead facilitating some exercises to explore connection with ourselves and others. Still, I understood that the sarcasm, the mocking and assuming the position of teaching the group rather than engaging with the group were efforts to protect himself. I respected that.

I understood the defensive behaviour but was pissed off at him projecting his fears onto the younger men, who had taken the risk of opening up and sharing vulnerably. If he had made the subtle distinction of saying, 'It is nice to see you guys sharing your emotions. Real men don't talk like this in *my* world,' it would have felt completely different from a sweeping statement that 'real men don't talk like this in *the* real world'.

Owning our experience by using 'I' or 'my' can be a simple, though not always easy, practice that can completely change how we relate to ourselves and others.

Consider the difference between some of these examples:

'You pissed me off when you showed up late.'

Becoming:

'I was disappointed when you showed up late.'

'Who doesn't like a few drinks in the evening to unwind?'

Becomes:

'I like a few drinks in the evening to unwind.'

'There aren't any good men out there.'

Becomes:

'I can't see any good men out there.'

—————— Humanising Our Parents ——————

Our early experiences with our parents or primary caregivers shape the expectations, communication styles and emotional responses for all our future relationships, and so a distorted or polarised view of our parents can result in us unknowingly applying that same polarised thinking to our partners, friends or other relationships. A key step in growing up psychologically involves taking our parents off the pedestal and out of the pit and choosing instead to humanise them. We can work to stop putting our parents above or below us, and instead put them alongside us as unique individuals on their own journey of life.

As we have discussed throughout this book, the nature of the mind is that it likes to polarise and put things in neat boxes. We often make the people in our lives heroes or villains, sinners or

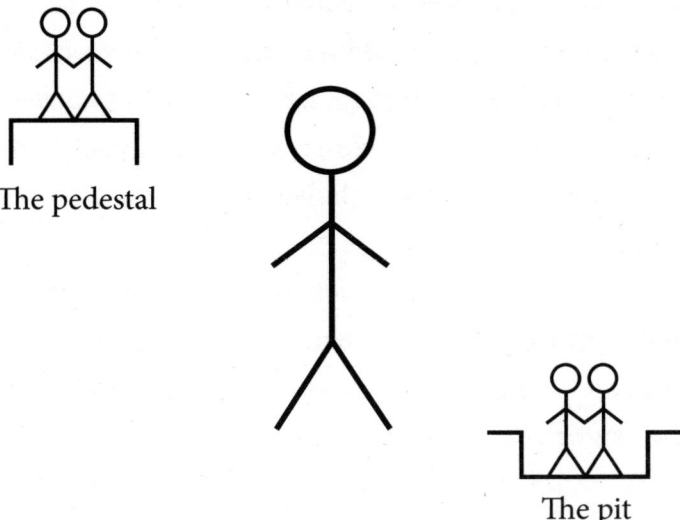

The pedestal

The pit

saints, and fail to see beyond the labels we have given them. I once read that 'your world will change and you will truly grow up the day you come to see your parents as children of other parents'. I believe there is a lot of truth in that statement. We cannot love someone we have polarised because we dehumanise them, placing them in a box and losing the ability to see them as unique, complex, multifaceted individuals, with their own hopes, fears, strengths and weaknesses. Polarising people prevents us from having genuine compassionate connections. It also leads to us comparing and holding ourselves to impossible standards as we try to be like them or be the opposite, depending on whether we have made them a hero or villain. Learning to see our parents as people shaped by their own life experiences can completely shift how we see and relate to them and to ourselves. Being able to hold the tension of opposites and being able to recognise both the shadow and light in ourselves and others is a true sign of emotional maturity.

Growing up, a close friend would frequently relay stories to us of his superhero father who could seemingly do no wrong. Many of the stories seemed a little far-fetched, maybe even completely made up, but none of us could help feeling a little envious of the relationship he reported having with his father. Toward our later teens the rebellious part of my friend crept in and his father became everything he did not want to be. His father probably hadn't changed a lot, but as my friend grew a little older he could see the flawed man and not just the perfect dad. Of course, no man or woman is perfect and so the higher the pedestal we place someone on, the greater their fall will be when they no longer meet our expectations.

Placing someone below us is equally dangerous and we fail to see their inherent worth as we overlook their complexities. A client who had judged his father for being impatient with him as a child later came to an understanding of the financial pressure he had been under at the time and saw the situation from a less polarised perspective.

As many of us grow older we come to a more balanced way of seeing our parents. We perhaps let go of resentments we had for unmet expectations in childhood or adolescence, recognising how many commitments and how much pressure our parents may have been juggling at the time. Or in retrospect we may begin to see cracks in the armour of the superhero parent who could do no wrong and notice some of the vulnerabilities or flaws we had previously overlooked. In seeing the human and not just the parent, we free ourselves from invisible cords that dictate how we engage in life. We can release the story of wanting to be just like them or nothing like them, and can instead be more of ourselves while also loving them without condition, as humans, not just our parents.

Consider the following exercise for humanising your parents. This exercise is to support seeing your parents as individuals, beyond their role as caretakers, even if they are no longer with you.

Humanising Your Parents

Step 1: Make Two Lists

Pedestal List: write down any of the ways you have placed your parents on a pedestal or made them larger than life. Include any of the qualities, achievements and actions that you admire or idolise in them. This list makes up all of the ways you look 'up' to your parents.

Pit List: next, write down all the ways you place your parents in the pit and see them as flawed or having failed. Include any of the qualities, mistakes or actions that have disappointed or hurt you. This list makes up all the ways you look 'down' on your parents.

Step 2: Humanise The Lists

As you look through each of your lists consider what the motivation or context for each quality, achievement, mistake or action may be. Take into account the upbringing they might have had, the personal values and worldview they may hold, the pressures they may have faced and the imperfections that come with being a human.

Step 3: Write Two Letters

Write letters to each of your parents (which you will not be sending) expressing your understanding of them as individuals. Acknowledge the ways in which you have put them on a pedestal or in the pit and express your recognition of their humanity. Use empathetic language and look to connect with their experiences, struggles and joys.

Step 4: Reflect

After completing the exercise check in with how you now feel toward your parents. Notice any subtle or not-so-subtle shifts that come from seeing them not as above or below you, but as other humans walking alongside you on this journey of life. You may choose to share some of your reflections with a therapist or close friend, or maybe even with your parents if it feels appropriate.

With this exercise some will be challenged and feel disloyalty or guilt at finding any flaws in their parents, while others will struggle to find anything that they admire in theirs.

For those who struggle to find any flaws, it is worth remembering that everyone has flaws and imperfections and it may be useful to reflect on times when your parents were tired, stressed or dealing with their own issues. These times can point to the vulnerabilities that are a part of being human rather than infallible figures. To point to their flaws is not to make them bad people; it is to recognise our shared humanity.

For those who struggle to find anything that they admire in their parents, it can be worth considering some of the challenges they may have had in their lives and how this might have fostered qualities such as resilience, determination or other admirable traits. It can also be useful to recall any early memories in which you felt loved, cared for or happy with your parents and consider some of the positive qualities in those scenarios that you may have overlooked.

Relationship Inventory

Philosopher George Santayana is quoted as saying, 'Those who cannot remember the past are condemned to repeat it.'

We can see this in a cultural or societal context, with common repetitive cycles repeated throughout history. We will also see it in our own lives in the patterns that are recurring for us in different areas of life, including the area of intimate relationships. Some are terrified of being alone, or feel a stigma or expectation that to be happy they must always be in an intimate relationship. Thus, rather than allowing some space to pause and reflect between relationships, many move from one relationship to another with barely a chance to take a breath and reflect on lessons learned or patterns replayed in their most recent dynamic. Inevitably they bring their old patterns into their new relationship and cycles continue to play out, leading to frustration and disconnection.

Consider: Playing Out Patterns

- What are the repetitive dynamics, frustrations or challenges that you have experienced in your relationships?
- What aspects of your past relationships have you carried with you into your most recent relationship dynamic?

Whether it's a familiar dynamic with partners, a consistent choice in the type of people we attract, or recurring challenges we face while in a relationship, our past relationships hold valuable insights if we are willing to hold a mirror up to them. When I reflect on my own relationship history over the years I see patterns of jumping in too quickly, overlooking my own needs and not communicating well, then growing frustrated that my partner 'doesn't understand me'. I also often notice myself feeling crowded and 'needing space'. Upon closer inspection I see that really what I am saying when I say I need space is 'I am afraid of you seeing certain aspects of me and so I need to create some distance so that I can hide what you might reject.'

Relationship Inventory

A relationship inventory can be a really useful exercise for extracting wisdom from your own lived experience.

Think of any significant romantic relationships you have had in your adult life and consider some of the following prompts.

- What have been the most common recurring relational challenges/dynamics for you?
- What things about your previous partners triggered you the most?
- What feelings did these triggers provoke?
- What judgements did you have about your partners?
- What have you projected onto your partners in the past?
- Where did you not live fully and blame them?
- How did you not show up fully in the relationship? Where did you withhold?

Reflecting on all your answers, what do you see as the recurring themes that have shown up consistently in relationships? How has the shadow played out for you? What do you need to keep an eye on in the future to ensure you do not stay stuck in these patterns?

As an added element to this type of exercise, John Wineland, a teacher I have learned a lot from, has suggested considering how our behaviour or attitude may have affected the other person. For example, if I have listed that a common dynamic in previous relationships has been me going into shutdown and not communicating when stressed or overwhelmed, I can consider how that might have impacted my partner. In this example I could say, 'When I shut down and stopped communicating, I can imagine that made them feel anxious and confused.'

Sexual Shadow

As with all other aspects of the human experience, our sex lives can be run from the shadows and be influenced by largely unconscious drivers. Diving into our sexual shadow can reveal desires, fears and vulnerabilities we have kept hidden or repressed alongside personal insecurities, fears around intimacy and societal taboos. When we are not consciously meeting our needs in life, we may find aspects of our shadow reaching out to fulfil those needs unconsciously through our sex lives. Perhaps we use sex as a form of stress relief, a source of validation or a tool to avoid uncomfortable feelings, as opposed to sex being an act of genuine connection, love and mutual pleasure.

For many of us, shame surrounded the areas of sex and nudity when we were growing up, and it's common for these feelings to linger into adulthood. Often, we find ourselves stuck in an inner teenager's mindset when it comes to sex and intimacy, holding onto outdated beliefs and insecurities from our formative years. It can be useful to reflect on the meanings we came to in our earliest sexual experiences, and the beliefs we formed about sex and about ourselves as sexual beings, then reflecting on how these beliefs continue to play out in our lives to this day. Where have we not grown up in the areas of sex and intimacy?

There are many ways we might see the shadow playing out in our sex lives, including:

- Reenacting trauma by choosing emotionally unavailable partners
- Sex being used as a distraction from deeper issues in relationships
- Avoidance of intimacy by pursuing only casual encounters
- Seeking validation through multiple sexual conquests
- Porn, sex or love addiction
- Porn being used as a means of expressing unspoken sexual desires and fantasies
- Sex being used to distract from emotional pain or to manage stress
- Sexuality being used to manipulate or gain power
- Confusing sexual desire with emotional connection

Consider: Secure Sex

- A useful question to consider is: how is sex different when your needs are met and you are coming from a secure place, versus when your needs are unmet and you lack that feeling of grounding and security?
- Reflect on these differences. Write down any patterns or behaviours you notice, aiming to bring unconscious drivers into conscious awareness.

Your Sexual Story

Reflect on your sexual journey from your first kiss to your most recent sexual experience. Write about it in the third person to give it a little distance and encourage objectivity and introspection.

Upon completion of the exercise, identify patterns or beliefs that may have emerged from your exploration. What have you learned about your sexual self?

Summary: Gold in the Shadow

- Those who choose to move past the power struggle relationship stage in a conscious way move to a commitment to 'conscious love'.

- As a result of projections and transference we often do not see the person in front of us in the present, but instead see them through the lens of our past.

- Only by revealing ourselves and our experience vulnerably and authentically can we achieve true connection and intimacy.

- An important aspect of growing up psychologically is humanising our parents or primary caregivers, acknowledging their strengths and weaknesses, their merits and flaws.

- Performing a relationship inventory is a good step in waking up to some of our patterns and recognising some of the ways our shadow is influencing the partners we choose, the conflicts we find ourselves in and the challenges that are recurring for us with intimate partners. Consider how sex is different when your needs are met and you are coming from a secure place, versus when your needs are unmet and you lack that feeling of grounding and security.

Incomplete Sentences

Read the beginning of each sentence aloud and allow yourself to complete the sentence spontaneously in an unfiltered way. After completing all the prompts you can jot down any insights or reflections that stand out to you.

- My shadow attraction draws me to people who are …
- The source of most of the conflict in my relationships is …
- I project my fears onto my partner when …
- The person I need to find closure with is …
- The parts of me I am most afraid to share in relationships are …
- My fears in a relationship show up when …
- My relationship with my sexuality is …
- To improve my relationship with my sexuality I can …

Journalling Prompts

1. What messages did you receive about love, relationships and intimacy during your childhood? Consider the implicit and explicit messages as well as the behaviours and attitudes modelled by your caregivers or observed in your family environment. How have these early lessons influenced your expectations and beliefs about love today? Are there aspects you would like to reconsider or redefine as you cultivate your own understanding of love?

2. Think about your past and current intimate relationships. Can you identify patterns in the way you relate to intimate partners? Are there recurring themes or dynamics that seem familiar? How might these patterns be connected to your early experiences with caregivers or influential figures in your life?

3. Consider the qualities or traits that attract you to others. Are there certain characteristics or behaviours that consistently draw you in? Reflect on what these attractions might reveal about your own desires, fears or unmet needs. How might these attractions reflect aspects of your shadow self that you may not fully acknowledge?

4. Recall a recent conflict or disagreement in a relationship. What emotions did it evoke in you? How did you respond, and why? Reflect on whether your reactions were influenced by past experiences or unresolved issues. How might addressing these underlying shadows help you navigate conflicts more effectively in the future?

5. Reflect on your tendencies in relationships. Do you often prioritise others' needs over your own? Are you uncomfortable setting boundaries or asserting your own desires? Explore instances where you might have felt overly responsible for others' happiness or wellbeing. How do these patterns relate to your sense of self-worth and autonomy? What steps can you take to cultivate healthier, more balanced relationships?

Ego Eradicator

This week I invite you to try an exercise from kundalini yoga called the 'Ego Eradicator', which, a little like the cold shower exercise shared earlier in the book, offers an embodiment practice to support staying open and present, not shutting down or reacting during moments of intensity – a valuable skill in the realm of relationships! Learning to be with intensity allows us to stay in connection rather than defaulting to protection while in the eye of the storm.

Begin by sitting comfortably with your spine straight. Raise your arms to a 60-degree angle, fingers curled into the pads of your palms, with thumbs pointing straight up. Close your eyes and focus on the space between your eyebrows.

Start a powerful breath of fire by inhaling and exhaling rapidly through your nose, keeping your breaths equal in length and your abdomen pumping rhythmically. Focus on the exhale and the inhale will happen by itself.

Continue this breath for 3 minutes, maintaining the arm position and the intensity of the breath. As you do this, notice any resistance or discomfort, and consciously choose to stay open and present to the intensity and sensations.

You may feel your back, your shoulders, your arms on fire and feel yourself wanting to collapse or drop your arms, but look to keep your heart open and proud, allowing yourself to practise staying open to discomfort and intensity, staying responsive rather than reactive.

After 3 minutes, inhale deeply, bringing your thumbs to touch above your head, fingers still curled, and hold the breath briefly. Exhale and slowly lower your arms, allowing yourself to sit quietly for a moment, feeling the effects of the exercise. Try this exercise at least three times in the coming week.

Afterword and Integration

'The big question is whether you are going to be able to say a hearty yes to your adventure.' Joseph Campbell

'The curious paradox is that when I accept myself just as I am, then I change.' Carl Rogers

As we come to the end of this exploration, we find ourselves, perhaps unexpectedly, at a beginning: the beginning of truly accepting all that we are.

Throughout this journey of understanding the shadow, my intention has been to serve as a gentle guide, inviting you to explore at a pace that feels right, with compassion for every step you take. I hope you have felt that gentle support as you delved into parts of yourself often left unexplored.

This journey isn't about achieving perfection or 'fixing' ourselves, but about embracing the present moment and accepting ourselves as we are. It can be tempting to wait to start living until we feel fully healed or to keep digging for more understanding or insight we think will secure our personal growth.

But this – right here – is life. This is where we begin.

Each chapter of our lives, no matter how uncertain or challenging, is meaningful and deserves our fullest presence. Life itself presents us with the perfect people, experiences and challenges to support our development and healing, if we only allow ourselves to meet them with an open heart.

Real transformation comes when we meet our lives this way, moving from merely thinking about change to fully embodying it. When we stay open to what each moment offers, we shift from understanding our experiences only cognitively to living them as embodied wisdom. The mind's need to 'solve' or 'fix' can keep us endlessly searching, yet the invitation here is to step into the wisdom already unfolding within us, to let life be the teacher. Our challenges, relationships and everyday experiences are part of the healing path, always guiding us back to wholeness. Often what we perceive as being 'in the way' is the way.

The shadow work we've undertaken together is an ongoing journey, one that asks us to walk forward with openness and courage, to lean toward our uncomfortable edges rather than away from them. Transformation arises not from rejecting our difficult parts but from embracing them as essential to who we are. In doing so, we create space for genuine growth and allow for a deeper relationship with life itself. Paradoxically, it is through self-acceptance that the path to transformation emerges.

As you move forward from here, may you continue to approach yourself with compassion and patience, knowing that every chapter, every feeling and every experience is part of your path. By welcoming life's gifts and challenges, we learn to integrate the wisdom they bring, becoming more authentic with each step. There will be moments of light and ease, as well as times of difficulty, but in each, you are becoming more whole.

The invitation is simply to keep saying yes to your life in all its beauty and complexity, honouring the fullness of your experience and allowing yourself to be truly transformed. This is not an ending but a step forward on a path of self-discovery, acceptance, and deep peace with yourself.

Thank you for sharing this part of your journey here. May it lead you to live with compassion, curiosity and playfulness, and a wholehearted embrace of who you are, right now.

Grá mór,

Pat

Acknowledgements

In writing the acknowledgments for this book, I'm reminded of the countless individuals who have helped me on this journey – those who have shown patience, insight, love and support.

I have deep gratitude for each person who has shaped my understanding and commitment to this work, even if they remain unnamed on this page.

Though space limits me from listing everyone, please know that each contribution has been invaluable. To those mentioned here, and to those whose names remain unspoken, your presence and influence have been felt deeply.

A big thank you to my parents, brothers, sister and close friends for your ongoing love, support and encouragement.

Thank you to Mark McCarthy, Marta Czubak, Nicola Herd, Niall Graham, Jason Best, Gill Carroll, Jack Simpson, Jordan Thornton, Prema McKeever, Wayne Cantwell, Carla Salvio and all my other colleagues and friends who provided feedback and support during the writing of this book.

Thank you to Sarah, Isabelle, Esther, Charlie, Fiona, Jane, Georgina and all of the team at Gill for your support and guidance in the writing of this book.

Thank you to my training partners at Durinho BJJ and anyone else I've shared the Jiu-Jitsu mats with while travelling these last few years.

Thank you to my students in the Journey the Breath facilitator programme and all the clients who have worked with me over the last 15 plus years. I have learned and continue to learn a lot from you all.

Listing all of my teachers and guides could fill a full book in itself but a notable thank you to Robert Masters, John Wineland, Byron Katie, Debbie Ford, Caroline Myss, Carl Jung, Robert Johnson, Julia Cameron, Gabor Maté, Alexander Lowen, Stan Grof, Rafia Morgan, Turiya Hanover, Devaraj Sandberg, David Berceli, Satyarthi Peloquin and Carl Rogers.

And to you, the reader, thank you for taking the time to engage with these words and for being open to exploring the depths of shadow work.